Sn

Pignight, Blowjob
More Light, Darwin's Flood

Pignight: 'Both through dialogue and the quality of imagination Wilson forces out uneasy and enormous laughter.' *Guardian*

Blowjob: 'The command of character is complete – and each is allowed a gloriously funny solemnity. It does mark a development of Wilson's view of the world – dangerous grotesques in the heart of cruelty; an extended form of naturalism.' *Guardian*

The Soul of the White Ant: 'Wilson's marvellous writing aims to make a violent poetry of his assembled images.' *Financial Times*

More Light: 'A striking succession of images, an intellectual breadth, and a non-stop whirlwind of surreal events and jokes that leave you breathless. This is Wilson at his most distinctive: a flamboyant showman, brilliantly resourceful.' *Time Out*
'Sometimes serious, sometimes facetious, and always intelligent, the skill of the writing lies in its light treatment of what ought to be weighty matters.' *Daily Telegraph*

Darwin's Flood: 'The pile-up of teeming ideas which infuses Wilson's play with wicked intelligence group Charles Darwin, Jesus, Friedrich Nietzsche and Mary Magdalene under one roof for a hilarious exploration of time and human personality (it *is* hilarious, honest).' *Evening Standard*
'The play is relentlessly funny, performing elegant magician's tricks with famous names like a pack of visiting cards.' *Sunday Times*

Snoo Wilson was born in Reading, he studied at the University of East Anglia and was a founding director of the Portable Theatre, Brighton and London. Wilson was script editor for the *Play for Today* series, BBC TV, he has been dramaturge for the RSC, director of the Scarab Theatre and has taught film script writing at the National Film School. In 1980 he was awarded a US/UK Bicentennial Fellowship and worked at Santa Cruz University and with the New York Theatre Studio in New York. In 1989 Wilson was Associate Professor, lecturing in play writing, at University College San Diego. With a writing career from the 1960s, Wilson's place as an important and distinguished playwright is confirmed in his many award-winning plays both in Britain and across America. He received the John Whiting Award in 1978 for *The Glad Hand*, the San Diego Theater Circle award in 1988 for *80 Days* and most recently the Eileen Anderson/Central Broadcasting Premiere Award for Best Night Out for *HRH*. Wilson has written films, libretti, radio plays and two novels. His libretti include an acclaimed adaptation of Offenbach's *Orpheus in the Underworld* for the English National Opera and the book for *80 Days* at the La Jolla Playhouse in California.

by the same author

Layby
The Pleasure Principle*
Vampire
The Number of the Beast
Flaming Bodies
The Everest Hotel
The Glad Hand
A Greenish Man
The Grass Widow*
The Bedbug
Moonshine
Sabina

NOVELS

Spaceache
Inside Babel
I, Crowley

*published by Methuen

SNOO WILSON

Plays: 1

Pignight
Blowjob
The Soul of the White Ant
More Light
Darwin's Flood

*Introduced by the author and
with forewords by the directors*

Methuen Drama

METHUEN CONTEMPORARY DRAMATISTS

1 3 5 7 9 10 8 6 4 2

This collection first published in Great Britain 1999
by Methuen Publishing Limited
215 Vauxhall Bridge Road, London SW1V 1EJ

Peribo (Pty) Ltd, 58 Beaumont Road, Mount Kuring-Gai,
NSW 2080, Australia, ACN 002 273 761
(for Australia and New Zealand)

ISBN 0 413 741 80X

A CIP catalogue record for this book is available from the British Library

Methuen Publishing Limited Reg. No. 3543167

Typeset by Deltatype, Birkenhead, Merseyside
Printed and bound in Great Britain by
Cox & Wyman Ltd, Reading, Berkshire

Contents

Chronology vii

Introduction ix

Foreword 3
PIGNIGHT 5

Foreword 37
BLOWJOB 39

Foreword 79
THE SOUL OF THE WHITE ANT 81

Foreword 123
MORE LIGHT 125

Foreword 191
DARWIN'S FLOOD 193

Snoo Wilson
Chronology

1971   *Pignight*, also directed. Leeds and London
         Blowjob, directed by David Hare. Edinburgh and London
         Layby, group play written with seven others, also directed. Edinburgh and London

1972   *Reason*, and a companion piece *Boswell and Johnson on the Shores of the Eternal Sea*. London, (Chicago in 1975)
         England's Ireland, with others, also directed. Amsterdam and London

1973   *Vampire*, first produced London, revised version London 1977 and New York 1979
         The Pleasure Principle, London

1974   *The Beast*, London, (New York 1977), revised version as *The Number of the Beast*, (London 1982)

1975   *The Everest Hotel*, also directed, London
         The Greenish Man, televised, (staged London 1978)

1976   *The Soul of the White Ant*, London

1977   *Elijah Disappearing*, London
         England-England, London

1978   *The Glad Hand*, London, winner of the John Whiting Award
         The Language of the Dead is Tongued with Fire, London

1979   *Flaming Bodies*, London

1980   *Spaceache*, Cheltenham and London

1981   *Salvation Now*, Seattle, USA

1982   *The Grass Widow*, Seattle, USA, (London 1983)

1983   *Our Lord of Lynchville*, New York, (then produced as *Lynchville* by the RSC in 1986)
         Loving Reno, New York and, also co-directed, London
         La Columbe, music by Gounod, adaptation of the libretto by Barbier and Carre, Buxton, Derbyshire and Sadler's Wells, London

1984   *Hamlyn*, Loughborough, Leicestershire

1985   *Orpheus in the Underworld*, music by
        Offenbach, adaptation of libretto by Crémieux
        and Halévy, London
1987   *More Light*, also co-directed, London
1988   *80 Days*, music and lyrics by Ray Davies, Califor-
        nia, USA
1992   *Walpurgis Nacht*, adaptation from Venedict Erofyev,
        London
1994   *Darwin's Flood*, London
        HRH, London, winner of Eileen Anderson/Cen-
        tral Broadcasting Premiere Award for Best Night
        Out
1995   *The Bedbug*, adaptation of play by Mayakovsky,
        London
1998   *Sabina*, London

Films

1985   *Shadey*, with Antony Sher and Billie Whitelaw
1993   *The Touch*, with Sarah Miles and Max Von Sydow

Novels

1983   *Spaceache*, later published in US (1987), Germany
        (1989)
1985   *Inside Babel*, sequel to *Spaceache*
1996   *I, Crowley*

Introduction

I was in my teens when I met the Russian cultural attaché. I had seen David Lean's recently released film, *Doctor Zhivago*. Finding myself nose to nose with censorship, greatly daring, I asked why Boris Pasternak's book, which had inspired the recent movie, was still banned in Russia. The attaché cocked his head as he gravely listened to the question from the spotty, English, public-school boy, and replied in measured tones, saying that Pasternak's book had not been released because it was 'not suitable for the majority of Russians'.

Censorship in this country was still in force at that time, though the sexual frontier was considered more dangerous than the political. When I began writing at university, new stage material had to be submitted to the Lord Chamberlain, who replied, beginning, 'The Comptroller of the Lord Chamberlain's Office *desires* me . . .' before going on to purge my text of lewd innuendo. I barely noticed when a few months later, these solemn rigmaroles guarding public order melted away in the heat of the sixties.

Almost four decades later, the mighty Russian Empire that towered so reliably and terrifyingly over childhood is gone, and my children are older than I was when I popped the question to the attaché. I myself have had thirty years of experience as a writer and playwright, living in a western liberal democracy, able to explore whatever material seems of personal and political import. I have been very lucky to have been able to follow a calling, however erratically, over such a length of time and I should use this opportunity to try to explain what I am trying to do in these plays and what makes them what they are.

To enlarge Wittgenstein's famous quote a little; the universe, rather than the world, is everything that is the question. We're all plugged into the universe whether we like it or not. Giordano Bruno, the hero of *More Light*, knew this when he wrote 'The guardians of my soul are wit and light.' We are not only the sum of our histories, but also the sum of our potential, which we can explore.

What the plays are 'about' are the stories themselves, but the paths of the stories are laid through the gardens of man's strange destiny through the ages, with a powerful curiosity as to how we go to where we are now and whether it is truly any different to the world say of the high Renaissance, or the world of the genial agnostic living just outside Bromley called Darwin, who in the middle of the nineteenth century tipped God out of his throne.

As to play-making: a full length play usually has seventeen thousand words to make a story happen in its particular universe. Some stories beg to occur and lend themselves easily to the telling; some give the storyteller the run around. I wrote the first draft of *Soul of The White Ant* in a day, but it took considerably longer to get it to feel right: to organise the surreal checks and balances, and ensure that it would be funny, internally consistent and alive.

My instinct in play-making is to provide a further viewpoint, to delight and amaze, to reach out beyond death and linear logic in a way which permits a dream resolution. *Darwin's Flood* and *More Light* have the same premise; they are imaginative arabesques danced on the ledge of their heroes' oblivion.

Some of the plays are accidents of politics. There was a period before the fall of apartheid in South Africa, where British writers were urged not to allow their plays to be done in South Africa. *Soul Of The White Ant* came out of an attempt to give a South African theatre a chance to do *Vampire*, with its creator, incorporating an Afrikaans-heavy third act. Dusty Hughes literally exhumed it from my bottom drawer, and Richard Romagnoli of the New York Theatre Studio gave it a brilliant second production. How would it play in Johannesburg? Would it make them laugh, too, now? It has of course never been done in South Africa, but a scene was revived with the original actors, some white-haired, twenty years later, for the Bush Theatre quarter-centenary. I felt so proud for everyone, accompanied by a continuing mild surprise that we were all inexplicably getting old.

Such a lot of technology has happened over the last thirty years that the past seems truly a different country, though war and taxes remain a constant. The price of air fares to America continues to fall even though continental drift has ordained that New York is some yards further away than when I began filling A4 for a living. When I finished the typescript of *Blowjob*, the cheapest way to copy it was for me to photograph the pages with my Praktica TSL, (then the pride of East German, Behind-the-Wall workmanship), and print the pages as large photographs. It was in this manner, that I tempted David Hare out of a brief self-imposed withdrawal from directing, with A3-sized pages of document paper – the smudgy photograph of a playscript.

When the Babylonian scribes discovered that they could record a world on their clay tablets, the world's resources changed. Now everything is changing again. One day, if the brain is wired to a spatially co-ordinated cortical neuro-linguistic scanner for the job of rendering an imaginative world, will the owner of the brain be a 'writer'? Who knows? We think we're getting smarter, but so much of it, apart from the ease of electronic cut-and-paste, is running on the spot. Never mind what happened to the aural history dramas before Babylon, my computer can't understand what computers were up to a mere ten years ago. Meanwhile global computer viruses threaten to torpedo its hard disk, descending uninvited from the Internet, like Tartars with drawn swords into a Russian *shtetl*.

Theatre is communal, words are its music, plays are individual Deep Memory variations on themes our preliterate ancestors drew on, I suspect. *Ur*-anthems, BC, Before Cuneiform, to recount to themselves what it was to be human. It was only ten thousand years ago we hearing these questions. Who are we? Where are we going? Here are some further variations on that ancient quest.

Snoo Wilson
London, 1999

Pignight

Foreword

Pignight was first directed by the author. I was a young dog, (or possibly, pig,) of twenty-one, and it was the first fully-scripted, professional play I had written; a ninety-minute comedy about a schizoid farm labourer who returns to the farm where he had been fostered. Smitty has problems with the pigs in his brain, and finally obeys their instructions to murder and eat the gangsters who have bought the farm from his step-parents. Dramatically minimalist, using a gun and some pig-masks, I sometimes think the construction of the play is like a skinless sausage: there is nothing obvious binding it together except the zeal of the nightmare, and the alarming jokes of a misperceived universe. There are not many topics suitable for this treatment, but possession by murderous entities is, I think, one.

When it went on tour, questions were asked in the House of Commons about the suitability of giving Arts Council money to such mimetic displays of depravity. The sawn-off shotgun used to set fire to drapes when it went off – it was easier to get firearms' licenses for such effects before The Troubles got under way – and I think we set fire to almost as many small theatres as David Hare's tour of *Blowjob*, a few months later. It was even a brief *succes de scandale* and John Calder published it which was lovely too. It's actually rather a spare piece, much fuller of scripted pauses than the writing I do now, though I remember resenting having to score the script a second time for endless pauses, when the original manuscript got lost. The character of Smitty was based on the newspaper story of a young German prisoner of war, who had been adopted by a lonely Welsh farming couple. Twenty years after the war his only connection with his previous life was his old regimental forage cap, which finally fell apart.

The tour ended up at the Young Vic theatre in London. The climax to the production mingled the illusion of cannibalism and cooking, but it was all lost on a Swiss theatre group, who watched the last night, but spoke no English. The English audience made their way out after the grisly end, looking rather green. But the Swiss actors, who I later learned had driven from Geneva without stopping for meals, descended quickly and quietly from the back of the theatre and ate the bread, margarine, and the 'human' liver that was still lightly frying on stage. I sometimes see Paul Freeman who played Mrs Mullen, and in our cups, we plan to remount the play.

Snoo Wilson, London, 1999

Pignight was first performed by the Portable Theatre playing at the Traverse Theatre, Edinburgh, the Young Vic Studio and the King's Head Theatre, London, with the following cast:

Roland Mullen	Darryl Kavann
Raymond Gibbs	Darryl Kavann
Jasmine Marchant	Paul Freeman
Mrs Mullen	Paul Freeman
Smitty	Peter Brenner
Voice of Bravington	Darryl Kavann

Directed by Snoo Wilson

The dog Robby was created by Supadogs of Islington

Note: It is important that the parts of Jasmine and Mrs Mullen be played by a man.

A hat and coat rack, the sort which can lie flat against the wall, is set behind a box wide enough for three at the back of the stage. The audience should be on three sides. There is a simple wooden table up front. The clothes for the various characters are hung on the coat rack. The various props are behind or inside the box, which should be accessible from the back.

The characters playing **Ray** *and* **Jasmine** *enter slowly, with conspiratorially furtive pleasure. They are wearing pigmasks which cover the top half only of their faces.* **Ray** *is carrying a* **Dog** *and wearing the riding coat which he wears as* **Mr Mullen**. **Jasmine** *is carrying a large multistriped golfing umbrella which she opens out and places over the hatrack.*

This is the signal for the start of the play.

She sits down under the umbrella on the box with an air of expectancy. **Ray** *takes the* **Dog** *with one paw up and tapdances with it assiduously. He invites* **Jasmine** *to join him. At first she refuses, then joins in the dance.*

They dance in a line facing the audience, each holding a paw. **Ray** *attempts a turn and the* **Dog** *drops to the floor. This accident suddenly ends the dance. They pick up the* **Dog** *and* **Ray** *offers it to the front row of the audience to stroke, a random two or three.* **Jasmine** *watches approvingly. On the last offer,* **Jasmine** *takes the* **Dog***, strokes it, offers it to one of the audience to stroke. As he reaches for it,* **Ray** *kicks it out of her hands.*

Smitty *enters from the back. He is wearing jeans, a leather coat, dispatch riders' boots and a German forage cap which he holds in his hand. He exhibits nervousness. There is a copy of a* Superman *comic or similar sticking out of his coat pocket.*

Ray *and* **Jasmine** *take the* **Dog** *and put it on the ground. They then push it in a slow arc across the floor towards* **Smitty***, both of them building up with low growls and snarls to an hysterical crescendo of yapping. The* **Dog** *stops about two foot short of* **Smitty***. They stand back and continue to yap hideously.*

Smitty *seizes a hayfork from the back of the stage and pitchforks the* **Dog***.* **Ray** *and* **Jasmine** *make suitable dying noises, briefly. Very shaken,* **Smitty** *sits down on the bench.*

Ray *gets out a small sack which is under the table at the front.* **Ray** *and* **Jasmine** *hold it out for* **Smitty** *and with great distaste he puts the* **Dog** *in on the end of the fork. He sits down, immediately passive again.*

Ray *and* **Jasmine** *go and sit on the small table at the front of the stage. A long pause.* **Ray** *feels his teeth diffidently. Pause. He speaks almost as if to himself:*

Ray   I got something stuck, (*Pause.*) in my teeth.

Jasmine *pulls him round to look in his mouth, then turns him away again.*

Jasmine (*disdainfully*)   Wallpaper.

Ray   I can't stand it.

Jasmine *pulls his mouth over and fiddles about in it. She stops, wipes her finger and clucks her tongue. Without turning around, she raises her voice to speak to* **Smitty**.

Jasmine   Tell us about yourself.

Ray (*helpfully*)   What did you have for breakfast?

Jasmine   Bubble and squeak?

They laugh covertly, then get off the chest and go and sit down, one each side of **Smitty** *on the box.* **Smitty** *speaks with unnatural precision. The correctness of the schizophrenic.*

Smitty   No thanks, I don't eat breakfast. I have a packed lunch which I make up myself of Spam and soft white bread and margarine. Afterwards I peel and eat an orange or apple. In the evenings I bicycle to the village and enjoy a steak and kidney pie in the public bar with half a pint of shandy. I give the orange and apple peel to the pigs. I cut my apple into quarters and take out the pips with the tip of the knife. I eat the rest of the core. For my room I have the use of the potting shed which has chintz curtains, made for me by Mrs Mullen. I am very much afraid of chintz dogs.

Jasmine (*vindictively*)   Murderer.

Jasmine *and* **Smitty** *go the table and pull out a bucket of kidneys from underneath. They eat some of them.* **Ray** *takes one from* **Jasmine** *as she is about to put it dripping, into her mouth. (Pear halves in red and blue dye for actors not hooked on raw offal.)*

Ray (*hideous interest*)   That's a nice one.

He eats it instead. Pause.

Smitty   Are you from Mr Khruschev?

They do not respond. Continue eating slowly.

From Mr Macmillan?

Pause.

From Mr Kennedy?

Pause.

Ray (*elaborately casual*)   He's dead, isn't he?

They tidy away the bowl and stand up straight. Facing audience again.

(*Terrible nonchalance.*) This is such a big thought, Smitty, that it's going to burst your head open. It's been decided that the pigs are going to take over from the human race.

Blackout. In the dark, the **Bravington** *actor takes a loud hailer which he swings, throughout the speech, the arc of the audience. The voice is a heavy Yorkshire accent, fat; he speaks in almost epiglottal whispers.*

Bravington   Yes, officer. I'm Mr Bravington. (*Pause.*) I bought the farm out of the kindness of my 'eart. I don't like to speak disrespectfully of the dead. (*Pause.*) Mr Mullen was a rotten farmer. You could tell. Three wagonloads of dead sherry bottles my men cleared out the back. I can't see what possible use they would be in evidence. (*Pause.*) Yes, officer, I did employ Raymond Gibbs. I'm afraid I can't tell you anything though, about Jasmine Marchant. Now would you kindly step aside, I would like to speak to – my solicitor. (*Pause.*) Er . . . yes. That is – a photograph of Mr Mullen.

Asthmatic breathing of **Roland**. *Culminates in groan. A flash of light shows* **Roland** *mounted on* **Jasmine** *who still has the pigmask on.* **Jasmine** *is crouched on the table.* **Roland** *is wearing a dirty riding mac, a flat cap and a pink eyepatch.*

A second flash. He has his hands up to shield his face.

Sounds of walking on gravel in the dark. A small fruit box which is kept under the table.

Roland *is walking in it. The steps cease.* **Roland** *speaks. It takes him time to get under way: he is numb drunk.*

Roland   Would the honourable member for Sleaford stand up, and give his maiden speech. In 1951 the polls were miscounted and Roland Mullen has been given a seat. After all. (*Pause. Dully.*) Hooray. (*Pause.*) A burst of excitement as he rises to speak. (*Pants. Then quite straight.*) He's only got one eye. One bullet lodged in the thorax and one in the cerebellum. He plugs his ionizer into the mains and takes a breath of fresh air. (*Inhales.*) I should like to tell you about farming. In farming, we're up to our necks in shit and I should like to ask you to cooperate. (*Pause.*) By not making waves. (*Pause.*) I feel that an old soldier like myself is entitled to a couple of jokes. How does a Frenchwoman hold her liquor? (*Pause.*) How? (*Pause.*) By the ears. (*Pause.*) The ears. (*Pause, then morosely.*) Oh – all right.

A slow dim-up starts. **Roland** *treads on something nasty and grunts in disgust. He puts the box away. Low and savage.*

My wife and I cannot stand the country. Barbed wire fences, a sea of chopped mud tarmacked in strips, drainage ditches with scum on them, a few small orchards dripping pesticides and the fen creeks rancid with ammonium nitrate. Thistles, nettles and blackthorn hedges to be abolished. Also, long and winding roads, cowpats, horse dung, dog shit and all stools. Rain. Sleet. Snow. Wind over four m.p.h. Weather of all kinds. Horses, donkeys, cows, all animals of the cloven hoof with the exception of the pig. The human race to be fed upon synthesised vitamins, hydrolised starch, and monosodium glutamate. (*Pause.*

Reasonable.) To show you what a miserable life it is I shall now read from my wife's diary. (*Deadpan hatred. He pulls out the diary. The light is now at half.*) 'I confide in my secret heart that R for Roland has started drinking again ... Blah blah farm in debt. (*He skims through.*) Deep shock ... despair ... a feeling of chilling peace. Mumble mumble ... Please burn this before ... (*Pause.*) Effort and pain ... wur wur ... (*A new page.*) Bach ... Schopenhauer prone my identity submit coarsened so little time and I be so little time and I life is hell. (*Pause. Feelingly.*) Life is hell.' (*Rallies.*) Here I am. Spavined with asthma. A one-eyed sclerotic living on a damp plain. Drunk. With memories of Vera Lynn. Sometimes sinking as low as British Ruby-type port. Peach wine. (*Pause. A terrible confession.*) Plum cordial. (*Pause. The pity floods out.*) The pigs in desperation, gnawing each other's curly tails, going hungry for *days.* (*Switches to anger.*) Because it is *not* otherwise! (*Pause.*) I can't get the labour. The German boy, the ex-prisoner of war my wife kept on, started killing the animals. Put him inside. Off his head. And my wife. Not now Roland not now. (*Fiercely.*) Never. (*Pause.*) So I went to the pigs for company. I had my favourites. Whispered sweet nothings in their ears. The boy didn't do anything for me. I went to the doctor and told him about my ... (*Pause.*). ... trouble. He gave me a little book on technique and told me not to let it get out of hand. The boy saw me doing it. He found out. Started killing the animals. Had him put away. (*Pause.*) Not that we didn't do anything for him. He was like a son to us. My wife taught him to read. She said, (*An expansive gesture of the arm. The light is now at full.*) 'Smitty, the whole of European literature now is at your command.' (*A fit of coughing.*) I would kindly like to finish before the honourable member pulls the plug of my ionizer out of the wall. You shall hear me. I shall come before you again and you shall hear me! (*Shouts.*) Silence! (*Pause. Ominous.*) Read your horoscope for the day. Touch wood. Debate seriously about entry into Europe. My horoscope predicted difficulties and a long sea voyage. (*Throwaway.*) A reference to a floating liver. (*Pause.*) I have been talking to the pigs and they know. The pigs are going to take over the earth.

Blackout.

In the dark, the voice of **Smitty**. *Heroic, precise.*

Smitty   Schnell, fort aus den Wäldern und in den Fluss hinein. Zhukove gewinnt immer Tankschlachten und diese wird keine Ausnahme. Leutnant, ich kann nicht weiter, ich bin der Sohn eines Artisten. (*Pause. Then with difficulty, as if reading. Unaccented.*) Ac-tually, you are coming into a patch of-good luck as your sign in Gem-ini is at a beautiful angle to the planet Uranus in your personal chart. This puts you in a roman-tic mood.

Roland   Sellout! Sold a rotten old farm to a man called Bravington, who brought ten thousand pounds along in a suitcase. Going to Australia with Mrs Mullen to start a new life. (*Curiously.*) Kangaroos . . .

Immediately, **Ray** *fires a sawn-off shotgun in the dark.* **Jasmine** *lights a match close to her face. She is standing on the table.*

Jasmine   Oh, there you are.

Ray *fires again.* **Jasmine** *drops the match.*

Jasmine   Did you hit it?

Ray   I can't see a fucking thing.

Jasmine   You might of hit it –

Ray   I was blind. You blinded me. I'll fucking cripple you –

Jasmine   Oh, sorry.

Ray (*at a loss*)   I fired up in the air – I think.

Jasmine   – Perhaps it was a flying one –

Ray   – A flying what? –

Jasmine   – It can't be deaf – you must of frightened it. Can you see the dog anywhere?

Ray (*acid*)   I had forgotten your dog was gun-shy.

Jasmine   I can't hear him barking anywhere –

Ray   Perhaps he isn't barking, then.

Jasmine   He usually does if he's excited.

Lights. **Jasmine** *is standing on the table.* **Ray** *is at the back with the sawn-off shotgun.* **Jasmine** *takes fright at the light.*

Jasmine   Ray – it might be coming back!

Ray (*at the end of tether*)   What did you see? In the pen?

Jasmine   I saw its eyes. Little red ones – hundreds of them in the flashlight.

Ray   About this high? (*Indicates* **Jasmine**.)

Jasmine   Yes, and they were moving –

Ray   Pigs. (*Pause.*) You saw pigs' eyes in the pigs' pen.

Jasmine   Ooh . . .

Ray (*savagely*)   Yeah, Oh. (*Pause.*) Look, I really don't think you can stay. I don't think that country life suits you.

Pause.

Jasmine (*upset*)   Ray, can you please call Robby.

Ray   There's only pigs outside. It's your dog.

Jasmine *turns away suddenly. Pointing in the direction she was looking, she screams.*

Jasmine   Aaaah! There – there it is! Through there! I saw it! It went past on two legs – two legs not four – it's a man!

Ray (*surly*)   I can't see anything.

Jasmine   Is it in the pens?

Ray *has had enough. He goes over and takes the gun barrel and pokes it through* **Jasmine**'s *legs; then, still holding it, starts to move round the table.* **Jasmine** *flusters even more.*

Jasmine   No – Ray – look don't – stop! Ray! Me tights!

Smitty *stands up from the box at the back holding his cap. As he stands up.*

Smitty   Hello, Mrs Mullen. Hello, Mr Mullen. I've been seeing friends in Sleaford.

Pause. They both turn, caught completely off guard.

Hello. (*Pause.*) I've been seeing friends. (*Pause.*) I'm sorry I'm late back.

He goes to the bucket of water by the table and takes off his jacket and T-shirt. He starts to wash. **Jasmine** *and* **Ray**, *appalled, back away. Long pause.*

Ray (*nervous, aggressive*)   Come to see Mr and Mrs Mullen? (*Pause.*) They've left the property and gone to Australia. Where d'you live?

Smitty (*simply*)   In the house at the bottom of the garden.

Ray   The property and the animals have been bought by Mr Bravington. D'you get what I'm driving at? (*Pause.*) I mean that things have changed a bit since you went on holiday. (*Pause.*) You went on holiday to Sleaford, you said. (*Pause.*)

Jasmine   Have you seen a little dog?

Smitty (*rattled*)   No, Mrs Mullen.

Ray   Mrs Mullen's gone now. I mean she isn't here any more. Like Mr Mullen. They both – goes off to Australia. It's Mr Bravington's farm now. (*Pause.*) Something wrong? Were you asked to come? By Mr Bravington?

Pause. **Ray** *has regained the ascendancy. During the following speech he takes the gun apart, lock stock and barrel, cleans it, and puts it back together again.*

Ray   Mr Bravington invests in farms. He has a pig-breeding scheme and this farm is now become part of it. The investors buy a sow and the litter is the dividend. It's a compound interest rate of four per cent per annum with a ceiling for the original dividend holders of forty-eight per

cent after twelve years. You heard of it? (*Pause.*) It's a
scheme which is multiplying in other fields as well as pig-
breeding. I mean, there's a limit to the amount of pork
you can take. But there's always the leather industry, which
leads into clothes and shoes, fancy goods: and battery
poulterers buy the bone for chicken meal. Gelatine gives
you a lead into the sweet industry. With the fat and the
lard you got a strong arm in the catering trade. Undercut
someone else's lard, make good with the frozen chicken,
and you're into foods, which is all packaging, really. (*Pause.*)
You know what goes inside the packages? (*Pause.*) Pork
chops, vacuum-sealed hams, black pudding reintroduced at
luxury prices. Freeze-dried giblets. British Home Stores,
Marks and Spencers, Tesco's, they're all negotiating for our
sausages. They're beautiful sausages as well. You wouldn't
be surprised to learn if he exported the pigshit. It's a busy
business – farming. (*Pause.*) Come for your things then?
(*Pause.*) You see, it's the stock Mr Bravington's interested in.
He can't afford to keep on casual labourers.

Smitty *finishes washing and stands up.*

Smitty   Thank you.

Ray   Er – Wass your name? –

Smitty   Smitty.

Ray   Smitty. Yeah. You could give us a few useful tips
like how the pigs are fed and that. What *do* pigs eat –
nowadays? Most of the swill seems to be ham sandwiches.

Smitty   Yes.

Ray   That's a bit kinky, isn't it? Don't they get a taste for
it?

Smitty   It comes from the construction camp.

Ray   Where they send the ham? Oh. Thanks. You been
with Mr and Mrs Mullen long?

Smitty   Since I was very young.

Ray   And Mr and Mrs Mullen didn't tell you they was

going away?

Smitty They didn't tell me.

Jasmine You haven't seen a little dog anywhere?

Ray (*evenly*) Shut up about that fucking dog.

Blackout.

Then a spot on forestage as **Ray** *and* **Jasmine** *sit down at the back.* **Smitty** *walks into the spot on the table and sits down. He takes the* **Dog** *half out of the sack and, sticking his fingers through the collar, dangles it like a ventriloquist's dummy. The* **Dog** *has a mouth into which sweets can be thrust and removed.*

Jasmine *and* **Ray** *put on pigmasks in the background. One of them should provide the* **Dog**'s *voice. Comic, epiglottal.*

Smitty *settles himself with the* **Dog**.

Dog I like sweeties.

Pause. It sniffs one of **Smitty**'s *pockets.*

You got some aniseed balls in your pocket. Can I have some?

Smitty *takes some out of his pocket and offers them to the* **Dog**. *He puts a few in the* **Dog**'s *mouth then.*

Dog *More* aniseed balls? I like Maltezers really. Quality Street. Milk chocolate Flake.

Smitty *is rattled.*

Smitty I've only got aniseed balls.

Dog (*disappointed*) Oooogh – all right –

Smitty *continues to stuff them down his throat. The action gradually starts to become hysterical.*

Dog Hang on a bit. I'll get indigestion – (*A threat.*) I'll get sick! I've changed my mind. I don't like aniseed balls. I like – er – Swiss chocolate – Fruit 'n Nut – Battenberg cake – Mars bars – Nuttall's Mintoes – jelly babies – Treets – Rimmer's Milk Chocolate Buttons – marizpan – sherbet licks – nougat – Refreshers –

Smitty *starts to strangle it.*

Dog   But I don't . . . like . . . aniseed . . .

Smitty *strangles it, then makes the* **Dog** *disgorge the aniseed balls with one move. They splatter on the floor. He then gently places the* **Dog** *on the table, kneels down and whispers to it.*

Smitty   Schnell, fort aus den Wäldern und in den Fluss hinein. Zhukove gewinnt immer Tankschlachten und diese wird keine Ausnahme. Leutnant, ich kann nicht weiter, ich bin der Sohn eines Artisten.

He leaves the **Dog** *and goes to sit between the other two on the bench.*

The lights go on to the back.

Ray (*a different voice*)   In the eighth dimension of the metatonic age, to the star cluster Tactar near Galaxy Aurax nine to the power of sixty-three light years from the solar system containing the planet Earth, Galactic Knight Kaarg telepaths his report. He has taken as his medium the body of Rudolf Van Vollenhoven, a human, the present dominant species, risen from and now observed to be retrogressing to the apes. Galactic Knight Kaarg reports through the eyes of his medium that the most suitable animal to take over the dominance of the earth under our supervision is the pig. Brave, resourceful, gregarious, intelligent and humble, their period of dominance shall be – indefinite.

Ray *and* **Jasmine** *hum the opening bars of Thus Spake Zarathustra.* **Smitty** *is agitated.*

Jasmine (*a different voice*)   Galactic Knight Kaarg has something to say.

Ray   There is nothing more to say. In twelve weeks the trap will be sprung and the pigs will rise as the men rose, suddenly and inexplicably. Dominance has nothing to do with the opposed thumb, or walking on two legs.

Smitty (*desperate*)   Mr and Mrs Mullen have sold the farm.
They've gone away. Someone called Mr Bravington is
going to take the pigs away and sell them for meat.

Pause. A gesture of introduction to the audience from **Jasmine**.

Jasmine   Bravington.

Blackout. **Bravington**'s *voice as before. This time he's teasing.*

Bravington   Hey hey hee hee. Come out from under
that bed, y'll get yer arse fluffy. (*Chuckles. Pause.*) I can't turn
the lights on. I told you before. It's a power cut. (*Pause.*)
'Ave some more bubbly. It's fizzin all over your lap. (*Pause.*)
How about that. I've asked for some angels on horseback
to be sent up. That's prunes wrapped in bacon. (*Pause.*) It's
a cocktail delicacy. (*Pause.*) They're called angels on
horseback because the prunes do a lot o' gallopin. Hey hee
hee.

A spot on the **Jasmine** *actor midstage, as* **Jasmine**. *She is
holding the* **Dog** *under one arm.*

Jasmine   I got to be at work in the morning.

Bravington   Take it off.

Jasmine (*quick as a flash*)   What?

Bravington (*drawls*)   The morning. (*Pause.*) I can't see
what's the matter with you.

Jasmine   I can't see what's the matter with *you.*

Bravington   There's nowt the matter with me.

Jasmine   You know bloody well.

Bravington   Oooh aye. (*Pause. He is counting notes.*) One,
two, three, four. In tens. (*Pause.*) 'Ang on, telephone.
Bravington here. 'Oo is it? (*Pause.*) No, I don't take advice
on how to run my businesses. (*Pause.*) What's yer name?
(*Pause.*) I don't sell my stock. I said I don't sell my stock.
(*Pause.*) I asked the switchboard not to put any calls
through. I'm not discussing anything tonight. Goodnight.
(*Pause.*) You'll do what? (*Pause.*) You're straight out of a

loony bin. Listen – one finger on my swine and they'll be
mixing you up in the swill inside of a week. I've got a
whole line of lumpy lads just dying to straighten you out.
You won't be the first to go. I'm not a violent man – just
don't try to blackmail me. (*The conversation finishes.*) I've been
threatened. Told what to do. I can hardly believe my ears.
(*Pause.*) One, two, three, four. In tens.

Jasmine You want to do business?

Bravington Aye.

Jasmine Forty pounds!

Bravington (*taken aback*) I cud've 'ad Lord Derby for not
much more.

Jasmine That's not a week's wages to you.

Bravington I don't see what that's got to do with it.

Jasmine Two fifty. And then not till I'm properly pissed.

Bravington (*at large*) Everyone's gone mad. (*Pause.*) 'Ere,
'ang on. I got a proposition.

Jasmine I'm turning it down.

Bravington I got this farm.

Jasmine (*does a little dance as she sings*)
Old McDonald had a farm -ei aye ei aye oh –
Two fifty –
And on this farm he had some pigs –
Is it a roll in the hay?

Bravington You know Ray Gibbs. He's going down to
the farm to look after some stock there till I can get it
slaughtered on the quiet. He's an 'ard man but I look after
'im. You keep him happy for the week, and you'll get your
money.

Jasmine He's a raving GBH man. He'll open me up
with the kitchen scissors.

Bravington He's on the other side of the fence. (*Pause.*)

Mostly.

Jasmine   Suppose he goes for me with the breadknife?

Bravington   I'll talk to him about it. Two fifty.

Jasmine (*suspicious*)   What's on this farm then?

Bravington   Swine.

Jasmine   They shitting ten bob bits then?

Bravington   There's two thousand of them in pens. I
know a lot of interested parties. I got to 'ave an 'ard man
there, make sure he stays there for the week.

Jasmine   I'll take Rob I think.

Bravington   No –

Jasmine   He's the dog.

Blackout. The spot.

Bravington   Oh, all right. The dog. I see. Hey hee hee.
The dog. Have some bubbly. Good old Rob. (*Pause.*) There
was this man, took 'is false teeth out to put them in
Steradent one night. 'Ere, 'e said to 'is wife, what's that
there stuck between me molars? That's 'am she said. 'Am,
'e said, 'am? 'Am? 'Aven't 'ad 'am for a *fortnight*. (*Laughs.*)

Lights up to show **Jasmine**, **Ray**, **Smitty** *on the bench with*
Jasmine *and* **Ray** *in pigmasks, as before.*

Smitty   Mr Bravington you would now kill?

Pause. **Ray** *nods.* **Jasmine** *shakes head.*

The lady and gentleman?

Pause. No response.

The lady who sells sweets?

Pause.

Mr and Mrs Mullen?

Jasmine   There will be no violence. There will be no

struggles. There will be no more wars. *We* want *you* to stop
the pigs being taken away from the farm. All we need is
three days.

Ray and **Jasmine** *take off their pigmasks and hang them on the*
stand. They walk away from **Smitty**. *(Note: If for any reason the*
play has to be played with an interval, this is the place to have it.
It's not advisable, though.)

Ray and **Jasmine** *are now themselves again.*

Ray You off then?

Pause.

I mean you're not employed by Mr Bravington, are you?

Pause.

Not employed to help on the farm. (*Helpfully.*) Mr
Bravington has not asked you to help on the farm.

Smitty No.

Ray But you'd like to help. (*Pause.*) If you want to stay
on and help, that's your business. I mean, I can't promise
you any money. Farm labourers don't get very much
anyway, do they? You on Schedule D? PAYE?

Smitty Mrs Mullen used to give me pay.

Ray And she paid your stamps. Insurance stamps. Eighty-
three and fourpence a week – she paid that, did she?
You're going to have to fend for yourself a bit now. Mr
Bravington can't afford – loss leaders. How much did Mrs
Mullen give you a week then?

Smitty Twenty –

Ray *whistles.*

Ray That's a lot of money.

Smitty – Shillings. Sometimes thirty.

Ray One pound ten a week? What a screw.

He slaps **Smitty** *on the back and walks away again.*

You'll be better off in the city, Smitty. Twenty-five pound a week as a labourer. (*Pause.*) Single, are you? Wise. I mean, it's not wise to get married. I mean, it's a mistake. Promise me you won't try it. Supporting a wife, when you're in the city. Kids sopping up your pay, with milk and orange juice. Babyfood. Bawling for fish and chips. Nappies at breakfast. (*Pause.*) You know much about slaughtering? (*Pause.*) I have this idea that Mr Bravington wants the animals dispatched as quickly as possible. I think he wants them out of here, by the day after tomorrow in fact. You must have done some pigs in your time. (*Pause.*) I don't like the sight of blood. Brings me out in a rash. Fur and feathers. Coverings and what's inside. Like dogs. The way they walk with tendons at the back of their legs. (*Confidential.*) She wants to know what I did with the dog. Thinks I had it. (*Working himself up.*) Dig it up, slip it in a graveyard with a little cross saying FIDO. (*Tantrum.*) Women are like that about animals! They can't leave them alone! (*Pause. Quizzical.*) Not English, are you? German. I'm not getting at you mind. It's just not – normal, to have foreigners in the country. Birmingham, Wolverhampton, Leeds – they're full of Micks and Darkies. But in the country . . .

Smitty   I am fond of the country. I am fond of the farm.

Ray   I don't know how you can stand it when the wind changes. Two thousand animals standing up to their bellies in shit waiting for the next hopper of ham sandwiches. I went into one of those hangars and I came out again. I had to. I was sick in the swill bucket. (*Pause.*) So you don't mind slaughtering.

Jasmine *catches hold of the tail end of the conversation and comes forward. Alarmed.*

Jasmine   Mr Bravington didn't say anything about you doing that.

Ray   Shut up.

Jasmine   He just wanted us to stay for the week.

Ray   He changed his mind.

Jasmine   He never told me.

Ray   It was when you were out.

Jasmine   I haven't been out.

Ray   He didn't tell you. That's all.

Jasmine   What about my money?

Ray   What about your money?

Jasmine   I'm going to phone Mr Bravington and find out.

Ray   No you are not.

Jasmine   I am.

Ray (*having lost it*)   Want me to lose my fucking temper?

*Jasmine gets up and thrusts **Ray** out of the way clumsily. He picks up the **Dog** sack and hits her on the face with it hard. She slowly puts her hand to her cheek. Pause.*

Jasmine (*shocked. The first thing she can think of*)   It's all wet. (*Looks at her hand.*) Pig.

*Tension relaxes. She goes and looks in the bag which **Ray** has put down on the table.*

Ray   As I was saying, Mr Bravington rang –

Jasmine (*a voice of icy calm*)   Look what you hit me with. (*She pulls the **Dog** out of the sack. Pause.*)

Ray (*uncomfortably*)   'Sa dog, isn't it?

Jasmine (*lips quivering*)   You hit me with Robby.

Ray (*retreating*)   That's not Robby. He was a fat little doggy. That one's all flat –

*Pause. **Jasmine** looks at **Robby**, heartbroken.*

Jasmine   Robby . . .

Ray (*to **Smitty***)   Found him run over in the road, did

you? (*To* **Jasmine**.) He found him run over in the road.
Now – put it back in the sack.

Jasmine (*advances on* **Ray** *with the sack outstretched*)   You did
it.

Ray   Look, he found him run over in the road. I didn't
have nothing to do with it. Don't come near me.

Jasmine *advances.*

Ray   Put that dog down, or I'll bottle you. It's nothing to
do with me.

Ray *is near the table, with* **Jasmine** *bearing down on him. He
snatches a beer bottle from underneath, and tries to break it on the
table. Fails. He takes* **Jasmine** *and they have a messy scuffle on
and round the table.*

They stop. **Ray** *is panting with excitement.*

Smitty *has a fit. The works. Goosesteps with arms at side, lying on
the floor. Rolls to and fro rigidly. Froths at the mouth.*

Smitty (*screams and grunts*)   Sturmtruppe Kommandant
Truppführer Hinelitzer, und die Jungen, ich meine die
Männer, and der Frontbreite, wir werden diesen Juden
schweine was lehren und ihre Vorhäute in ihre Arshlöcher
Stecken, ihnen zeigen, wie es eigentlich gemacht wird. So
ist's ja richtig ganz prima –

Ray *and* **Jasmine** *are helpless with laughter. They have abandoned
their fight.*

Blackout.

Pause.

The voice of **Mrs Mullen**. *Genteel North Riding.*

Mrs Mullen   Hölderlin . . . (*Pause.*) . . . was a true
romantic poet. He went mad. He fell in love with the wife
of the family he tutored in Bordeaux. He was so young.
(*Pause.*) His novel is about Ancient Greece. Although he
had never been there, it is said that he recreated the
landscape – perfectly. It is about the love of two young

men ... (*Pause.*) ... that was too perfect to last. (*Pause.*)
Somewhere ... (*Pause.*) ... in France, there was a
colonnade of reproductions of the great statues in a garden.
One night, people looked out and saw a person fondling
them. They went out, but he ran away. (*Pause.*) I am sure
it was Hölderlin.

Lights.

Mr Mullen *and* **Mrs Mullen** *in Mullen costume. They have
linked arms. They hold the umbrella above them. They sway from side
to side.*

Roland *toots like a departing steamer. They wave stiffly to the
audience. They drop their hands.*

Mrs Mullen *leans forward to speak.*

Mrs Mullen   We taught the boy all we could. He loved
the open life. He came to the farm, quite late, in 1945.
Roland had been invalided out and was busy with
landgirls. We had terrible trouble with the Americans on
the airfield. Twice they landed Flying Fortresses in the
fields, and damaged the stock. (*Pause.*) We always farmed
pigs, even in the difficult years. We didn't have many
prisoners working on the farm, so they became ... (*A
flashing smile.*) ... quite like friends. It was only natural that
Smitty should stay. He was so young, he can't have been
more than twelve or thirteen when he came to us. (*Pause.
Confidential.*) I think it was terrible, the way Hitler sent them
out to fight so young, at the end. We were very busy in
those early years but I always set aside half an hour –
when I could – to teach him to read. I don't think Roland
ever forgave him for being quite so ... (*Pause.*) ...
German. Roland was never the same after his lobotomy,
became morose and didn't talk very much. One day he
found the boy killing a pig. It was then that we had to
commit him to a mental institution. When he came out a
month later he was at it again. We had to put him in care
for good. (*Pause.*) A Mr Bravington rang up and offered us
a ridiculous price for the farm. I accepted, on Roland's
behalf, and decided to go to Australia for his sake as much

as my own. (*Pause.*) Smitty was educationally severely
subnormal. He had forgotten all his German, and really
learnt very little English, although he spoke it well enough.
(*Pause.*) After we crossed the line, Roland was drunk at
breakfast and said he heard grunts all day.

Roland (*still numb drunk*) Flying fishes . . . (*Pauses. Lyrical.*)
. . . up and down in the water. Thought the
phosphorescence was a herd of swine, following the boat.
(*Pause.*) Fell off the stern. (*Pause. Pleasure.*) Residual lead from
bullets lodged in thorax and cranium, poisoned sharks' fin
soup served up in Hong Kong, leading to war with
Chinese.

Roland *goes and gets the straitjacket and starts to put it on the
unprotesting* **Smitty** *at the back.*

Mrs Mullen Smitty was very sweet. I mean, he was
almost dog-like in his affection. But you can't go on like
that. (*Pause.*) He was ill. (*Pause. Emphatic.*) He wasn't like
other people.

Roland *to* **Smitty** *in a low voice.*

Roland How does a Frenchwoman hold her liquor?
Mmm?

Mrs Mullen I got married in Australia to the vice-
chairman of a soup company. (*Disappointment.*) We were
divorced after six months. (*Bravely.*) I took a small flat in
Melbourne. (*She folds the umbrella as she says the last sentence.*)
The gas cooker exploded.

Roland *and* **Mrs Mullen** *sit each side of* **Smitty** *on the
bench.*

Smitty (*neutrally*) Van Vollenhoven, Rudolf Willem
Kristian de Broek. Born Zorst, near Cologne. Five years
primary school, failed entrance to gymnasium.
Educationally subnormal. One year infantry division
Eastern front. Deserted. Recaptured. Six weeks suicide
squad. Deserted. Came home. Semitic population of Zorst
killed in Dachau, antisemitic by high explosives

manufactured in Essen, Coventry, and Tucson, Arizona.
Lived in Zorst through winter, off roots and people.
Captured by English. (*Tone changes slightly.*) Now I have a
packed lunch which I make myself of Thursday, bread and
Spam. Mr Mullen is very kind and gives me war books.
Mrs Mullen is very kind and gives me poetry. Oh to be in
England now that spring is here. Du Liebe Gott here I am
stinking sweat and hot. Also in the shop Mr Mullen buys
the Adventures of the Incredible Hulk, fighting on the side
of right.

During the following speech, **Roland** *puts a pigmask on* **Smitty**
and pulls his trousers down, then leads him forward to the table.

Mrs Mullen   I think the European tradition of Culture is
– terribly important. I have a Belgian aunt. We could have
retired to France or Portugal, but Roland would have had
difficulties with the language.

Pause. She ignores what is going on with **Roland** *and* **Smitty**.

And is there honey still for tea. (*Pause.*) On Poppy Day, I
always used to take Smitty with me, collecting for the Haig
fund for the disabled.

Roland *bends* **Smitty** *over on the table. Bows over him from
behind. They freeze, looking straight ahead.*

Mrs Mullen   During the war, American officers used to
come to tea. How cute, they used to say. I was very
friendly with one young officer. We shared a love of
Dvorak's New World Symphony. (*She tries to hum a few bars
from the beginning of The Emperor Concerto. Fails.*) Anyway. He
was a terribly sensitive young man, although deeply
patriotic. One night, he broke down and told me he was a
homosexual. Roland couldn't stand him. Roland and I
were never compatible. (*Pause.*) We never had – any
children. (*Pause.*) It was so unfortunate, that Smitty should
turn out so strange. (*Despair.*) We had no alternative, but to
put him in a home.

Blackout.

Bravington, *in the middle of an argument.*

Bravington I know it's an 'ard world. I'm no soft. Feel
my stomach. You may think that's fat. (*Grunts.*) I told yer.
It's like punching a tank turret. (*Pause.*) I were a wrestler in
Blackpool before I were rich, and famous. You got to look
after yourself, because no one's going to do it for you.
Either do it yourself, or bend over, and get your own
membranes stretched. (*Pause.*) My own father taught me
that when I were twelve. Piss off. He said. (*Pause.*) I respect
him for that.

In the dark, **Ray** *and* **Jasmine** *sing the opening bars of Thus
Spake Zarathustra banging their feet on the floor for the drums.*

Lights.

They have the pigmasks on. They are seated each side of **Smitty**
who still has his straitjacket on.

Smitty In the eighth dimension of the metatonic age, to
the star cluster Tactar near Galaxy Aurax, Galactic Knight
Kaarg telepaths his report. (*A strain.*) Great difficulties. (*Back
to normal.*) Galactic Knight Kaarg reports transference out of
Sunny Acres Farm to Sleaford Hospital for the Mentally
Disabled. Severe depression of medium and low cerebral
activity. In ward for permanent residents containing
numerous catatonic cases, four deteriorated schizophrenics,
five cases of premature senility and incontinence, a
paralysed mongol, a manic depressive paralysed from the
waist down by a suicide jump, a 22-year-old male
psychopath who holds conversations with the smile he has
painted on his penis. In the ward also two thirteen-year-old
twins committed indefinitely for the planned death of a
neighbour's infant.

On the right bed eighteen inches away is an Irish labourer
with *delirium tremens* who thinks he is Parnell. On the left
bed eighteen inches away, a human cabbage in the middle
of a brainstorm.

Rudolf Van Vollenhoven, educationally subnormal,
committed indefinitely for repeated random attacks on

animals. The patient is subject to fits and is under heavy
sedation.

Jasmine ⎤ Uppa uppa uppa uppa uppa.
Ray ⎟ Found in bed with Kitty O'Shea. The ruination
⎟ of Ireland and my political career. Threw my
⎦ life away.

Smitty   There are still thousands of them left. They're all
over the country. They're going to take over the world.
We'll be put in slaughter houses. Hung up by a hook
through the Achilles tendon. Gutted. Headless.

Jasmine (*cosily*)   We're only here on a visit. Down there
in the locked wards are the real patients. They feed them
through a hatch with gauntlets. It's a curious sort of
creature. Vicious. Unpredictable. (*Pause.*) Mr and Mrs
Mullen have gone to Australia. You'll never see them
again. There are two other people on the farm. They're
going to sell the pigs to be slaughtered. We don't want
that. We want you to stop them.

Smitty   Mr and Mrs Mullen have not gone away.

Ray (*stifles a laugh*)   They thought you were – off your
head – (*Laughs.*) They rang for someone to take you away.
You'd killed eight pigs.

Smitty   You were going to kill Mr and Mrs Mullen.

Ray   There's no question of that now. They've gone
away. The people you deal with will be strangers. Not like
us. You won't have to do anything to them if they go
away. (*He fiddles with his mask and produces with great apparent
agony a complete set of false teeth from his mouth.*) See! (*Holds them
up. The triumphant conjuror.*) My teeth! (*He snaps them.*) See my
incisors? See my molars? We're omnivorous, like humans.
Good for fruit off trees, rotten apples and acorns. Grubbing
up the earth for trace minerals. (*Pitiful.*) We suffer from
iron shortages too. Also cold and heat, are neurotic when
over-crowded. (*Pause.*) When our heads are boiled, the
cartilage goes to gelatine and the rest makes brawn. Just
like yours. (*Pause.*) The brain is impervious to cold and

heat. Saw a hole in your cranium, stub my fag out on it, and you wouldn't feel a thing.

Puts the teeth in **Smitty***'s cap and puts it on his head. They start to take the strait-jacket off.*

Now we'll help you to get out of here. If you help us. And if you don't help us.

The straitjacket is off. They hang it up.

You won't know it's happening. But in three minutes, we'll eat your brain.

Blackout.

In the dark, **Jasmine** *and* **Bravington**.

Jasmine   I'll tell your fortune.

Bravington   Don't be so soft. Hey hee hee.

Jasmine (sotto voce)   Christ, you got bad breath. (*Pause. Clearly.*) You'll come to a bad end. You'll have four wives.

Bravington   Three down and one to go.

Jasmine   You'll die of cancer. The throat and the genitals are particularly vulnerable.

Bravington   Cock and balls. Aye. Have to look after them. (*Pause.*) I got everything I want. The conversation of friends and the enjoyment of lovely objects. The last touch of a personal valet. I have become a patron of the arts. Large, anonymous donations to the Library Theatre in Manchester, The Liverpool Everyman, and the North Riding and Durham Fund for the Dependants of Crippled Miners. (*Pause. Luxuriously.*) And I 'aven't got bad breath.

Lights.

Ray *and* **Jasmine** *back as themselves.* **Ray** *is standing. So is* **Smitty**.

Smitty   Has Mr Bravington rung?

Pause.

Ray (*hostile*) He has.

Jasmine No, he hasn't. (*Pause.*) When did he ring then?

Ray When you were out.

Jasmine I haven't been out.

Ray Looking for the dog.

Jasmine You were out as well then –

Ray – I came back –

Jasmine You can't have been out for very long. I didn't hear the phone go. Why didn't you look for the dog a bit longer?

Ray It wasn't a very long conversation that we had.

Jasmine Did you ask him?

Ray I did –

Jasmine About Smitty – what did he say?

Pause.

Ray (*to* **Smitty**) Come for your things then?

Jasmine Did he say he could stay?

Ray He did not –

Jasmine You told him all about it and he said no? You told him he had nowhere to go? (*Pause.*) I think that's awful. I think he might have given him a chance. You didn't tell him the full story. (*Bitingly.*) I mean he hasn't got a wife and kids or anything. I bet you made it up out of spite.

Ray *takes* **Jasmine** *and twists her arm in a half-nelson over the offal bucket. Forces her on her hands and knees. Then takes her by the hair.*

Ray Shut your fucking hole or I'll get violent.

Jasmine (*panicking*) No don't do this. Don't. Ouch. I'll do anything. I can do things for you – I'm not an amateur –

(*Screams.*) I'll dress up like Smitty –

Ray *is horrified. He releases and stands back.*

Ray You'll do what?

Jasmine (*gets up and tidies herself*) That's all he wants. All this hard man stuff doesn't mean a thing. He's a bumfucker, a nance. He carries pictures in his wallet of Pricks I Have Known. A man's man. You'd like it with Alsatian dogs and boys with boots on. Why d'you have to break him down first? 'Cos you're a fucking psycho who can only get a hard on when you've scared the other person shitless.

Ray *wants to strangle her but containing himself he picks up a kidney and shoves it down the back of her neck. Strides to the box and sits down facing away.*

Pause.

Jasmine *speaks in a conversational tone.*

Jasmine It's cold. What was it, Smitty, did you see what it was? It wasn't a rat, was it? He *knows* I can't stand rats – (*Pause; then suddenly screams.*) Get it out – (*Jumps up and down. The kidney falls through. She continues.*)

Smitty *picks it up and throws it in the rubbish tray under the table.*

Pause.

Jasmine Oh. It was one of them. Ta. (*Pause.*) He's a walking suppository. (*Screams at* **Ray***'s back.*) Stuff it in! Pull it out! (*She tries to reach the back of the dress with her hand to unzip it.*) Fuck. Look, can you do it.

Smitty *does it and she shoves the sponge into his hand. He makes no attempt to wash her. She leads him to the table.*

Jasmine Here, I'll lie on the table, it'll be easier.

Quite calmly **Smitty** *washes her back.*

Take my advice. Get out now. He gets violent when he's

had his whack. (*Pause.*) That's lovely. (*Pause.*) Doesn't like to think of it. Him and his wife and kids. (*Pause.*) Three more days. Then I'm back to hairdressing. (*Pause.*) I think I'll move down to London.

Smitty Why are you staying?

Jasmine I bin paid. Half before and half after. It wasn't my idea. I mean the way Ray feels about it we'd all be much safer if he had a nice clean pig. (*Pause.*) But he really fancies himself. That thing with the bottle – he saw that on the telly once.

Smitty You're staying.

Jasmine I'll have to. I mean, I'm a freelance. I'm not his wife.

Smitty You are not his wife?

Jasmine No! I'm on the game ... (*Pause.*) Mr Bravington pays for me to be here to keep him happy. You didn't know that? (*Pause.*) Are you going now? He'll calm down in a bit. I wouldn't mind having somebody else around. I don't mind all that stuff with raspberry jam and that, but what if he turned? (*Pause.*) I get scared in the dark too. Rats and things. I can't think why people live in the country. Ray doesn't mind it. He doesn't mind where he is. He spends half his time inside. (*Anecdotal.*) The last time he was sent down the judge said he was an 'incorrigible ruffian'. Ray said he farted then and the judge added two years to his sentence. (*Laughs.*) Two years for farting! (*Subdued.*) And five for GBH. He just decided one day that he was going to be a hard man. (*Pause.*) If you hear me yelling in the night, rush in and shove a broomstick up his arse. That'll divide his loyalties. (*Pause.*) The Mullens all right to you, were they? I mean they didn't tie you to the wall and make you perform with teddy bears or anything?

Smitty Mrs Mullen was kind to me. Mr Mullen asked me once, but I said no.

Jasmine And you got up the lady of the house?

Smitty *shakes head.*

Jasmine   Nothing? No spin-off from thirty bob a week
and the use of the potting shed? Never mind. I started with
a rotten bloody lot. Business was two pounds reduced to
thirty bob. But you don't have to stop at that. With a bit
of effort, you can make yourself independent.

Pause. The washing has finished.

You off then?

Smitty *picks up the sack and holds it out to* **Jasmine**.

Jasmine   It's all right. You go and see your friends in
Sleaford. I'll kick him in the balls, or something.

Smitty   This your dog?

Jasmine   Robby in the sack? Yeah.

Smitty   I killed it. (*Pause.*) With a fork.

Jasmine *takes the sack and ferrets in it.*

Jasmine   Ray –

Ray *comes back from the box. Pause.*

Ray   That's your dog.

Jasmine   Smitty says he killed it.

Ray   You did what with it?

Smitty   It was asking for chocolates.

Jasmine   Hang on a bit. (*Pause.*) It's not Robby.

Ray   So it's not your dog. I told you.

Jasmine   Robby was plump.

Ray   So it's not your dog.

Jasmine   No – Robby had a different expression . . .
(*Pause.*) He may be still alive. Lost . . . Ray, do you think
you could phone the police?

Ray *is shocked.*

Ray   Could I? Ring the men in blue? You must be off your head girl.

Jasmine   We haven't done anything wrong –

Ray (*definitively*)   I'm wanted.

Jasmine (*pleading*)   Not really –

Ray   What do you know about it?

Jasmine   Ray –

Ray   I'm hungry. (*Goes and sits on the table, facing audience.*)

Jasmine   There are some kidneys – Ray –

Ray (*shouts*)   I can't stand fucking kidneys!

Jasmine *puts the* **Dog** *back in the sack. Lull.* **Ray** *picks his nose, humming 'Strangers in the Night'.*

Behind them, ignored, **Smitty** *goes and loads the gun at the box. He closes the breech.*

Ray (*jocular, facing away*)   So Smitty killed the little dog, did he? Perhaps Smitty would like to go out and do in a pig, for supper. (*Pause.*) My uncle was a master butcher. A craftsman with the poleaxe. Used to drop it – right here. (*Touches the back of his neck with his hand quickly.*)

Blackout.

In the dark.

But it's dicy with pigs. They got so much fat on them.

The gun fires twice in the dark. A brief wordless scuffle in between.

Smitty *lights a portable gas ring which he takes out of the box on the table. By this light, and the spot at barest minimum, he cuts out the kidneys of the other two actors who are lying in the shadow of the table.*

He puts butter in the pan and drops a kidney in, when the smell of cooking has spread out from the stage he turns the gas fire off and the actors exit.

Bravington (*in the dark*)   There's a limit to the amount of pork you can take. But there's always the leather industry, which leads into clothes and shoes, luxury goods, battery poulterers buy the bone for chicken meal, gelatine gives you a lead into the sweet industry. With the fat and the chicken you got a strong arm into catering. Undercut someone else's lard, make good and you're into frozen foods which is mostly packaging. And you know what goes inside the packages. Pork. Ham. Bacon. Tripe. Trotters in jelly. Black pudding and freeze-dried giblets, reintroduced at the top of the range for fancy prices.

Blowjob

Foreword

Looking back, I would say the reason I was drawn to Snoo's plays was because, at a time in the 1970s when everyone else appeared to be intensely serious-minded, here was a dramatist who achieved his effects by making great jokes. I'm not sure anyone quite knew what to do with them, because the spirit of the day veered towards denunciation and excoriation, and Snoo veered towards making you laugh.

The humour, of course, was mordant and it was highly original. Snoo's brain hummed with ideas. You would call him fertile, rather than austere. The problem for the director was that if you asked Snoo to re-write he tended to give you twice as much as you had already. The quality was fine. It was just the quantity which could be overwhelming. On his manuscripts, bubbles in green ink would snake down the sides of the pages, until finally they over-covered the original text. Rewrites, usually introduced to make things simpler, quite often made them more complicated.

Blowjob was, if you like, a classic fringe play. When the fire was lit in the safe, then less hardy members of the audience dived for the exit. We were well used to watching them leave. In those days, they were always leaving, and for all sorts of reasons. Fear of fire was as good as any. We did *Blowjob* in the rough-and-ready manner of the day, making the production look as scrappy and improvised as possible, so that in our eyes it looked 'real'.

Only with *The Pleasure Principle* did we find a more accomplished style. There was lovely comic playing from Dinsdale Landen and Julie Covington, and I set out to mediate between the wildness of Snoo's imagination and what a regular Royal Court audience expected from an evening in the theatre. The play was a huge success, but I know Snoo felt that my approach – asking for the satisfactions of plot and character – had somehow watered him down. Naturally, I didn't think of the process as compromise. I thought of it as a means of opening him up. But, for one reason or another, that's where the experiment ended for both of us. I was reading it the other day and the play's blissful humour still makes me laugh, in retrospect.

David Hare, London, 1999

Blowjob was first performed at the Edinburgh Festival in 1971, with the following cast:

Dave	Miles Reitherman
Mo	Dennis Lawson
Cottrell	Constantin de Goguel
McVittie	Constantin de Goguel
Moira	Margot Lester

Directed by Dusty Hughes

Act One

Dave *and* **Mo** *are sitting round a table which overflows with bottles of beer and emptied cans.*

They are dressed as skinheads. Braces, short hair, boots.

On the other side of the table, **McVittie**, *facing them. A much older man, coming on for forty, with a tweedy suit and a poor toupee. They are all slightly drunk,* **Mo** *the younger skinhead more so than anyone.*

Suddenly **Dave** *gets up and leaves the stage.*

McVittie *seizes the opportunity to chat up* **Mo**.

McVittie It's curious, isn't it, this tradition of working men's clubs in the North. I find –

Mo (*sloppy belligerency*) Some mornings I wake up and I think life's pretty cruel. Nobody got their fucking thumb on the scale for me. If I had an E-type and lots of birds it would be all right. (*Pause.*) Dave and I went on this Spanish holiday. For a laugh. He was the one pulled all the birds. Even the ones who couldn't speak much English. (*Vicious.*) If they had they'd a found out how thick he was. I was at school with him. (*Pause.*) You know. (*Pause.*) We ... used to spend time passing water in the inkwells.

Looks intensely at **McVittie** *to gauge the effect of this.* **McVittie** *shifts minutely.*

That was about the only thing that caught on there. We got thrown out at the same time for wanking in the back row. It was a boring lesson, one for slow readers or something and we were ... (*Pause.*) ... wanking to pass the time. (*Bitter.*) It had to be me that was caught. (*Righteous.*) We weren't wanking each other or anything disgusting like that. So I left and did this and that.
Then my old man got drunk and disorderly for the forty-second time and did a gas-meter in Woolwich. He made

such a noise that they sent six coppers round and he . . .
(*Pause.*) . . . bit several of them in the truncheon. Face was
right out to here. (*Holds hands in front of face.*) Eyes like
button holes. I don't mind.
I mean but it doesn't exactly give you a flying start as a
Greek ship owner, does it. They used to come round every
time someone stole a fucking banana from the wogshop. So
you get used to it. Being a villain. I mean we're meant to
be up here on a job – we dress as a bird and his bloke –
less suspicious – Dave's idea – but if he gets much more
pissed he'll pass out and we'll go back to London – we had
another plan to do a bank in Peterborough –

McVittie (*stopping the flow*)   – I work as a security
policeman. (*Pause.*) For the other side as it were. (*Sweetly.*)
Now I'm like you, I like to think of myself as a humane
person –

Mo   I don't do that!

McVittie   – I'm sure you do – I wouldn't hurt a fly . . .
I've got a dog which I have to take round with me in the
van – it gives me asthma because I'm allergic to its fur and
if I let it off the lead it's uncontrollably savage . . . but I
don't want that, and you don't want that – it's our *lives*
that are wrong . . .

He takes **Mo**'s *hand who slowly withdraws it.*

What are you doing now?

Mo (*instantly suspicious*)   You said you were going on duty
in a couple of hours.

McVittie (*changing tack*)   No, I don't mean . . . I mean . . .
what's your *job*?

Mo (*intransigent*)   I'm a fucking skinhead, aren't I?

McVittie   No – how do you earn your living?

Pause.

Mo   Er . . . 'prentice catering supervisor . . .

McVittie You have hobbies . . . in your spare time?

Mo Yeah, I do drag acts.

Dave *re-enters with a crate of beer. He stands by the table with it. They look at him.*

McVittie David . . . you look a wee bit pasty.

Dave I'm fine. (*A proof of rude health.*) I been sick twice. Clear the table.

He slides the crate onto the table which sends the bottles and cans onto the floor.

McVittie *goes down on hands and knees and starts to pick them up.*

Dave *sits down with* **Mo**.

Mo (*secretly to* **Dave**) He's a poof.

They both laugh.

McVittie (*from the floor*) It's curious, isn't it, this tradition of working men's clubs in the North. I find them a very useful entertainment. I've got to go on duty in a few minutes – they fill in the time very nicely. If I had to rely on ordinary pubs, they'd all be closed now.
Except for the illegal ones of course.

He sits at the table again. **Dave** *opens a bottle of beer for* **Mo**, *and one for himself. He ignores* **McVittie** *and winks at* **Mo**.

Dave What's the time?

Mo Half past twelve.

Dave Time you was getting ready.

Mo All right I'll just nip off.

Dave (*mock expansive*) No! No – stay here. He's changing for his drag act you see. I mean, the ladies or the gents, whichever one he goes in he comes out wrong . . .

Mo I don't think I'm doing it.

Kicks **Dave** *under the table. Nods at* **McVittie**.

Dave What's that?

Mo I said I don't feel well. I don't feel like doing my act tonight.

Dave Why's that?

Mo I just don't want to do it. – Dave – I told him something I shouldn't – I don't feel right for it –

Dave We didn't come up all this way for nothing – so get better. (*Turns to* **McVittie**.) If he doesn't get better I'll just split his nostril.

Mo There's a very good reason why I can't do it Dave. (*Hysterical.*) But I can't tell you here. I mean it's not that I don't want to do it, it's just that it's the wrong time to do it, we should come up and do it next weekend.

Dave It'll be too late.

Mo Dave I want to have a little word with you outside. I said something about the job by mistake –

Dave (*shouts*) Well I'm not leaving my crate! (*Slaps it. Looks briefly at* **McVittie**.) Sorry, er, wassyour name, did you want a drink.

McVittie Thank you kindly.

Dave *gives him an unopened bottle and stands up. Walks so that* **Mo** *is between him and the crate.*

Dave (*producing knife*) I think I'm going to practise a bit of knife-throwing at the crate.

Mo (*seeing the danger*) Look no – Dave – it's all right – I'll get dressed . . .

Dave *sits down quick as a flash. Plays with the knife carelessly.* **Mo** *starts to change and tries to make it unobtrusive by remaining seated.*

An unpleasant pause till he has half his costume on. **Dave** *picks out a matchstick from the ashtray and does out his ears with it.*

Dave (*singing* sotto voce)   Are you going . . . to San
Francisco . . . be sure to wear . . . flowers in your hair.

Another long pause.

Ah well . . . (*To* **Mo**.) All right there?

Mo *is putting on his stockings. Renewed embarrassment.* **McVittie**
plays with his unopened bottle.

McVittie   Ah well . . . (*Pawky irony.*) Four months to Burns
Night . . .

Dave   Oh yes?

McVittie   I was born in Aberdeen, then my family
moved to Glasgow, then Inverkeithing, then Jedburgh . . .

Mo   Where's the fucking wig? (*Searches in box.*)

Dave   Underneath.

McVittie   Does Maurice get much work in this line?

Dave   He's learning.

McVittie   Has he been an artiste for very long?

Dave   'Ere, what's the time Mo?

Mo *is making up.* **Dave** *pulls his wrist over and looks at it.*

Mo   Leave off.

McVittie   I think I'll be popping off now. It's been
pleasant talking to you boys.

Mo   It's no good, Dave, I can't find it.

McVittie   I hope to catch up with your act sometime,
Maurice.

Dave   We'll have to go soon.

McVittie *is standing.*

Dave   You haven't drunk your beer.

McVittie   Er, no.

Dave   Something wrong with it?

McVittie   Oh no . . .

Dave (*standing*)   Would you like perhaps two Babychams in a pint glass with a cherry?

McVittie (*cannot ignore this, offended*)   Goodnight to both of you. (*Turns to go.*)

Dave   Just one moment.

McVittie *stops.* **Dave** *goes up close and takes* **McVittie**'s *wig off from the temple, revealing a mostly bald skull. Holds it out backwards to* **Mo**.

Dave   Mo – This one do?

Mo *looks up briefly then down again, deciding to stay out of it.*

Dave   Sorry about that. (*hands it back to* **McVittie** *with an ingenuous smile.*)

McVittie (*flatly, with great dignity*)   It's just my foolish pride.

As he says this, the lights go down to red and green on **Mo** *finishing changing into drag. The line is a cue for the music which is the song,* 'Mr Blowjob' © *by Nick and Tony Bicat.*

During the song, the table is struck.

> Blew into town
> Ugly woman
> Breathing bad breath sign
> Dropping capsules in her gravy
> Drinking sour wine
> Mr Blowjob how she suffers
> Suffers for the sins of man
> She got boils
> She got scabies
> But she does the best a man can
>
> Ma ma
> Marmalady
> Ma ma
> Marmalady

She's my lady marmalade

Blew into town
Evil preacher
Lifts his black dress high
Wears mascara on his eyebrow
Smiles as I go by
Mr Blowjob how she suffers
Suffers for the sins of man
She got boils
She got ague
But she does the best a man can.

Chorus.

Blew into town
Ugly ugly
Blew into town
Ugly ugly

Etc. and fade.

The stage is divided into two areas. One is a builder's yard, the other is the interior of a house abutting the yard.

They are divided by the lighting.

Neither of them can be seen yet.

In front of them both, **Dave** *changes into a dark suit, white shirt open at the neck, and takes* **Mo***'s arm. They look now like a young working-class couple out for the evening.* **Mo** *is wearing gloves.*

Dave   You're a bit of all right

Mo (*falling into the part*)   You won't take no for an answer.

Dave   Come along. Terrible thing for a girl to be late.

Dave *puts his arm round* **Mo***'s shoulder.* **Mo** *brushes him off.* **Dave** *does it again.*

Dave   Pick up your bag.

Mo *picks up a large bag full of tools.* **Dave** *exits and* **Mo** *follows him off slightly unsteady on high heels.*

Blackout. Pause.

Moira's Voice   It's very much farther from the ground than she thought. She's got vertigo. You'll have to help her down –

Pause.

I'm not going back to the old job – posting shit through letterboxes ... We've all got this straitjacket of conformity on us. I mean it cramps our potential. Cramps everyone's *style . . .*

The lights go up on the stage right area, which is inside **Leonard Cottrell***'s house. A house underneath a railway arch. Very shabby. In the background a bath up against the back wall. The foreground littered with the rubbish of an old recluse.*

In mid-foreground, **Dave** *and* **Mo** *working on a safe which is turned away from the audience.* **Dave** *is fiddling with it.* **Mo** *has a cloth roll of tools which he passes to* **Dave** *like a surgeon's assistant.*

Dave   Pliers.

Mo *passes him the pliers.*

Dave   Couple of hairpins.

Mo *takes them out of his wig and passes them over. Pause.*

Dave   Rat's tail. (*Pause.*) Rat's tail *file.*

Mo *hands him a rat's tail file.*

Mo   Sorry.

Dave   Watchmaker's number three.

Mo *hands him a small screwdriver.*
Pause. **Dave** *fiddles.*

Dave   What plug's the Black and Decker got?

Mo   Square. (*Pause.*) Shit. Black shit and corruption.

Dave (*as if to a child*)   That's no good here – all the plugs are five amps round.

Mo That's why I said! I know! I looked!

Dave (*a put down*) Good. (*Goes back to work.*)

Mo There's no number three. I give you a number two.

Dave Where's little old Mr Cottrell gone?

Mo I put him in the back room. (*Stands and kicks the safe with an attempt at casual authority.*) I think we're going to have to take this one back with us.

Dave Good. (*Pause.*) I hope you didn't bump about with him too much. (*Pause.*) We don't want the neighbours in. (*Pause.*) You cleaned up in here?

Mo Yeh.

Dave (*picks up hammer, covered in blood and hair at the end*) You said you cleaned up in here. Can you give the hammer a wipe.

Mo Yeh all right.

The light dies on them.

Sound cue of goods train going slowly overhead. The sound fades.

Light spot on **Cottrell**. *He is lying in the bath. He slowly comes up above the rim to be visible. All that can be seen of him is a head. The rest is a pile of rags, in the bath.*

This will enable the **Cottrell** *actor to remain in the* **McVittie** *uniform and double as* **McVittie**.

He wears a blood-stained handkerchief on his head tied at the four corners. His mouth is very red. He has a ludicrously pert and alert expression. He darts his eyes from side to side. He talks like an old queen, at great speed.

Cottrell Come on, train. (*Suppressed laugh.*) Rastus at the station – come away from the side of that platform or the train'll suck you off – come on, train. (*Laughs swiftly.*)

Of course the really *lovely* part about living in Birkenhead is ... (*Sing-song.*) You're *so near* the *sea* ... The bays. The boys. The boys in the bay. Swimming and fishing and swimming like fishes. I love my little room underneath the arches. (*Sings.*)

Underneath the arches ... (*Stops.*)

I wouldn't know where to go if ... Bamber Obridge used to say about the boys in the bay, 'If you can't join them, beat them.' (*Laughs.*) Bamber was a conchie. People used to send him white feathers almost every week. Bamber's brother was very badly shell-shocked. He's still alive. He stays in the back room listening to Strauss and Wagner. (*Laughs.*) Bamber died from liver trouble. He spoke French extremely well. He had a sister too. He last saw her in 1933 when she was walking out with one of Mosley's Blackshirts. All five foot of him. (*Laughs.*) So much for politics.

The trains are crossing the bridge again slowly. Sound effect.

That's cars. Cars for export. Wolseleys and Rileys from Cowley, er, Fords, some from Dagenham but mostly from the Midlands, and Hillman Imps from depressed industrial areas of Scotland. On the left-hand side of the house, that'd be going south, Chevrolet, Pontiac, Volvo, corn oil ... They park on the bridge sometimes and you can hear their engines revving ... (*Lyrical.*) ... up and down (*Imitates the sound, tongue wagging in hollow mouth.*) Come on train. (*Pause.*) I do read the newspapers. I keep up to date. Up to the minute. There's the Mersey tunnel and that mole they used to dig it, wriggling and wriggling through the clay to get to the other side. And when it gets there, it'll only have to turn round and come back. (*Cheeps through his teeth to an imaginary cat.*) What do you want? Leonard hasn't got any milk. Leonard hasn't got anything for you ... I'm relatively wealthy but I live a very modest life. (*Pause.*) I invented cat's-eyes. Simple – self-cleaning reflectors. I've saved millions of lives. The last time I was out in it, the countryside was full of them.

I have four colour televisions. I don't hold with curtains or carpets. No ornamentation. Just my savings and a small picture. The savings are for the cat when I pass on –

(*Pause.*) off ... and the picture is a photograph taken in 1904. Underneath is the title, 'Our Visit to London'. It's of myself and a couple of friends. We bicycled up to London from Suffolk. (*Awed.*) In those days, you could get supper, a bed for the night and a girl if you wanted, breakfast, the run of the orchard afterwards and fill your pockets with apples, for two and sixpence. (*Pause.*) Nowadays, I don't do so much. If it weren't for the televisions, I think I'd sleep ... (*Close to tears.*) And from what I hear, they seem to have built over the orchard – (*Starts to speak very quickly.*) And another thing – a small – minute – contact print, half-frame snapshot slightly blurred of myself and a friend, summer, New Brighton, about the same time. But he was called away to South America, unknown to me, sailed from Liverpool – in many ways I have found it difficult to live anywhere except where his feet last –

The light goes off and he stops speaking.

The light goes up on the builder's yard section of the stage. Sand, planks, scaffolding. On top of the scaffolding **Moira** *is seated looking down at* **McVittie**.

McVittie *is wandering around, embarrassed. He carries a walkie-talkie. He coughs meaningfully. He shoots his cuffs. He looks at his watch. Blows his nose.*

Long pause.

McVittie ⎱ Would you mind telling me –
Moira ⎰ It's a terrible thing. (*Pause.*) It's a terrible thing for a girl to be a wall. It makes you so tall.

McVittie (*helpful*)   D'you want to come down?

Moira (*shakes head violently, eyes shut. Derisive laugh*)   You must be joking. You couldn't possibly reach up and – no, *really*. I'll have to stay up here until some real help comes.

McVittie   You know – this yard – they've got dogs in it. Security.

Moira   That's all right. I like dogs.

McVittie Yes but they won't like you.

Moira They can't reach. It's too far down. (*Pause.*) Do you believe in reincarnation?

McVittie *laughs in a confused way.*

Moira I do. I had a long talk about it with a petrol pump attendant the other day. Do you know, his skin was brown and pink in blotches, like a dog? I'm certain we all come back one way or the other. D'you think Jesus believed in linear time? I mean, d'you really think he spent three days in hell?
Sartre thinks hell is ourselves.
I made a list of the diseases Jesus suffered from.
Depersonalisation, derealisation, autism, nihilistic delusions, delusions of persecution, and omnipotence, auditory hallucinations and end of the world fantasies.
He's a classic, well-documented case of psychotic behaviour. I suppose you still think I'm sick.

McVittie I think Jesus was pretty sick!

Moira That's very interesting. (*Flatly.*) Do you like me?

McVittie I'd like you a lot better if you got down and out of the yard like a good wee girl.

Moira That's grammatically manipulative. That was my critical self speaking. My negative self wants to comply but I won't let it. (*Wistfully.*) My child image . . .

McVittie Well, would all of you like to come to some sort of agreement?

Moira No. (*Pause.*) That's why she's *on* the wall. The wall she sat on so that all the people could say –
'Look! She's sitting on the – (*Pause.*) Fence. Her mind's sitting on the fence.' And they'd feel sorry for her. An outward and visible sign. Of an – inside.

McVittie Look, I've got an eight stone Alsatian in the van. I'll lead him up the steps and he'll make your mind up for you if you like.

Moira   I thought they were trained to hold, not to chase.

McVittie   Look, the best thing is, I call the police.

No response from **Moira**. **McVittie** *gets the aerial on his walkie-talkie up and switches it on. It is important that a real walkie-talkie is used.*

Voice W/T   ... And the man said, ding fucking dong.

Laughter on W/T. Several people.

McVittie (*annoyed*)   Hello. 429. Hello.

Voice W/T (*oblivious*)   Doris is blushing –

Doris' Voice W/T (*excited garble*)   Oh no I'm not –

Voice W/T   Doris ... have you heard the one about Nick the Greek?

McVittie   429 Graham McVittie calling from Bevan's Yard. Hello. 429 calling, McVittie, Bevan's yard. Request police assistance.

Another Voice W/T   Oh God, it's the queen of the arsehole bandits ...

McVittie (*distressed*)   Er ...

1st Voice W/T (*overfriendly*)   Graham! Me old mate, how are you?

McVittie   I'm fine. Request –

Moira *suddenly gets down and watches him.*

1st Voice W/T   You're a bit early aren't you? How's Rover?

McVittie   Rover's fine –

1st Voice W/T   Let him say a little word. Just a little woof.

2nd Voice W/T   Ask him if –

1st Voice W/T   Here give me the mike. The story of Nick the Greek, broadcast on wonderful Radio One worker's playtime, from Birkenhead.

2nd Voice W/T (*great speed*)   A man came in from work
and found his wife in bed with a fella so he pops down
under the bed while the two of them are looking at him.
'Ere says the wife, what yer doing, and the man says, I'm
looking for that poor bugger's white stick and his dog –

1st Voice W/T   The story of Nick the Greek. Was the
cook on a boat. A sailor took a job on this boat, they said,
you know if you ever fancy a lay, try Nick the Greek. And
the man said, I don't want it with a bloke. Six months at
sea, he was really horny, going round with a boner all day.
One day he swallowed his pride, went below to the galley
and asked for Nick the Greek.
There was this cook, a huge fat greasy bloke with big
nostrils.

– Are you Nick the Greek?
– I am Nick the Greek.
– Forty drachmas?
– Yeah, forty drachmas. Put it right there.

Nick the Greek taps his nostril. This fellow thought, Christ,
but you know, six months at sea. So, he whipped it out
and slipped it in.

It was all right. Nothing special. But all right. He wanted it
so badly still that he paid another forty drachmas for the
other nostril. They got talking afterwards. Nick the Greek
said.

– You haven't got clap have you?
– No.
– Syphilis? Cystitis? Gonorrhoea?
– No no no said the man.

What you got to do Graham is place your right forefinger
on your right nostril. Now sniff.

McVittie *does this. Long pause. Muffled titter from W/T.*

Now put your left forefinger on your left nostril. Now sniff.
(*Pause.*) That's a really good joke now isn't it? Don't it

make you laugh? What was that you said about assistance?

McVittie (*sourly*) The panic's over.

He switches off and puts the radio back in the breast coat of his uniform.

Moira *has been listening intently. They face each other.*

Moira I heard that. (*Pause.*) Do you know the one about the queer who went to the front of a bus queue and barged in front of someone and they said, get out of here or I'll shove this umbrella up your arse, and the queer didn't move and they did and the queer said, lovely, now open it out.

A man in a pub told me that, he was drunk and trying to pick me up. He had a fat girl from Bradford with him who was writing all the jokes down.

Pause.

McVittie Are you going to leave the yard now?

Moira Mao Tse-tung says, that in two thousand years we're all going to look a bit stupid. (*Simply.*) Yes.

Blackout

From **Cottrell**'s *half of the stage* **Dave** *lights a blowlamp near the safe. The* **Cottrell** *actor is getting ready.*

Dave The lugs. I skewed the lugs. They're made out of soft stuff, white metal in these cheap old safes. They use it for bearings now. It's easy to machine. Now what I'm going to do now that the numerals have jammed ...
(*Pumps up blowlamp so it roars and plays it on a lemonade bottle held in other hand.*) The mechanism's got this thick cast-iron collar round the outside for protection. Very strong, very brittle. I apply heat to one side only.
(*He is demonstrating with the bottle.*)

It breaks.

The bottle breaks. **Dave** *turns the blowlamp off.*

Mo   When you hit him −

Cottrell (*from the dark*)   Oh . . . (*Shocked by grisly ecstacy.*)
You boys . . . you boys . . . don't just turn me over and let
me be . . . Don't . . . oh, tell me, what it is you're doing to
me . . . I must know . . .

Dave (*shouts in the dark*)   I don't think we got any message
for the elderly and infirm, Mr Cottrell, but if you really
want to know, it's a claw hammer the other way round . . .

Spot on **Cottrell** *in the bath.*

Cottrell (*assertive*)   Oh, life, life. The story of Jean-Paul the
French gigolo.

A gigolo always used to ask his mistresses for a scout's
penknife in addition to payment. He stored these knives in
the bottom of a chest of drawers. Things for opening
bottles, taking the stones out of horses' hooves . . .
One mistress he made love to regularly, she got used to the
request and even brought him the knife beforehand one
day.
He was busy when she came in

  − Shall I put it in the bottom drawer for you dear?
  − Oh, if you would, kindly.

She opened the drawer, to find it full of penknives.

  − What on earth do you want *these* for?
  − Ah, said the gigolo. When I am old, and not able to
  work any longer, what wouldn't a little boy do for one
  of these?

(*A chill gravity*) Quand je serais vieillard . . .

Blackout.

Moira (*in the dark*)   They have this hospital for beautiful
people, beautiful people who have personality problems. In
ordinary situations they're particularly vulnerable to
personality disintegration because other mentally unstable,
unsuitable people tend to fall in love with them.

Lights in the **Cottrell** *house area.* **Dave** *and* **Mo** *are watching* **Cottrell** *in the bath.*

Dave He's watching you Mo. (*Pause.*) Mr Cottrell. Mr Cottrell.

No response.

We can't get into your safe, Mr Cottrell, we don't know the number . . .

Mo (*indignant at this* volte face) Well after all you done to it!

Dave Hush. (*Pause. Leans over* **Cottrell**.) Mr Cottrell. Can you hear me? Are you there, Mr Cottrell?

Cottrell *dribbles from the mouth and* **Dave** *wipes it away with his sleeve.*

Dave Mo, walk around in front of him. (*Looks carefully at* **Cottrell**) His eyes are following you . . .

Mo *does a careless mannequin turn, hand on hip.*

Cottrell Heyuuurn . . .

Dave (*delighted*) Whey-hey! Now we know you're alive, Mr Cottrell! When we got the safe open, we'll send for an ambulance. But until then we're going to be here.

Mo *is walking up and down rather faster in front of him.*

Dave What I want you to do is to say yes, or grunt as best you able, when I say the first digit right. Right? Now, keep the figures clear in your mind.

One – two – three – four – five – six – seven

This is the cue for the music.*

The lights go to red and green as before.

Mo *picks up speed in front of* **Cottrell** *and does a strip to the audience.*

The false boobs and the wig taken off on the final chord. A bow to the audience, then blackout.

*(A note on the music. The Portable production, which

David Hare directed, used 'The night they raided Minsky's', which is admirable for strippers but has a mainstream luxurious quality which is rather too richly furnished for Cottrell's essentially stingey imagination. It should be as ersatz as 'I'd like to teach the world to sing'.)

Act Two

Cottrell's *half of the stage lit.* **Dave** *and* **Mo** *are leaning on the safe.* **Mo** *is dressed again.*

Tableau.

Cottrell *has disappeared into the bath again.* **Dave** *is worried for the first time.*

Dave Mo, I shouldn't have used the blowlamp. It's fused some of the numerals together. (*Pause.*) But he didn't say anything, did he?

Mo *shakes his head.*

Dave Look – I saw this acetylene torch in the yard – the cylinders are padlocked so's you can't take it away. I know all about them because I worked in a garage. The hottest part is just above the blue flame. When you turn it on, heats up the metal so when the flame blows on it the bit you want to cut just burns away. Disappears. (*Pulls at safe.*) Come on.

Mo It's a bit heavy, innit?

Dave You can help me down with it.

They both leave the safe and go and stare in the bath tub.

Dave *leans on the end and takes a screwdriver out, and teases something in the tub with an abstracted concentration.*

A strong brief irregular drumming from inside. They both step back quickly. **Dave** *wipes the screwdriver on his trousers and inhales through pursed lips.*

Dave Look, go out and see if there's anyone in the yard.

Mo Why don't you?

Dave There's only one thing they'll pick you up for.

Mo You didn't have to hit him.

Dave Now what's that got to do with it?

Mo A lot if I'm accomplice to third degree.

Dave As far as anyone knows, it's not you.

Mo (*snapping false boobs*) This lot stand up under a search?

Dave It won't get that far.

Mo You're a fucking booby. (*He kicks the safe impotently.*) How many times you hit him?

Dave All right, I went a bit wild.

Mo (*close to hysteria, points*) They're coming through the top of his head!

Dave (*confident*) No, they are not! (*Peers in the bath.*)

Mo You're not doing it for the money. You enjoy it.

Dave It's the money you stupid cunt. I'll only do a job if the money's right.

Mo Then why aren't you touting for abortions at Heathrow – you could pull in two hundred a week.

Dave I'd still have to get up in the morning – drive down the M4. (*Suddenly an access of humour.*) I think Mr Cottrell's still quite lively – pull him out of the bath and tickle his arse with a feather.

Mo Dave – when he went down his eyes rolled around and he shook.

Dave Sounds like the black and white minstrels.

Mo Don't you be so fucking funny either.

They face each other.

Dave, I know he's dead, honest. I worked in an abattoir, a slaughterhouse and they had a thing like an eggwhisk and they put it in and turned it round – I just think we ought to leave –

Dave Are you frightened?

Mo (*lying*) No, I am not frightened.

Dave Well, neither am I.

Mo   I still think we ought to leave.

Dave   And why's that?

Mo   You'll get thirty years!

Dave   Two more ways. I got two more ways to break the safe. It's just not sensible to leave now, seeing we come so far. I mean just because you feel like going a bit yellow for five minutes . . .

Mo (*pointing to bath*)   He's dead!

Dave   No he isn't. He's thinking. My God, what an arse – (*Pinches* **Mo***'s arse.*) That's what he's thinking.

Blackout. In the dark, **McVittie** *talks into the W/T.*

McVittie   McVittie. 429 Frank McVittie Central Securities at Bevan's yard, Quay Street, Rockferry, Birkenhead. I have no incident to report. The shutters are secured out of reach. I have tried the doors manually and made an inspection of the yard. I shall drive to the Tranmere Rovers football ground and make a pedestrian inspection of the Bebington Building precincts with Rufus.
With the dog. The next report will be at 2.45 precisely. I conclude this report at 1.59.45 seconds.

Lights on in the yard section. **Moira** *is still up on the scaffolding. She is staring down intently at* **McVittie** *who is primly lowering the aerial on his W/T.*

Moira   I went down south. To be an au pair. I went to a teacher's training college. I got pregnant. I didn't like the people. Where's your dog?

McVittie   Oh . . . (*Stares at her hopelessly. Gets a packet of St Moritz out, takes the cellophane off and puts them away again.*)

Moira   I came back. (*Simply.*) I'm always coming back. I've got this third eye. (*Fingers forehead.*) You see, I see this big ratcatcher in front of me.

McVittie (*dully*)   A ratcatcher. Oh aye.

Moira   In front of me. With his hands open. And he's got a dog.

McVittie (*spirited attempt at irony*)   A dog.

Moira   It's a ratcatcher's dog with three legs and a bristly back. On a chain. A lavatory chain. Yeah, a shithouse chain and he's coming to get me – (*Screams briefly and turns her head to one side. Pause.*)

McVittie   Indeed.

Moira   I don't know how it strikes you but sometimes I feel so terribly *old*. (*She howls it. Pause. Then hurried, apologetic*) I think, if you don't mind, I'll have a conversation with my friend. (*She blows her nose.*) You got a cold coming on. (*Changes.*)

  – Yes –
  – What you crying like that for –
  – Was I crying I didn't know I was crying –
  – Yes you were crying –

(*Suddenly escalates.*) What do you fucking know about it? Six months after I failed my 11-plus I got bunked up! Sitting around all day with your arse in a fucking bucket of cream – (*Pause. Flatly.*) She says she's only talking because you won't join in. She'd be quite happy to remain silent.

McVittie (*shifting hopelessly*)   Look –

Moira   The problem will appear rather different to you. I'm sorry to trouble you with it in many ways, but there have been periods of my life when I have *lost* several days. They're dead to me.
Also, sometimes, in the mornings, around nine o'clock I'm worried about death. (*Breathless* diminuendo.) Sometimes I think I could give it the red carpet treatment and sometimes it's of no use at all. My father's a coal merchant but he's not dirty.

McVittie (*into W/T*)   Hello. Hello. Hello.

Moira   Why don't they answer you?

McVittie (*savage regard for the truth*)   Because round about this time Jamie and Doris usually have it off in the control room and they don't like people listening in.

Moira   Going to get your dog?

McVittie (*turns*)   Yes.

Moira produces a box of matches with a flourish and starts to rattle them.

Moira   Tara!

McVittie   Oh no.

Moira   I'll only set fire to the place if you go away.

She lights a match and lets it drop to the floor, then another, then another.

McVittie *stubs them out with his heel. Takes out cigarettes.*

Moira (*sees them*)   Ah. If you give me one cigarette I'll give you the matches.

McVittie *throws one up. It misses. He throws another one up.* **Moira** *catches the third and breaks off the filter and lights it. She throws the matches down.*

Moira   What are you waiting for? Get the dog.

McVittie   For you to finish.

Moira   Oh! I'm sorry . . .

She breaks off the burning tip. It drops down.
McVittie *extinguishes it. She crumbles the cigarette and stuffs it in her mouth, then spits it out messily.*

Moira (*childlike*)   Finished! (*Pause.*) I think you must have a terribly interesting job. (*Pause.*) Of course, property's meaningless. (*A sudden yell.*) If you set your dog on me you'll rot in Hell!

McVittie (*at the end of his tether*)   I'm doing a dull job for thirty pounds a week and I don't like dogs. I might have been testing car bonnets or working in a public library but I'm not. I don't want to chew anyone's balls off for that amount of money, and I'd rather they left mine alone.

Moira   Is that why you left Rover behind?

McVittie   Rufus. Of course property's meaningless. And literacy's obsolete, and the wheel. I'll agree to anything you say. Just get down. And which ever one I'm speaking to can tell the others.

Moira   The classic schizophrenic has a democracy of three, but in my mind it's like fruit flies.
I've always been interested in public service, it was only natural that when I left school I should go and work socially. It came as quite a shock that in Liverpool and all over the country there are children being raised in deprived conditions for dead-end jobs. Families of five in one or two rooms without money for the gasman or windows.
No electricity. No one at the council interested in these people's lives. Sometimes I think the people themselves aren't . . .
What we were *trying* to do was to stop the pattern of underachievement repeating itself . . . Of course, that's a bourgeois interim measure. In Bootle there was a case of two subnormal marrieds employed on low-grade manual labour by the council . . . the woman refused sterilisation and the man refused a vasectomy . . . They went on breeding . . . The children learnt to reproduce the parents' behaviour patterns. Other experience did not impinge.

Long pause. She starts to chuckle quietly. She speaks to **McVittie** *in a totally different tone. Honest appeal.*

She says – (*Pause.*) You are shorter. Shorter than she would like you to be. (*Pause.*) But she is not happy in herself. (*Pause.*) She feels she will not live – a very long time. She feels she is losing her bloom. She says she is afraid you find her unattractive. (*Pause.*) She says she has seen you before. She wants to stroke your hair. Hold your cheek and lick the crust from your eyes. Turn her little finger in your ear. She wants you to press her stomach in gently with your thumbs. Move her kneecap inside the skin when she is lying down and make squares on her breast with lipstick and mascara. (*Pause.*) She'll bring you off any way you like.

Long pause. **McVittie** *looks away.*

Moira *takes off her tights and puts her head inside one leg as far up as it will go, squashing her features up.*

Moira   All right. I'm going. You don't have to tell me.

Blackout.

A flat hard tone.

Negative identity.

Cottrell (*a terrible cry*)   Pussy! Pussy! Puss!

McVittie (*through W/T*)   429 Frank McVittie from Bevan's yard. I have had some delay as I have been dealing with mentally disturbed person potential arsonist. I relieved the suspect of a box of matches. The suspect has gone in the direction of Arch Street.
Do not advise; inform police.

Lights up in **Cottrell** *section.* **Dave** *and* **Mo** *have the safe between them.* **Moira** *has just come in. She still has the stocking over her head.*

Tableau.

Dave (*stunned*)   How you goin' . . . ?

Moira   Hello. (*She takes the stocking off.*)

Dave   Just set this down a moment will you?

They put the safe down.

Borrow your coat.

Takes **Mo***'s coat and covers where* **Cottrell***'s head is in the bath. Returns to safe and turns to face* **Moira***.*

This is a private house. Can we help you?

Moira   You haven't got a glass of water have you?

Dave (*instantly*)   No. (*Pause.*)

Mo   We got some tea . . .

Dave   Having a teabreak, are we?

Mo   Yes.

Dave   Oh! Does anyone want a sandwich. (*Sarcasm.*) I mean I made some before we came out.

Moira   I couldn't drink tea. It'd be too hot. I suppose you haven't got any water at all.

Dave   This is a condemned property. The Water Board came along and turned it off.

Moira   A condemned, meaningless property . . .

Dave *and* **Mo** *are sitting on the safe watching* **Moira**. *She goes towards the covered bath.*

Dave *moves to head her off.*

Dave   I shouldn't sit there if I were you.

Moira *turns a tap on and off. No water.*

Moira   Am I disturbing you?

Dave   No . . . we were just . . . moving this old box outside.

Moira   I have this trouble with my mind. I want to go round and talk to people in the middle of the night. My body swells, the palms of my hand go the size of whales . . .

She goes to the safe and sits next to **Mo**. *Licks a finger and wipes the mascara from under one of his eyes.*

She whispers in his ear and he smiles nervously.

Moira (*at large*)   Have you got a cigarette?

Dave (*roughly*)   What she said?

Mo   Nothing.

Dave (*to* **Moira**)   No.

Moira *runs her hand up* **Mo**'s *back. He fidgets and looks away. She slides her finger behind his ear.*

Moira   Does that make your hackles rise.

Mo (*neutrally*)   Yes.

Moira   Houseman never used to think of poetry when he

was shaving because it brought all his bristles up. (*Pause.*) I think I'll stay here all night. (*She whispers again.*)

Dave What she said this time?

Mo Asked if you were my boyfriend.

Dave No I'm not. I'm her brother. Tell her we're busy.

Moira *takes* **Mo**'s *hand.*

Moira There's a gap between your headline and your lifeline. It means you can't express things very well. The line of Mercury's very broken up – you'll always have financial trouble. It's likely that you'll go on a long journey in the near future . . .

Dave What's a long journey! I been across the Atlantic thirty-six times on grain barges – does that show!

Pushes his hand between them. **Moira** *ignores him.*

Moira Rome . . . Constantinople . . . you've *had* the happiest years of your life . . .

She leads his hand to her leg. **Mo** *removes it.*

Oh – I'm sorry. (*She puts her tights on again.*) Stupid . . .

Dave We're doing a very important job. A very dangerous job. You're a bit loose in the head aren't you?

Moira (*meekly*) Yes.

Dave *goes to tool kit and pulls out a box full of cotton wool. Opens it. Two sticks of gelignite in the middle. He holds it out to* **Moira**.

Dave Touch it.

She touches it.

It's sweating. Old gelignite. Unstable. It might go off at any time. (*Pause.*) I don't want nutters fucking around me, they might just set it off. Now we're going down to the yard with the box. You are going to piss off and not tell anyone about it.

Moira Yes, of course. I'm sorry to bother you . . . If there's anything . . .

Dave You just piss off out. Right?

Dave and Mo lift the safe up with the tools on top.

Dave Up the gunners. (*To* **Moira**.) You go downstairs, and don't look behind, you'll turn into a pumpkin.

Three second fade as they follow her out with the safe. **McVittie***'s voice comes in over the top of it.*

McVittie W/T Frank McVittie 429 Arch Street.
Investigating potential arsonist I mentioned earlier. I am inside number 63 which backs onto Bevan's yard. I have reason to believe that she . . .

A pause in the dark.

There's someone asleep in the bath . . . the boots of an old tramp.

Hello . . . He's got a coat over his head. Hello. Oh. (*He retches.*)

Lights. He is on his knees by the bath. His cap is off. He has been sick on the floor. He is searching on the floor for something.

Moira, *at the entrance again as at the start of the previous scene, is watching him. The safe of course is gone.*

Moira What you lost?

McVittie Contact lens.

Moira They're expensive, aren't they?

McVittie There's nothing meaner than an Aberdonian Jew.

Moira (*very fast*) There was a boy and girl in here before. I fell in love with the girl immediately. She was completely ravishing. I wanted to cup her breasts in my hands. I don't think she was interested though. Hardly a sophisticate. But oh, she knew. A little wisp of hair tucked inside her ear – such a casual way of standing – hardly a thing going on inside her mind – she looked so like me.
Oh, I'd be the mirror of course. Ridiculous to think that this coarse flesh . . . I'd be the thinking half, parting her lips with my mind going round and through her body.

The hair by the temple – the blue veins underneath the skin – I can imagine her in bed, biting her thumb, crossing her tongue with her hair – (*She goes and looks inside the tub. Absently.*) I must concentrate on exteriors ... I've had enough of bleak internal landscapes ... dead marsh grass ... brown castles ... grey sky ... (*Peers closely.*) The colour's superb.

McVittie *reaches over suddenly and slaps her. She cowers over the tub and almost falls in.*

Moira   I was watching the flies on his lids – the different patterns – the red and the brown ... It's beautiful. I try to write poems about them, but they come out all bloody.

McVittie   I don't think you're daft any more.

Moira   *You* don't think *I'm* daft any more.

McVittie (*trying it on*)   You've come to realise the harsh terms of reality.

Moira (*still where she fell*)   Oh, don't misunderstand me. I'm just as much for the abolition of present society as anyone. (*Bravely.*) Tomorrow, perhaps, the revolution? It'd have to be a worldwide one – but that would be comparatively easy – the Negro is so much more spontaneous than us ... I'm sure you're right to insist that so-called innocence of perception is actually raddled with sophistication. Do you believe in a life force?

McVittie   Do you believe in Father Christmas?

Moira   You believe that things should be represented as they are.

McVittie   I do that. Nasty.

Moira   I thought we had something in common. But it's incidental.

McVittie   What have we got to say to each other?

Moira   If you want to talk to the others, they're in the yard. (*Pause.*) I'll tell you what happened. I met the boy and the girl in the yard. Scenes of extensive debauch. They both had me at

once. Bliss. After such knowledge. (*Nods to* **Cottrell**.) They
referred me to him. They gave me the weapon. It was a length
of three foot, twenty-four-gauge copper piping beaten flat at
one end and weighted. I came up the stairs (*Ecstatic*.) And it
was like a feather in my hand.
I opened the door and there he was. Either dead, or sleeping
with his mouth open. I waited to see if he would stick his
tongue out to catch the flies. He didn't so I hit several times
about the cranium with a (*Pause*.) blunt instrument. (*Pause*.) But
this was long, long ago . . .

McVittie *feels the ankle.*

McVittie   The body's still warm.

Moira   In which case I really have no option –

*She fumbles in her bag and produces a razor in a plastic holder. Holds it
against her wrist. Looks at* **McVittie** *and transfers it to her jugular vein.
Holds it an inch away.*

Moira (*deadpan*)   Jugular glugular.

McVittie (*quick as a flash*)   Glasgow joke.

Moira   Quick. (*Drops hand.*)

McVittie   Man standing outside St Enoch Station. Two
o'clock in the morning. Two fellers come out by the
underground. One of them's doubled over with his face in his
hands.

– Eh – Jimmie – can you tell us the way to the Royal
Infirmary. Graeme's got himself cut up by the Wee Free.

– Oh, I can, says your man. – Up to Queen Street, right, left
at Springburn Road, and it's on your right.

The feller who's down suddenly reaches up and slashes our
man right across the face. (*Sideways arm swipe*.) Says, – On your
way then.

Moira   That's very good. (*She raises her hand again.*)

McVittie   Oh, they're sporting in Glasgow. They blunt the
meat axes.

Moira *looks at the razor and suddenly throws it down carelessly.*

Moira   It's an old blade.

Three second fade.

Cottrell (*in the dark*)   I have no opinions, nothing to look forward to, nothing to look back to. Even when edited. Hounds of spring on winter's traces. A long quarrel with tenderness and the smell of geraniums. When they want chickens to stay in one place for films, they tie black cotton thread between their legs. No one can see it. They just stand there. Peck peck peck. That's what it's been like. The Kop. Red Cheshire sandstone. Houses and trains. Rushed meeting with Cumberland lorry drivers. (*Like station announcer.*) This is Carlisle. This is Carlisle. This is Carlisle.

Mo (*in the dark*)   The door. The bloody girl's shut the door.

Dave (*calm*)   Lyle's golden syrup. Smear it over the pane. Near the handle. Sheet brown paper. Hit it with a hammer. Reach through and release from the other side. Breaking and entering. (*Pause. A dying hiss of gas.*) Cylinders empty. Never mind. Safe down. Plan two. Watch-very-carefully Mo. Hold the other stick of gelly.

Mo   It's all sticky.

Dave   It is all sticky. Yes. Now you see the way. As I turn the base the soft portion disappears into the crack. It builds up in the well behind the hinges. Thumb. (*Pause.*) Pack it down.

Mo   Is it really unstable?

Dave   If you don't know how to use it. Just don't hold it too tight and you'll be safe as houses.

Suddenly the burglar alarm in the yard goes off very loud.

Mo   Dave –

Dave   No one takes any notice of those. They go off just like that –

Mo   There's a fucking copper down there with a dog –

Dave   Over here – quick –

The bell stops.

In the dark, the sound of **McVittie** *and a dog approaching. Sniffings and panting and a chain clinking.*

McVittie   What have you got in your mouth, you dumb beast? Here give it here –

A tremendous explosion.

Pause.

McVittie (*a terrible cry*)   Oh Lord, Lord, why persecutest thou me?

Lights. **McVittie** *is on one of the heaps of rubbish. His arm has been blown off. His other arm is still holding the lead with a few lumps of bloody fur on the end. He has blood all over his face.*

Moira *is perched in the scaffolding unseen by them, watching.*

Dave *and* **Mo** *slowly emerge from a corner where they have been cowering.*

Dave (*fiercely*)   Where's that stick?

Mo *holds out his hands hopelessly.* **Dave** *looks around petulantly and sees* **McVittie**.

Dave   Fuck . . .

Mo *starts to laugh uncontrollably, his hand over his mouth. Sits down on safe.*

Dave (*coldly*)   Share the joke.

Mo (*helpless with laughter*)   We went in there . . . he came along with the dog . . . when all of a sudden I felt this wet nose in my hand . . . sniffing, then the dog had a lick at the stick . . . you told me not to hold it too tight . . . he must have thought I was giving it to him – he carried it off to chew . . .

Dave   So what's happened to my other stick of gelly?

Mo (*waves arms*)   Pucgh!

Dave (*in an effort to bring some order*)   I didn't do this one. (**Mo** *immediately sobers down.*) You're lucky the other lot didn't go up – sympathetic detonation. You're a cock-sucking liability!

Mo   It was a mistake, I mean . . . I was holding the stuff in my hand . . .

Dave   You should know! The glycerine's sweet – they keep them hungry – (*Desperate.*) It's common sense – When it gets sticky –

Mo (*sudden realisation*)   Hadn't we ought to go? The noise . . .

Dave *is working on the safe again. Alarm clock and batteries in circuit with wires.*

Dave   This is not a residential area. Down by the river. It's two o'clock. One shift's coming off in quarter of an hour. If they do get any phone calls, they'll tell them it was a car backfiring on Chester Road or whatever it's called.

Goes back to work. **Mo** *starts unbuttoning his blouse.*

Dave   What you doing?

Mo   Nothing.

Dave   You're not getting undressed.

Mo   I'm getting dressed.

Dave   Put that back on.

Mo *is undecided. Wanders about without his blouse on.* **Dave** *hands him a wire.*

Dave   Strip half an inch clean off that. And not in your teeth.

Mo *wanders about the stage doing this. Stops and looks at* **McVittie**.

Mo   The man who sold you the job had the same hands.

Dave   Olly Wetherall.

Mo   Why didn't he come up and do it himself if he knew about Cottrell?

Dave   He didn't have a car this weekend.

Suddenly **Mo** *starts to weep silently.* **Dave** *has finished setting up the safe.*

Dave (*roughly*)   Get your clothes on Mo.

Mo   I'm frightened ...

Dave   I've set the safe for five minutes.

He puts the tools in **Mo**'s *bag and gives it to him.*

We'll go out to the car. Drive it round the front of the yard. If someone comes we can play courting couples. Come on.

Dave *has to physically help* **Mo** *off the stage and on with his blouse. A sudden access of protection.*

Steady there ... hold my hand ... that's right.

They exit.

The alarm clock ticks away. **Moira** *watches it, swings her feet from the scaffolding.*

Moira (*sings*)   Come on Jesus, Joseph and Mary
To which religion do you belong.

She starts to make herself up.

The inner self is occupied in fantasy and in observation, (*She talks to her reflection quietly.*) transcendent, unembodied, never to be grasped, pinpointed, trapped, possessed. Its aim is to be pure subject ... We see a model child, an ideal husband, an industrious clerk ... the façade becomes more and more stereotyped and on the façade, bizarre characteristics occur ... mutton daggers ...

She suddenly empties the contents of her bag over the stage. They splatter and spread. She takes off her shoes and drops them down.

Then she gets down. **Dave** *has left a large roll of insulating tape on the safe. She makes no attempt to do anything to the safe, but takes the tape and taking one of* **McVittie**'s *shoes and a sock off, ties one end round his big toe and the other to the ladder some ten feet away, both at six inches above the ground.*

Walks on it as if it were a tightrope. Rolls her tongue like a drum.

Brrrrrrr . . . . . . (*Pause.*) The big top. No net. Above and below.
No rosin on the feet. They can cut the wire at any time and
send you into the Crab nebulae, star clusters, strange
galaxies . . .

She gets to **McVittie** *and pulls his walkie-talkie out. Turns it on.*

W/T Voice   429 Frank McVittie. Hello. Calling 429.
There's been reports of an explosion in your area near Bevan's
Yard – can you investigate . . . Frank – Salford Arson Division
have sent a man over – they're holding a couple they found
outside – can you identify the girl –

Moira *turns it off. Silence.*

She makes up **McVittie** *from the contents of her scattered bag. Gives him
false eyelashes and tries to put his wig back on straight. Puts deodorant on
his jacket carelessly. Then draws his trousers to the knee.*

McVittie (*coming round*)   Eh . . . (*Weakly.*) . . . What yer
doing . . .

Moira *is cleaning her teeth crouched over him.*

Moira (*sweetly*)   Playing. (*Pause.*) The raging violin for those in
love, and the culturally deprived.

McVittie (*weak*)   You . . . slovenly . . .

Moira   It was going to be a treat. (*She paints a Cupid's bow on
his thigh, kisses it and draws his trousers up again.*) Why did you have
to spoil it?

McVittie   What's with the dog?

Moira   There's a bit of it around somewhere.

Moira *takes his hand and kisses it during this speech, once for each
disease.*

McVittie   I'm not a lover of dogs. Rufus was a skinful of
diseases. Slipped shoulder. Dropped elbow. Strained sacro-
iliac joint. Knocked-up toe. Track leg. Hard pad. Distemper.
Worms. A bruised cannonbone. (*Pause.*) Are my eyes very bad?

Moira (*peers*)   Very.

She gets up. Goes to the safe and calmly tears the wires out of the circuit.

Pause.

She pulls at the door, and rather stickily it opens.

She takes one of **McVittie***'s cigarettes and goes back to the safe. Takes a pound note out and lights it. Lights the cigarette with it and throws the burning note into the safe, which has smoke capsules in it and it begins to smoke.*

She gets out another razor and goes to **McVittie***, and carefully slices his jugular upstage away from the audience. Her hands come away covered in blood.*

Moira (*to herself*)   Sopping . . .

She tries to clean up with a tiny handkerchief which gets covered as well.

McVittie (*weak*)   What you . . . ?

Moira   Jugular glugular. (*She puts cigarette in his mouth.*) On your way. (*Pause.*) You're not inhaling . . .

McVittie (*weak*)   No. I don't smoke. Actually. It gives me bronchitis. I do have some asthmatic cigarettes . . .

Moira (*concerned*)   I didn't know you had a *condition*.

McVittie   It's just a constriction of the chest, sometimes leading to inflammation of the lungs . . . It's a bit like pleurisy . . . Sir Noel Coward had pleurisy. (*Pause.*) But it's better now. (*Pause.*) There's a scene from a homosexual novel I started reading in Orly –

Moira   No, I think you should really save your strength. I'll talk. I think it's disgraceful the way they make wild horses into pet food –

McVittie   Oh shit. Shut up.

Moira   Or – what's the difference between babies and letter boxes? You can't eat letter boxes. I think if we exchanged clothes it would be the highest compliment. How does it feel, what does it feel like to be dying?

McVittie   Obscene.

Moira   And when you're dead, you can come into my mind and stay there. And life is a true saying, and worthy of all men to be received. And you believe that at least at some time you've been unquestionably happy – like wrestling in fresh fish –

McVittie *does not respond.* **Moira** *gets up and lights a fresh cigarette and puts it in his mouth, then leaves the stage.*

Sound cue, 'Mr Blowjob'.

Blackout.

The Soul of the White Ant

Foreword

Snoo found an early draft in a bottom drawer (a third act for a putative South African production of *Vampire*) when I was pestering him for something to direct. At the time Athol Fugard's noble (and soon to be Nobel) dramas of South African life were tickling Aykbourn-saturated London's guilty conscience. This play cheekily deconstructed Fugard. Out of rewrites and rehearsals, a surreal, hilarious and rather compassionate thing emerged. Fugard, tipped-off no doubt that someone was taking the piss, came to an early show, sat there open-mouthed and confessed he was enthralled.

The termite-eaten (and apparently shat-on) bar was quite the filthiest set I have worked on. Lynda Marchal (La Plante as she is now) played Mabel as a kind of dangerous, Afrikaans Hilda Baker. Simon Callow based Pieter de Groot on a warthog (Drama Centre graduates were always animals). Clive Merrison as the racist junkie Marais transmuted from earth-covered hobo to white-suited angel – thrilling. Nick Ball went on to be *Hazell*, written by a future manager of the England football team.

We progressed to Amsterdam. The Dutch thought it was a melodrama set in a gold mine. They couldn't decode the thick Afrikaner dialect we had worked so hard to perfect. Years later I produced it in America when I was teaching at an Ivy League College. The irony escaped them completely. Which was somehow reassuring.

Dusty Hughes
London, 1999

The Soul of the White Ant was first performed at the Soho Poly Theatre on 2 February 1979, with the following cast:

Pieter de Groot	Simon Callow
Julius	Nicholas Ball
Mabel de Wet	Linda Marchal
Edith	Janet Amsden
June	Pat Hassell
Eugene Marais	Clive Merrison

Directed by Dusty Hughes
Designed by Di Seymour
Music by Tim Thomas

There are four sets, but they can all be accommodated in one environment by lighting selectively. The surroundings should be shabby, filthy even, so one scene blends into the other without difficulty. Stage Right, a mirror, a basin, a lavatory, a door. This is the womens' lavatory of the local newspaper. Centre stage, another entrance with plastic strips. This serves as the entrance to **Mabel***'s bar, and the entrance to the Club. Stage Left,* **Mabel***'s bar, with two stools in front of it, shabby, minimal, a battered jukebox to one side. Termite damage and dust everywhere.*

Party noises off. Joe Loss Orchestra. **Edith**, **June**. *Lavatory. Evening gowns. They're making up. Door opens.*

Male Voice Sorry.

Door closes. Door opens. **Mabel** *comes in. Drunk. Carrying a huge bowl of trifle. She puts it down.*

Edith How long did it take you to make that?

June Oh! Is it sherry trifle? Can I taste some?

Edith What a lot. Are you sure they'll eat it all?

Mabel I want them to.

June Oh they will if Mabel made it. Mabel makes terrific trifle.

Edith They've got a lot of meat out there.

June What d'you mean?

Mabel This is for afters.

June Nice.

Mabel I got the recipe from *Woman*.

June Which woman?

Mabel *Woman*, you know. The magazine.

June Oh.

Edith Not *Woman's Own*.

Mabel No that's a different magazine. There's another

bowl in the car. Will you look after it for me?

Edith   No one's going to steal it in here.

June   They might spoil the look of it.

Mabel   It's got my wedding ring in it. I dropped it in.

Edith   By mistake?

Mabel   When I was making it.

June   That's awful! Suppose someone swallowed it?

Edith   You could tell everybody to chew it properly.

June   Oh I am sorry. Can we get it out without ruining the pattern on top?

Mabel   That's it. And it's set now. They're not so nice when the jelly's all broken up. I didn't realise it had gone until . . . I must have dropped it in when I was chopping up the fruit. Then I got distracted . . . the boy came in . . . he stayed . . . and it was set before I knew what happened . . . Back in a minute. (*Exits.*)

Edith   What a stupid old cow. I bet it's not even in there. She gets pissed in her own bar and *reels* in . . . smell her breath?

June   It's a sherry trifle.

Door opens. A **Man** *pukes through the door.*

Announcer (*voice through door, amplified announcement*)   . . . number is an excuse-me dance. Take your partners for an excuse-me dance. Then there'll be a raffle for the printers' and typesetters' charitable trust . . .

The **Man** *has been wearing a party bobble-hat. He falls onto stage, puking, and crawls out. Door closes.*

Male Voice   Sorry. Never again.

Edith   Pieter on the sports column fancies me.

June   Oh yes. He's nice.

Edith Ah. We could do doubles. Me and Pieter, you and Julius.

June I can't see me going out with Julius much longer.

Edith I thought he was nice.

June His heart's in the right place, but he's dull.

Edith Well look at Mabel. She made a dreadful mistake marrying that travelling salesman. At least you'd have him home a lot of the time.

June Mabel wanted to train to be a biologist.

Edith Why?

June She wanted to be a biologist.

Edith She makes a poor show of running the bar. Come on, Mabel! I want to *dance*! (*Sings.*) 'I could have danced all night . . .' What are we going to do?

June We'll do doubles. I don't mind really. It's just . . . Julius is so sure he's right and I don't know if I could live with it.

Edith Grab it while you can. If you don't somebody else will.

June Is that why you want me to do doubles then?

Edith I . . .

June I want to stay friends with you.

Edith You're very kind.

She kisses **June**. **Mabel** *comes on with second bowl, hands wet.*

Mabel I found it! This one hadn't quite set so I dug around at the bottom – and I found it. Isn't that terrific. Shall we take them in? Neither of you are – I must have had too much sherry –

June Go on.

Mabel Thinking of getting married?

Edith   Why d'you ask?

Mabel   Well it was an innocent question. People pass remarks in bars ... I just wondered if you know, how happy I am now, what a weight of anxiety has been lifted off me – the joys of marriage. I feel so happy. If I'd lost it and my husband came back, he'd have half killed me! He says I drink too much. Do I? You don't think I drink too much do I?

June   No.

Edith   How much do you drink?

Mabel   No more than a man. But I think that's too much. I'm so pleased. I ... you know how things get on top of you, especially when he's away, I find it so difficult. I read a book on Queen Elizabeth and do you know I really felt sorry for her at the end. She's dying, right, and she says – 'Bit by bit, all the fabric of my reign is beginning to fall asunder ...' Poor queen.

Blackout. Tribal drumming and singing. Slow lights up on **Mabel**'s *bar.* **Mabel** *behind bar scrubbing round hidden body under newspaper;* **Pieter** *enters, goes to bar.*

Pieter   Pooh, flies! Why do they have a cake at kaffir weddings? To keep the flies off the bride. When are you going to get your screen door mended, Mabel? I'm joking really. Did you know I'm on the run? We've got a new Letters Editor who insisted that we put in a piece which says that the Interior is inefficiently farmed! He won't last. Another beer, Mabel! (*She puts one on the bar.* **Pieter** *swats a fly on his head with open palm.*) Unabashed criticism staring out of the page in bad Afrikaans ... Hey, little feller, you weren't fast enough were you? (*Wipes fly off hand.*) And they say journalists are burnt out at 35. I'm waiting for the big break. Go into film production. See my name in lights. I'm writing the definitive book on phrenology. That's the bumps on your head – did you know that, Mabel?

Mabel (*indistinct*)   Yes.

Pieter That's why they shave convicts' heads. Now you have a long, egg-shaped skull, Mabel. It's difficult to tell unless you shave people's heads. That's why they shave convicts' heads – they can sort out the troublemakers. You see it might explain why you dropped your bowl of trifle at the newspaper's Xmas ball. Mind you, it's more complicated than that. But if you're trained, you just have to lift a hat to read a character study. This is my bump of genius. (*Searches*.). All the characteristics of white races are in the bones round their heads. Blacks have a different measuring system. And of course that means that it's very important to know if any of your white bumps are in fact black bumps in disguise, and thus possess a quite different meaning. I wanted to run a feature on it – Edith for instance has got a head of which the frontal development on a native would mean passive, moronic stupidity. But it's all right on her. The matrix changes for sex, and race. So it's complicated. Why isn't there a film industry here? The weather's as good as California. We don't need the Americans. The Trek to the Interior with John Wayne. Voortrekkers. Mabel what are you doing? Has that husband of yours developed indelible puke?

Mabel (*muffled*) He's away.

Pieter Why can't the houseboy do it?

Mabel He's been taken in.

Pieter I'm not surprised the way he carries on. I've seen him treat that passbook as if it were a piece of old newspaper. Leaves it lying around when he goes out. Who does he think he is? Prince Charles? I hope they knock some sense into them. I told Julius about the bumps. I had him diving round the natives with a tape measure for six months. It proved several major points. There were one or two genetic freaks, one or two closet whites there ... He's getting very keen on sending them back where they come from at the moment – looks chunky and official in the report book. That's the one criticism, you know, I have of the passbook system – if they send him back to – where

does he come from – Maseru? Is it Maseru? They
shouldn't send them back to Maseru for misdemeanours –
they should just dock their wages. Or – here's a good idea.
All the people in the country have a share in the gold
mines. Right. And every time you have a native who
misdemeans himself, you send him to the gold mines for
punishment, and make him give you all the gold he finds,
and you pay him with a tiny bit of it, and with the rest
you get a washing machine, stretched-bodied Mercedes with
air-conditioning, and a brand new set of the Encyclopaedia
Britannica, so that anything the boys ask you, you can tell
them. Teach them how to get jiggers out from under their
toes, without local anaesthetic, I expect they know that one
already. The structure of complex atoms. Einstein's theory
of relativity. Aristotle's model of the physical world. How
much protein there is in peanuts and soya beans. The
world's longest oil tanker. The theory behind the Council
of Trent and papal infallibility. You could turn houseboys
into really interesting people. We could really give the
paper a boost. Some of the farmers round here, you know,
are as thick as pigshit. If you'll pardon my Swahili. You
could seize the opportunity to slip in a few polysyllables in
the news from abroad column. When one of our leading
ladies caused a stir abroad by referring to the 'characteristic
disgusting odour' of the negro, I wanted to run it as a
headline, but we had to make it comprehensible to the
average farmer, so it just came out as 'smell'.

Mabel   Pieter darling.

Pieter   You know what I'd like right now? I'd like to
walk out of this stinking arsehole and go into the Jo'burg
Bunny Club, and spend the next thirty-six hours with a
Bunny girl with a 36B cup. A white rabbit. I am just about
the only guy in the whole country who doesn't want to
hump something black. And you know why? Because it's a
typical vicious *liberal's* fantasy. I shouldn't say this, if you
take away all those people who've had some sort of sex, or
maybe a dream, a night-time pollution about the black
races – if you purged the nation, took them away, the

place would be like the Kalahari. So it's just as well it doesn't happen. Call me old-fashioned if you like. I think when you get a wife, you shouldn't let anyone else near her. That's what I'm going to do when I get married. Verwoerd knew that.

Marais *comes in and sits down; wearing slouch hat, white suit. Totally covered, head to toe, with earth. In shock.* **Pieter** *talks excitedly to him.*

Pieter Look at it this way. The film starts with the ox-carts rolling into the dawn. Decent ordinary Afrikaans who ask for nothing more than to be left alone, make the great trek into the interior, away from the interfering British, to waste a few Zulu armies. You could make a great film about it, with Glenda Jackson or Robert Shaw. It could be called 'Blood River', or 'Blood Knowledge' or 'Blood'. I mean nothing snobbish. I read this book on the Boer War, called 'How I arrested Winston Churchill' or something. The bloke only wanted the English to win! Those Hammer horror films – we could do better than that!

Marais Excuse me.

Pieter A drink?

Marais Yah – yah.

Pieter *(shouts)* Beer! What did you say your name was?

Marais Excuse me. Yes. Yes. Marais. *(Drinks all beer.)*

Pieter You like beer, hmm? Another?

Marais Excuse me, yes.

Pieter *(takes beer out)* Is that your head or your arse, Mabel? Do you know I'm the only phrenologist in the whole of the Transvaal who can still stand after four six-packs? Are you from around here? I said: 'Are you from Excelsis?'

Marais No. *(Spits earth out.)*

Pieter That's right. You're not, I know just about

everybody. It was a polite question. You might have heard of us. We had an investigation a few months back. The cops, God rest them, had been investigating several coloureds from outside the city boundaries, and four fell out of windows while being questioned, and died. And then some bright Van de Merwe back in Central Office starts objecting because the police station is a fucking bungalow. Pardon my Zulu.

Marais *washes dirt off his hands with lager.*

Pieter   It's a lie, I mean everyone knows you have to put something on paper. It's a lie but then you lie when you fill in an insurance form. I mean who leaves their car locked in a locked garage? Do you drive?

Marais *shakes head.*

Pieter   Working on the by-pass, yiss?

Marais *makes a non-commital gesture.* **Marais** *lurches over to jukebox.*

Pieter   They've got some smashing darkie rhythms on there. When it works!

Marais *grips the jukebox. The jukebox lights, plays a few bars and then goes out.* **Marais** *lets go. Turns.*

Pieter (*holding out beer*)   Wash your face this round?

Marais (*almost normal now*)   No, no, really.

Pieter   Why not?

Marais   I can't drink very much.

Pieter   Bad liver?

Marais   White ants.

Pieter   Well I'll have one!

Marais (*pause*)   My name is Eugene Marais. I wrote a book about the white ant. I wrote it in Afrikaans and Maeterlink stole my ideas. Bluebirds . . . white ants . . .

Pieter   What was the idea?

Marais   White ants.

Pieter   Ah, fuck, termites. 'Orrible things, aren't they?

Marais   The ants build upwards with their tiny claws and spittle, and put up a wall. Then the earth becomes too much . . . and then . . . smash down . . . no shape. 'The soul of the white ant does not know proportion.' (*Pleased with having remembered it, now quite normal.*)

Pieter   Oh, I see. It might make the gardening column I suppose . . .

Marais   (*sits with* **Pieter** *at the bar*)   In the dry season I have seen the tunnel they dig, running sixty feet down the walls of a demolished house.

Pieter   Oh really. That *would* definitely make the gardening column.

Marais   The're digging for gold . . . between each pair of feelers, a drop from the water table to keep the fungus gardens sprouting and keep the queen cool. Gigantic queen. A great sack of birth. Your house is infested with termites. They consume the porch and the walls. The windows fall down. What d'you do if you want to stop them. (*Pause.*) You dig for the mother. They're insatiable. Mahogany desk, shingles from the roof, you've got to dig for the mother. Cecil Rhodes had his bath made of granite so they couldn't carry it away. He had leather wallpaper in Groot Schuur so they couldn't use it for their fungus gardens. (*They both laugh.*) If you want to stop them, you've got to finish her off, the queen. Early days, I found a house on the veldt, deserted, joists of air, a good storm would have blown it away. They were about to take it down. I wanted to find out where she was. I pleaded, I paid, for three days for them to stand by, waiting, and we found this great mother engine in a hollow under the hearth of the house, pumping away.

Pieter   Well. It's a curiosity. Who'd want to steal that?

Marais   The truth is, the truth that I found and wrote down in good Afrikaans, which was stolen from me by that Belgian, is that all these million creatures, all these workers, warriors, and nurses and gardeners, are in fact a single body. They all dig for the mother. They water the gardens. If you destroy the mother, they know, and they run off out of doors. Pseudoneuropterous. Difficult word to get into Afrikaans. Farmer's language.

Pieter   Ja, ja. Try writing an editorial . . .

Marais   Imagine. When you're dead, the eyes, legs, teeth, liver, brains, pancreas and tongue, walk out on their own and turn to dust in the heat. I'm dead. (*Pause.*) I was proud of our country.

Pieter (*oblivious*)   We had the best rugby side in the Southern Hemisphere. And we will again.

Marais   When I was young I fell in love with a girl who played tennis. She had a serve like a man's. Her mother approved of me. And then I found out she was Jewish.

Pieter   Don't you feel the Jew makes a valuable contribution?

Marais   Wrong antheap. What am I doing here? Can't quite catch it . . .

Pieter   D'you hear that, Mabel? He's got a new name for the bar! The Antheap.

Mabel   Ach, Pieter. (*Rustles paper.*)

Marais   Ssh! Termites.

Pieter   Very quietly . . . Mr Marais, since you mentioned tennis . . . When are England sending us a cricket team? Why are they holding off? Are they waiting for Boycott to come back from the dead?

Marais (*stands*)   I have to go.

Pieter   Do we have termites? (**Marais** *picks up and drops a handful of dust.*) Jeez, Mabel, we're coming apart.

Marais   I work east of Francistown, and the water table's sinking. Artesian wells and the long summer. We're very badly stretched. I have to go and dig.

Pieter   You were buried by mistake and began to think you were a termite?

Marais   You can come with me and dig for the mother.

Pieter   No, I really work with my brain. This is my office.

Marais   Look.

Pieter   What's that?

Marais   I'm showing you the antheap. Look.

Pieter (*shocked*)   D.t.'s again?

Marais   No . . .

Pieter (*grabbing the last straws of rationality*)   How d'you do that trick? (*Approaches* **Marais**' *cupped hands.*) They're quite intelligent-looking close up. There's a funny looking feller. Hey! Shorty! Can you hear me?

Marais   That man is Dr Verwoerd. Professor of Applied Psychology at Stellenbosch University. He now journeys up the vertical slope with a drop of water hooked between his claws, which he's not allowed to drink. He wears himself out and the wind grates the dried up bits to dust. He is born and begins again as another termite. Dr Verwoerd digs. The great Undoena spends his life underground. (*Takes his hands away.*) Now. Dig for mother. (*He goes.*)

Pieter   Mabel, does that guy come in here often?

Mabel   Who?

Pieter   Feller by the name of Eugene Marais. Looks as if he's been wrestling with a hippo. (*Cups his hands and peers into them.*) The beer's warm, Mabel. Your mind's not on the job!

Mabel   Sorry, Pieter. The truth is I wish I were dead.

Pieter   There's a smell in here.

Mabel   The smell. That's my houseboy. I shot him.

Pieter (*professional*)   Let's have a look.

Mabel   Well you could but . . . I shot him in the head, so it's a bit *messy*, you know, no use for what you'd want, precise measurements and so on.

Pieter   When did this take place?

Mabel   Couple of days ago.

Pieter (*looks over the counter*)   It's a good job I'm a hardened reporter.

Mabel   I shot him in my room, but it's cooler in here.

Pieter   What have you done about it?

Mabel   I phoned the police this morning.

Pieter   When?

Mabel   When I woke up this morning I had a dream which upset me, I want to get the whole business off my chest.

Pieter   I see.

Enter **Julius**

Here comes the cavalry.

Julius   Yes.

Pieter   Somewhat after the last reel.

Julius   Those who wish to criticise the police should write to their local newspaper enclosing their full name, address and telephone number.

Pieter   I am intrigued to hear from Mabel that she rang the police station concerning an *incident* at eight this morning, and here you are at ten past four!

Julius   I did not log Mrs de Wet's call. I understood this to be a routine matter. Nothing for you here, Pieter.

Pieter   I'm there at every car accident before the chickens have stopped yelling their heads off . . .

Julius   Ach ja schmoel!

Pieter   Very well, sergeant. I'll shut my gob; even though you cheated at geography. The first police officer in Excelsis who's made an effort to stop trailing his knuckles on the ground . . .

Julius   Are you ready to answer a few questions, Mrs de Wet?

Mabel   Yiss.

Pieter   You'll be an Inspector yet, Jules . . . even though you lost the electrodes up that nigger's arse.

Julius   I understand he threw himself in front of your car. Is that correct?

Mabel   I haven't got a car.

Julius   *Mr* de Wet's car?

Mabel   He's away. I don't drive.

Julius   Did you hire a car?

Mabel   It happened inside.

Julius   (*loyally*)   You must have backed the car into the porch.

Mabel   He was my houseboy. I shot him.

Pause. **Julius** *gets out pencil.*

Julius   I'll just write down self-defence.

Mabel   (*vacuous*)   There are some of his belongings in here. (*Goes to freezer behind bar.*)

Julius   Are you reporting this?

Pieter   Not in detail. Her husband's away . . .

Pause. **Mabel** *fiddling in freezer.*

Julius   Do you know what the cause of the sickness of our nation is? Little white babies, the future rulers of our nation, architects, schoolteachers, prison governors, being dangled and fondled and coming into daily contact with the black races. Sick, sick, sick, and it's catching.

Pieter   Rape?

Julius   Of course, he's got his pants off.

Mabel   Could you put these on a train for me? (**Mabel** *takes out a lot of square Tupperware containers.*) For his wife, in Maseru.

Pieter   You're not going to put him in a food freezer!

Pieter *tastes the mixture, interested.*

Julius   Hang on, Mabel, don't spoil your food. We'll parcel him up and get him out of the way for you.

Mabel   Oh, it's not food. He couldn't have his wife here so I agreed to keep it in the deep-freeze till he made enough money to send it. His . . . you know. For making children . . .

Pieter *realises what he's been eating.*

Mabel   It was my suggestion . . . I used to be keen on biology, you can keep semen at sub-zero temperatures indefinitely. He was very upset when I first suggested it. Wouldn't speak to me for days. Finally he came round to it. This bit's frozen peas, beans, carrots and pork chops, and this bit's his racial inheritance.

Pieter   Ach, Mabel . . .

Pieter *goes out hurriedly.*

Mabel   He never had enough money for postage, and then I lost his wife's address. He was a sweet boy. If only I had a bigger freezer. But with all the special offers downtown . . . he never laid a finger on me . . . Where could I cool the beer? Nobody likes warm beer . . . and the freezer's almost full . . . I was alone . . . the freezer was filling up. At any moment a glint could come into his eye . . .

Julius   Could you tell me the exact circumstances of his death?

Mabel   I . . . put my dress back on and went and got the twelve-bore.

Julius   You were in the room when he . . . manipulated?

Mabel   I was always on the other side of the room. I had a chair ready like . . . a lion tamer d'you know?

Julius (sotto voce)   With your clothes off?

Pieter *comes back in.*

Mabel   Well this cotton dress is so unflattering; crimplene. It needs cleaning. The boy always used to iron my things, but that needs a woman's touch really, don't you think? He was always that little bit clumsy when I was in the room . . . shy . . . (*Breaking down a little.*) Poor little tadpoles. All alone with only fear for company.

Julius *mimes straitjacket to* **Pieter**. **Julius** *collects the containers.*

Julius   For Christ's sake let's sling it all in the river.

Mabel   Not the food as well.

Julius   Madam, it's contaminated.

Mabel   What can I do now?

Julius   Clean the gun, huh?

Julius *and* **Pieter** *go out with food and parcels.*

Mabel (*to corpse*)   Mucky pup. You are a mucky pup. (*Giggles.*) When I was on a P & O cruise once, they'd offer one a South African lager, and I heard an English woman say – 'No, thanks, I'll have a British'. And the steward said, 'Very good, madam.' And she said, 'It's not that I mind the regime, it's just that I don't like to drink stuff that's had those dirty black hands on it . . .' (*Shrieks with laughter.*)

Fast fade.

Club scene. Just the front stage lit. **Julius** *alone. Sounds of distant dancing.* **June** *comes in with two extravagant looking cocktails.*

June   Here's your pink flamingo.

Julius   Christ. I should have asked for beer. Where's the change?

June   There isn't any.

Julius   What!

She sits down. **Julius** *is standing.*

June   Have you got the car working?

Julius   Not yet.

June   Will it go?

Julius   Of course.

June   Somebody offered me a lift.

Julius   You didn't accept?

June   No! Because I knew you'd be annoyed!

Julius   I'm more annoyed if I do take you!

June   I don't see why you should be. You don't like to see me on stage.

Julius   No. And they're wife-swappers at that club where we're meant to be going.

June   Well we're still going aren't we? Look, if I could be certain I wouldn't go.

Julius   I'm not certain.

June   D'you not love me?

Julius   When I see you holding a microphone in front of all those drunken farmers, I'm worried about your safety.

June   That's ridiculous. Why don't you have the courage to say I don't want you to do it because I'm *jealous*.

Julius I'm not jealous.

June It's quite normal. Will you take me, jealous Jules?

Julius When?

June Now!

Enter **Pieter** *and* **Edith**, **Pieter**'s *arms too tight round her.*

Edith Pieter, leave off. We're in the light.

Pieter (*pseudo officious*) Very good, madam. Sorry. Evening officer. Had no intention of frightening the horses.

Edith What horses?

Pieter Got your car mended I see, Jules.

Julius I thought I had.

Pieter Well, you wiped all the muddy paw marks off the boot anyhow.

Julius The sump's cracked.

Pieter Serious.

Edith We could take a lift with someone else.

Julius I don't know, maybe we can't go. I thought I could repair it myself.

Pieter It's not as if labour costs are prohibitive.

June He's economising.

Julius We'll go.

Edith What's he saving for?

Julius If you don't mind stopping every few miles to pour oil in.

Pieter Stop anywhere you like.

Julius Otherwise it rips the guts out of the engine . . . It's only done 6,000 too.

June You sure?

Julius Sure, I'll take you.

June I can go with someone else.

Julius (*fierce*) No! (*Exits.*)

Pieter Come on, girls. That's an interesting-looking drink.

June It's a flamingo. (*Offers him glass.*) You can have it if you like.

Pieter Anyone spat in it? (*Pause.*) I've done worse things in my time. (*Drinks.*)

Edith Tell Julius to bring the car round to the front.

Pieter Yes, ma'am.

Edith We don't want to wait here all night. Don't spend all night saying goodbye to everybody.

Pieter They won't see me. I'll pass like a ghost through the club room. (*He goes.*)

Edith Who asked you to sing?

June A man who was in for piles at the hospital.

Edith Is that where we're going? To his club?

June That's right.

Edith To hear you sing . . .

June I used to do Ruth Etting numbers when I was pushing the anaesthetist's trolley. That's how I developed diaphragm control.

Edith You don't use a diaphragm.

June No – here . . . (*Holds **Edith**'s diaphragm.*) Breath in – suck it down. That's your diaphragm.

Edith Would you like to sing – professionally?

June I can't afford the time, or the lessons.

Edith But if there was a big fat promoter in the audience

– would you say 'no' to him?

June   Then I might change my mind.

Edith   Julius wouldn't mind?

June   I'm not happy with Julius.

Edith   It takes a lot of self-restraint for a police officer to let his fiancée sing, mix with dubious characters and that.

June   Well let him break it off then.

Edith   You bold girl.

June   I think half of it's the uniform.

Edith   He *is* handsome.

June   He's older than he looks.

Edith   He once went out with my sister.

June   Really?

Edith   A long time ago.

June   What happened?

Edith   Oh, she gave him the boot.

June   Why? (*Pause.*) Tell me, please, Edith.

Edith   He drove her home one night and she asked him in, and he said he didn't want to, just wanted to sit in the car and have her suck his cock.

June   We ought to go.

Edith   Has he asked you to?

June   Yiss.

Edith   What did you say?

June   I don't mind.

Edith   She said it was because he doesn't like men and women undressing.

June   That's right.

Edith   And you don't mind?

June   There are worse things in life.

Edith   What's it like?

June   ... Salt ...

Mabel *comes on.*

Mabel   Ye are the salt of the earth.

June   Hello, Mabel.

Mabel   But if the salt have lost its savour, wherewith shall it be salted him? Salt ... Lot's wife – you know Lot's wife – Wham – ! Turned into a pillar of salt as soon as she turned round. To look at the cities of Sodom and Gomorrah. And what was she doing to deserve punishment? I ask you that. I'm just about pooped out. Has what I've been saying to you made any sense? Sometimes the world seems like a dirty laundry basket, unmentionable stains. Well, I mean, bits of you go one way, bits go the other, how can you maintain your integrity before God? You just have to follow your desires through to the end.

Edith   June wants to be a singer.

Mabel   What's stopping her?

June   I don't know how to get started.

Mabel   Yeah. I know how it is. The one thing I want to do with the whole of my being is to kill David. My husband – you know? And I never seem to get round to it. Hold the axe over him at night if he's snoring – and damn you! Damn you! Damn you! I damn nearly killed him but – ach suss – I don't fancy running away, or staying. I can't tell you how much I despise him. And that man's a part of me. Meant to be. I'd like to – you know – chop it off. And one day I just might. (*Recovers.*) Or – people disappear! Did you know that? Elijah disappeared. He went for a walk with his friend Elisha, and was taken up in a firey chariot, and when Elisha came back from the veldt they said –

'Where's your friend?' (*Secretive.*) And they sent out a search party, but they never found him.

Blackout. Pink spots on **June**. *She sings a blues number.*

June   River Song
You promised me sunshine after rain,
That love would come and fill me with sweet pain.

River Song
You got me wanting something that's all mine,
I need to taste the honey and the wine.

So many days have blown away,
With just a sad goodbye,
Footprints wasted in the sand,
My river has run dry.

River Song
The words you sing to me are dark and deep,
I'm on my own my secrets will have to keep.

So many days have blown away with
With just a sad goodbye,
Footprints wasted in the sand,
My river has run dry.

River Song
I hear your music deep down in my heart,
But I've been used so bad ... I don't know where
to start.

Blackout. Night noises. Moonlight front of stage. **Pieter** *smoking a cigarette.* **Edith** *comes on.* **Pieter** *puts an arm round her shoulders.*

Pieter   (*pause*) Glorious night, isn't it? Almost worth being broken down. Unless we're killed by leopards or extremists of course.

Edith   Julius needs a hand. He's under the car.

Pieter   Good old Jules. Tearing at the world with his bare hands again.

Edith   Go on.

Pieter   Give us a kiss, Edith.

Edith   Go and mend the car.

Pieter   The moonlight ... makes you so attractive that I
... (*He is kissing up her arm.*)

Edith (*not unkindly*)   Go on, you idiot.

Pieter   If anything happens, – yell. Lions you know.

Edith   I'll be all right. June's just up the road.

June *comes on.*

June   Pieter!

Pieter   No honestly. I'm not surprised we broke down
here. It's like the Bermuda triangle. Sixty-five per cent of
all single vehicle accidents happen over this stretch. Cars
break down with weird electrical problems. There's
probably a force field or something surrounding the whole
area. In fact, I'm thinking of writing a book about it.

Edith   After your one on phrenology.

Pieter   Er yes ... Bumps on your head followed by
bumps on the road ... (*Exits.*)

June   Mabel said it was an unlucky road. That's why she
wouldn't travel with us.

Edith   Christ! What rubbish! She got sick of stopping
every two minutes, there's not room for three in the back
of a Volks, and she got offered a lift home by a single
man.

June   Oh!

Edith   I can't *believe* that anyone could be so naive as you.

June   I'm just lazy.

Edith   You want people to like you too much. But d'you
believe what they say? Course not.

June   You're right. No. I didn't believe what Mabel said
– half believed it 'cos I wasn't listening. (*Pause.*) I hoped it

was true. I was listening. I must have been.

Edith   How do you know?

June   Yes I was.

Edith (*triumph*)   There! Underneath you're suspicious, just like everybody else.

June   What of?

Edith   There you go *again*. (*Pause.*) Are you going to go on with Julius? He won't let you sing again.

June   I know he doesn't like it.

Edith   Thinks you'll end up in a coloured club.

June   He's no reason to think that.

Edith *waggles her fingers against her lips.*

June   Edith, don't! Please!

Edith (*delighted*)   You sound just like my mother! All right I won't.

Julius *comes on. Oil all over his face and forearms. It should look like a black face, a big white stripe for the mouth.*

Julius   All right, everyone, back in the car.

June   Julius! You gave us a fright.

Julius   I fixed it.

Pieter *comes in.*

Pieter   Good old Jules. We'll split the dry-cleaning bill if you get us home. Not that you'd mind walking.

Julius   I would.

Pieter   Oh no you wouldn't.

Julius   I would!

Pieter (*Al Jolson*)   I'd walk a million miles for one of your smiles – My Mammy –

Girls exit laughing.

Julius   Suss − I don't know why you're so full of jokes.
It's going to bush out the fucking engine.

Pieter   Well, why don't we walk.

Julius (*looks to see girls are away*)   There's a nasty crash
down the road. I don't want June to see it.

Pieter   Yeah. Hey, but she sees stiffs every day in the
hospital. No, you're right. I wouldn't want Edith to see it
either.

Julius   Seen it?

Pieter   Yes. Fucking ants everywhere. There was only
about six stone of him left, and he must have been a big
man.

Julius   Yes. What was it?

Pieter   White Opel Kadette.

Julius   A man?

Pieter   Yes. (*Takes a pork-pie hat out of his pocket, scrumpled,
bloodstains.*)

Julius   Why did he leave the road?

Pieter   Well, it is the Bermuda triangle round here, you
know.

Julius   Ach for pissing out sideways −

Pieter   Shall I tell you? It's a coherent curve from the
road till it hits the first antheap, and then the car was
obviously flung sideways and up and started to roll, righted
itself once and finished with all four legs in the air. Either
he went to sleep − in which case he would have woken up
in the 50 metres − or he had a heart attack. Course, now
we'll never know. Or he had a blow-out.

Julius   Radials?

Pieter   Poor white. Crossplys. (*Pause.*) It's Mabel's old man.

Julius I thought so.

Pieter He had a blow-out. I checked all the tyres – as much as I could. The little bastards are treating everything as if it was a take-away meal. And both offside tyres have been frayed on the inside.

Julius Mabel getting at them with a hack-saw when he's home?

Pieter He's been away.

Julius That's true. Couldn't have been that.

Pieter Except he's pointed in the wrong direction. He's been home – right? And then he's left Excelsis again, when he goes into the Bermuda triangle and crash.

Julius Ah . . . *fuck*.

Pieter You think there might be another investigation?

Julius Yes.

Pieter You got Mabel to sign the statement.

Julius Yes . . . But you know what she's like – she never memorised it.

Pieter (*claps him on the back*) Never mind. What you got to worry about, I don't know. I'm not going to say anything. As far as I'm concerned the fat slob must have had a heart attack when driving home drunk.

Julius Yes.

Pieter A junker hero's death.

Julius Yes.

Pieter Could you lend me 50 rand to the end of the month?

Julius What for?

Pieter I'll pay it back this time.

Julius   No, that's blackmail.

Pieter   Who's to know. I'll pay it all back.

Julius   What do you want it for?

Pieter   I want to get (*Mysterious.*) a crossbow.

Julius   What?

Pieter   I'm going to find out the truth about the
Bermuda triangle. I'll need some protection from terrorists,
you know. I'll pay you back at the end of the month.
Course you won't need it then.

Julius   What!

Pieter   Well June'll be a star by then. No she won't, just
a little joke. On at 12.00 tomorrow are you? I'll come to
your place after breakfast?

Julius   All right! All fucking right!

Turns. **Pieter** *imitates an ape behind* **Julius**'s *back.* **Julius** *turns
round.* **Pieter** *straightens up as the lights go off.*

June, **Edith**, *lavatory. Mourning gear.*

Edith   I'm late.

June   Well, we're both late.

Edith   No, my period's late.

June   So's mine.

Edith   Oh? Have you been . . .

June   No worse luck . . . have you?

Edith   Never . . . not recently.

June   I've never been to a funeral before.

Edith   Are you nervous? Do you believe that story?

June   Which?

Edith   The one that's going the rounds.

June   Is it about my Julius?

Edith   No! He hasn't done anything like that. Apparently he and Pieter tipped a whole deep-freeze in the river. That's what all those carrots were doing, floating down when we were having a dip.

June   What a waste!

Edith   Mabel kept something else in the deep-freeze.

June   Trifle?

Edith   Her houseboy used to masturbate into the icebox and she'd save it.

June   That's why the river was so slimy. Is that why we're late?

Edith   It doesn't bear thinking about.

June   She really was mad. I thought she just had the d.t.'s. Oh, how *awful*. Her husband knew?

Edith   You're the only person I've told. That houseboy incident upset her . . . You can't touch pitch, you know, and not be defiled. (*Pause.*) I wish I had a skin like yours.

June   It goes very dry, late on.

Edith   Mine's so oily.

June   It looks better in the end. Just be thankful you're not black.

Edith   I bloody am!

June   No – I mean . . . the boys, when they get acne, the little curly, squiggly, black hairs grow back into the skin and cause infection. They come to the hospital sometimes, poor things.

Edith   Is your hair curly at all?

June (*definitive*)   No.

Edith   My Pieter's a phrenologist.

June   I thought he was a reporter.

Edith   He can tell how intelligent a person is by the bumps on his head. He goes to the mortuary and measures them when no one's looking.

June   Why?

Edith   He's researching into miscegenation.

June   I don't want mine measured.

Edith   Oh! Don't worry . . . you know Mabel's houseboy, well he measured his skull, and it was the skull of a genius.

June   Stupid!

Edith   It was! That's what Pieter says.

June   Anyone would see . . .

Edith   The whole purpose of his genius showed him where his place was, right? Time for the funeral.

Mabel *comes in. Widow's weeds. Upset.*

June   There, there, Mabel. (*Clasping her.*) Sit down for a bit.

Mabel   The . . . oh would one of you girls get me a drink?

June   I'll get it. (*Exits.*)

Mabel   Oh . . . God, we were just about to start – I couldn't see you girls anywhere, and we can't get out of the town.

Edith   Why?

Mabel   They've sealed off the roads. Someone's robbed the bank.

Edith   Is it connected with your husband's death?

Mabel   I don't know what's connected with what anymore . . . No! . . . David always used to drive flat out when he'd drunk a bit, it was pure bad luck he struck an antheap. He's probably smiling down on us now . . .

Edith   It was a straight road.

Mabel   Don't . . . persecute me . . . I have enough trouble thinking of him at the last judgement rising from the grave with a steering wheel poked through his chest. I *told* him he drank too much.

Edith   Poor Mabel, it's really been a week of disasters.

Mabel   He never listened . . . people never listen. We could make that bar into a really nice place, but he'd never let ladies in. Dozens of ladies from all over town, and their beaux could've . . . but I can't start again on my own.

Edith   Yes you can.

Mabel   How?

Edith   June and I will be your first lady customers. Since you were so kind to invite us to the funeral . . .

Mabel   You're very sweet.

June *comes back with a glass of sherry.*

June   Here we are.

Edith   To Mabel's bar. (*A toast.*) Us girls stick together.

June   To Mabel's bar.

Mabel *drinks.*

Edith   Come on, let's go. They must have finished robbing the bank by now.

Julius *and* **Pieter** *burst in.*

Julius   On the floor everyone!

Edith *screams at sight of gun.* **Julius** *forces* **June** *and* **Edith** *down.*

Edith   Pieter! What's going on? It's wet.

Pieter   Look! There's no window in here.

June   What's it about?

Julius   Sorry, girls, just thinking of your safety.

Edith   This is the *ladies*.

Pieter   Seen anyone?

Edith   No.

Julius   A gunman has just raided the Central Bank.

June   What does he look like?

Julius   He's white.

June   And short or tall?

Pieter   He took around 50 kilos of gold, ran down the road for a mile.

Julius   Jesus, he must be a fucking weightlifter. Excuse me. A big strong fellow.

Edith (*bitter*)   Don't mind us.

Pieter   I think perhaps the women and children should go to the print room.

Julius   Keep lying down! Anything might happen!

Pieter *finds a door upstage next to entrance.*

Pieter (*rattling handle*)   Locked.

Julius   Anyone you ladies know in there?

Edith   Unless . . . no.

Julius   Back, everybody!

All get up and move away.

Stay calm. (*Sidles up to door.*) Come on out with your hands up. I shall count to three then blow the lock off. One, two . . .

Pieter   Try the key, Jules.

Julius *unlocks the door, then pulls the door open. Nothing. A blank* *wall.*

Mabel   Look ... Couldn't we get on with the funeral please. I made some trifle ...

Pieter   Suppose he tries to get out in the coffin, Jules?

Julius   Yes ... Just give it twenty minutes while I search the rest of the building. OK? Stay in here. (*Exits.*)

Pieter (*pleased*)   This is the first time I've been in a white woman's lavatory.

Edith   Planning to make it a long stay?

Pieter   If you'll excuse my apparent rudeness, I'll go. (*Exits.*)

Mabel   Ach, *men*. They don't care about doing something the right way.

Edith   They don't think about Mabel's feelings at all.

June   Yiss.

Mabel   At this rate it'll be a week before they get around to putting poor David in the ground. And there's no record, nothing to pass on, no children ... you see I was pregnant, twice, and each time I got rid of it. (*Pause.*)

June   How?

Mabel   There's a commercial traveller, sells fertiliser the rest of the time. Used to be a medical student ...

Edith   That sounds risky.

Mabel   I couldn't afford to go to Jo'burg, and when I got there I wouldn't know where to start. Which of you two in trouble?

June   Me.

Edith   And me.

Mabel   I'll see if I've got his address ... why don't you get married, you've both got boyfriends?

June   We . . .

Mabel   (*grogging out*)   It burns the heart . . .

Edith   I don't think we should tell her how we got pregnant.

Mabel   To kill life.

Mabel *subsides onto the lavatory seat.*

June   It wouldn't be fair in her condition.

Mabel   Still we've all got to go in the front line from time to time . . .

Edith   I'm frightened.

Mabel *starts to snore. Funeral music. Fast fade.*

Mabel's *bar. Enter* **Mabel** *using squirter containing arsenic powder. She is wearing a mask. Disappears behind counter.* **Marais** *comes in. Clean. Clean white suit, briefcase. Dusts shoes. Rings bell on bar.* **Mabel** *appears.*

Marais   I'll have a vodka and tonic.

Mabel   (*pause*)   I think we're short on tonics.

Marais   Vodka and tomato?

Mabel   (*pause*)   The delivery's *late*. Or, did it come yesterday, but . . .

Marais   Vodka?

Mabel   Er . . . no.

Marais   Beer?

Mabel   That we can do. Nice cold beer. Would you like a glass?

Marais   (*polite*)   Only if you have one.

Mabel   (*gives him one*)   Nice clean glass there. Sorry about the mess. My husband's dead and I'm dusting for termites.

Marais   What d'you use? Arsenic?

Mabel   Vikane. It's deadly. There's a jukebox over there, with some American records. My husband was fond of . . .

Marais *goes over and studies jukebox with her.* **June** *and* **Edith** *come in with little overnight cases. They sit at a table.*

Mabel   Welcome.

June   How do'you do, Mabel.

Mabel   Sweet bags . . .

Edith   We didn't know if we had to spend the night away.

Mabel *exits absent-mindedly.*

June (*to* **Edith**)   Is that him?

Edith   Where's he going to do it?

June   He might have a car.

Edith   A car. Oh God.

June   Isn't Mabel going to introduce us?

Edith   Psst!

They go over to him. **Marais** *turns round.*

Marais (*slow, precise, slightly amused*)   Nature is never random. But also never intentional. Even when she goes along with our intentions. Whatever we do demonstrates yet another law of Nature. So how do you choose when to stop controlling, since you can't control *everything*? How do you learn reverence for the act of surrender? Mmmm? How can you render the best obedient service to your country?

Edith   Are you saying we should have it?

June   Can you get rid of it? You see we think they might be the wrong colour.

Pieter *enters.*

Pieter   Excuse me. This isn't a bar for women.

June   Yiss it is.

Pieter   Edith, this is not a bar for women.

Edith   Mabel's changed that.

Pieter   It's not up to her. It's in the licence. It's a men only bar!

June   Mabel wants us here.

Pieter   I don't care! If she doesn't keep to her licence she could get closed down!

Edith   I'm talking with this gentleman.

Pieter   Who is he anyway? Hey, you . . . you were in here a few days ago.

Marais   Do I owe you a drink?

Edith   I'll buy you one.

Pieter   Look, I just don't want to see you here, and what's more, it's the law. You don't want Mabel's licence taken away, do you?

Mabel *sweeps in.*

Mabel   What's that?

Pieter   You've got to get them out, Mabel. The laws about unaccompanied women are there for their protection . . . This guy's a nut! You don't want to talk to him.

Mabel   It's my bar and I'll have who I like in here.

Pieter   You can't.

Mabel   One more word out of you and you're barred.

Pieter   Futsak!

Mabel   Get out! Go on! Get out!

Pieter   I haven't had my beer yet, Mabel.

Mabel   You haven't paid for it!

Pieter   Keep your fucking beer then!

Mabel *fronts him.* **Pieter** *exits hurriedly.*

Marais (*precise, quiet – to* **June** *and* **Edith**)   Nature provides intelligence only enough for day-to-day tasks. Every problem must have a solution, or it cannot enter into society.

June   Do you want to go outside and talk?

Edith   We've got the money.

Pieter *enters with* **Julius**.

Julius   Mrs de Wet, can I see certification that your bar may entertain unaccompanied women?

Mabel *fidgets in piles of dust.*

Marais   I loved my country and it killed me. How do you think I feel *now*?

Pieter   You'll catch it.

Mabel   I've got it somewhere. (*Finds it.*)

Pieter   Let's hope it's not out of date.

Julius *reads it.*

Mabel   It doesn't say anything about men only.

Julius   No.

Pieter   Oh!

Julius   Mrs de Wet, that is correct.

Pieter   Is it out of date?

Julius   No. (*He keeps looking.*) Can I see your entertainment licence, Mrs de Wet?

Mabel   *Entertainment*?

Julius   You have a mechanical reproducer of dance music here. Are you licenced for dancing?

Mabel   Dancing?

Julius   There is a fine.

Mabel *runs over to the jukebox and hacks through the flex with an axe. The jukebox dies with a flash and a crackle.*

Mabel   It doesn't work. (*Triumph.*)

Julius   All right we'll forget it.

Mabel   You can take it. I don't want it. I've always been persecuted, and tried to put a brave face on it ... but I don't care anymore! People whispering in bars ... 'David killed himself when he heard Mabel had been doing it with the houseboy.' Well it's not true! He never knew! I was never found out when he was alive! Nobody told him! His death was an accident! A tragedy! It had nothing to do with me! And now you try and persecute me again! Because I'm different!

Julius   Mabel, look ... *nobody* ... Pieter and I ... told *nobody* about the freezer. It's a secret. Promise. Nobody knows.

Mabel   You told David.

Julius   We didn't. Promise.

Mabel   I'm going to kill myself. And this time I'm going to do it properly. (*Exits.*)

Julius   Could you girls go and look after her.

Edith   What do you mean? Stop her?

Julius   Yah.

June (*goes off*)   Mabel!

Edith *exits.*

Julius   Can they handle it?

Pieter   Women trouble ... best sorted out amongst themselves. Just don't get involved, Jules. The man in the white suit owes me a beer. It's your round.

Marais *gets out a huge wad of notes, like a pint mug.*

Julius   Just a moment. You from round here?

Marais *scratches his head.*

How d'you get all that money?

Marais   Bridge, Canasta. Patience.

Julius (*going over*)   Would you mind if I borrowed your notes for a few minutes?

Marais   My pleasure.

Julius (*goes to phone on bar – dials. To* **Pieter**)   Could you sort of stand unobtrusively in the doorway?

Pieter (*steals over*)   Like a little mouse.

Marais *in the middle, quietly injects himself with a syringe, away from the audience.*

Julius   Hello? Van de Merwe? Got the list of banknotes stolen from the Transvaal bank? Ready? Ten rand ... C 445 5677, C 446 5964, C 330 4395, C 990 0044. (*Covers the phone.*) That sergeant's so green with envy, I can practically hear him having a miscarriage ... Yes, Mabel's bar. Right away. Just one piggy truck. (*Phone down.*) Right ... (*Frisks* **Marais** *quickly.*) Well, what's your name.

Marais   Eugene Marais.

Edith *and* **June** *bring a soaking, dead* **Mabel** *in.*

Edith   She hid from us in the water-butt. We found her because ...

June   We could see her heels sticking out.

Julius *starts artificial respiration ineptly.*

Edith   Can you bring her round?

Julius   Her heart's stopped.

Vigorous agonising, pumping.

Edith   I wouldn't know what to do.

June   They taught us at the hospital. But it was all theory.

Pieter   I'll get an ambulance. (*Phone rings – picks it up.*)
Yes. OK. Thank you, I'll tell him. (*Phone down – dials again.*)
It's engaged. (*Dials again.*) It's ringing. (*Rings for ages.* **Julius**
pumps.)

Julius   Can you see what I'm doing, Pieter? Can you
follow it? Blow air in, let it come out in a natural
breathing rhythm, OK? (*Pushes* **Pieter** *onto it.* **Pieter** *clumsy,
reluctant.* **Julius** *stands by* **Marais**.) Right don't want you
rushing off.

Marais   That's all right. I'm not going anywhere.

Pieter (*breaking rhythm*)   Oh, Jules, by the bye, the police
station phoned through. It wasn't notes he took, it was gold
bars.

Julius   Shit. Well I don't know how they expect me to
get married on my present pay. (*Pushes* **Pieter** *off.*) Dummy.
(*He works away.*)

Marais   She's dead.

Julius *still working.*

Edith   Is she dead?

June   She was upside down. She does look . . .

Julius *slows down.*

Marais   You're doing it wrong. You've got to exhaust the
fluid from the lungs first. (*He does it.*)

Mabel *blows out a great mouthful of water and under* **Marais**'
hands begins to breathe. She revives. All cheer.

Julius   Mabel, are you all right? You're alive, Mabel. (*To*
Marais.) Thanks and well done. Sorry about the notes
business.

Marais   That's perfectly all right. You keep them.

Mabel   I had a *dream* . . . As I swam in the boundless
river . . .

Julius (*jocular*)   I thought it was the water-butt.

Mabel   This man played and sung and treated me courteously, and made such sweet orchestras that I never wished to return, because this world has such a harsh, discordant sound.

Tableau. **Marais** *collects his things and moves softly to the jukebox. He touches it and it comes to life. It plays Fats Domino's 'Blueberry Hill'. All watch as he bows to them elegantly and exits, touching* **Edith***'s stomach as he goes.*

Edith (*delighted*)   My period's started!

More Light

Foreword

At drama school I had noticed the name Snoo Wilson listed as stage manager for a Portable Theatre production (Howard Brenton's *Christie in Love*, perhaps), and it stuck in my mind – stage managers were more usually called Andrew, Jocko or Claire in those days.

Two years later I was an embryonic Artistic Director at the Bush theatre – shabby home of 'grubby thrusters', as termed by the theatrical establishment – and producing Snoo's *The Soul of the White Ant* which Dusty Hughes brought us from the Soho Poly. And so started Snoo's long association with the Bush, which eventually led to my becoming his occasional director.

More Light still bears the imprint of the original commissioners, the RSC, and it is a shame they didn't produce it, preferably in tandem with *A Midsummer Night's Dream*, a play with which it strongly resonates.

Casting a female Shakespeare into the Elizabethan melange of Dee and Kelly (echoes of Prospero/Caliban), Queen Elizabeth herself (Titania) and the lusty, celestial barmaid (Mistress Quickly? Doll Tearsheet?) brings us to Viola and Rosalind and the Bard's constant cross-dressing and AC/DC tendencies. This leads us to the delightful possibilities of his/her lifetime impersonation, the glove-making and W.H. and on and on into the abyss of academic thesis land.

Abiding memories of our production of *More Light* are of the Bush's frequent 'star', Stuart Wilson, as the Pope, erupting out of the floor of the Bush – an obvious impossibility given the structure of the building (and what a tech that was!) – in full pursuit of Bruno, followed by the scarab, climbing with sweet inevitability up the spiral of Robin Don's magical set to impact astonishingly against the sun.

Simon Stokes
Plymouth, 1999

More Light was first performed at the Bush Theatre on 16 February, 1987 with the following cast:

Pope	Stuart Wilson
Dee	Christopher Guinee
Kelly	Ronan Vibert
Queen Elizabeth	Irina Brook
Bruno	Karl Johnson
Shakespeare	Lizzy McInnerny
Barmaid	Caroline Holdaway

Directed by Simon Stokes and Snoo Wilson
Designed by Robin Don
Costumes by Susan Long
Lighting by Paul Denby
Sound by Nicole Griffiths

Note: The part of Shakespeare is played by a woman.

Act One

The **Pope**, *richly and ceremoniously caparisoned in purple speaks to the audience. All around him is dark.*

Pope   There was no doubt he was dangerous. So dangerous we had to ensure the papers of his prosecution did not fall into the wrong hands, and be used later by the Church's enemies. So now I think we will be safe. But then at the hour of my own death I begin to imagine impossibilities. That Bruno has somehow escaped from us. Or that his trial papers have not been destroyed. I burnt them myself. But I cannot be certain in this my last fever whether these essential precautions have been put into effect. There were foolish rumours earlier, of course. Someone who wanted to make trouble would repeat some old wives' tale about how he had been seen walking the streets of his birthplace, Nola. But I spoke with many sober witnesses who saw him perish in the flame and smoke. It is ridiculous to entertain the thought that, in the sight of all as he was, he could have slipped away from the procession. But I still had a strange feeling that the matter of his death had not been entirely resolved. I even wondered if I would go to hell for burning him. As I lie dying I begin to go over the case in my mind again. That was a mistake. Dreams and delusions begin to intervene with the memory of my confessed and purified soul, and in the mounting panic, words issue from my mouth which I know I did not speak.

I feel the fit upon me once again.

In my worst nightmares I could always come to earth by asking – where am I? But this one I cannot escape from so easily. It is in vain that I try to wake from the diabolic landscape with its twisted logic and complete disregard for my own good character. Step by step I am trapped in Bruno's infernal machine, the Theatre of Magical Memory. This is how it always begins.

I dream that Elizabeth, the northern sorceress is consulting her dark prophets at the onset of her reign of terror. The torrent of the might-have-been begins to flood. Pray to St Peter that we do not founder before reaching the proven firmness of the further shore. Pray, all of you. Evil is abroad!

Elizabeth I *is being affirmed at the outset of her reign by her magical adviser,* **Dr Dee**, *on a black and white chequered floor. Music.*

Present: **Elizabeth**, **Dee**, **Kelly**.

Elizabeth *has a red wig, tall, with a white powdered face, and body naked.*

Dr Dee *is dressed in contemporary scholastic or magical outfit. A raunchy, near-naked, shaven-headed* **Kelly** *crouches over the calculations and the astrological zodiac on the floor.* **Dee** *and* **Kelly** *prepare* **Elizabeth** *as the focus of the universe. She sits in the centre of the zodiac with the sun in one hand, the moon in the other.* **Kelly** *manages to be craven and lecherous all at once.* **Dee** *is scholastic.*

Dee   I am Dr Dee, this is my assistant, Kelly. Your Majesty, I am honoured you have chosen us for a consultation.

Kelly   The angels all rejoice as well!

Elizabeth   I have asked Lord Walsingham to keep this meeting from the gaze and record of my future subjects. (*Pause.*) It is for protection of the realm.

Dee   An outstanding subject to broach with the angelic host. We should dignify the request with the outward accoutrements of your sincere wish.

Kelly *comes forward with a gold cloak for* **Elizabeth** *and proceeds to wrap it around her.*

Kelly   What kind of protection did Your Royal Highness have in mind?

Elizabeth   Divine.

Kelly Dr Dee and I can only undertake to negotiate with the lower orders, dominions, principalities and powers.

Elizabeth Why not God direct?

Kelly The divine light in which his presence is bathed would destroy the supplicants. Even his appointees.

Elizabeth What if I prayed?

Dee If prayer was enough you would not be here, Your Majesty. Do you wish to continue to honour us by taking instruction or will you dispense with our service?

Elizabeth I'll stay.

Kelly *dressing* **Elizabeth**.

Kelly I pray for you. Dr Dee prays for you. His wife and the rest of the country is praying for you. If prayer was everything we'd all be in heaven by now, married and gone to bed all together. That's what happens in heaven. An angel told me that if we should be like them, we should hold all our wives in common. But that won't happen here. Not for you anyway. Let's have a look at your hand, see if you're of a sensual disposition.

Elizabeth I know I am not.

Kelly I kiss the narrow virgin hand of my lady, monarch of all our rocky coasts, monarch of forests fair, monarch of all the stews.

Takes hand.

Dee It is time to begin.

Kelly With this cloak, you out-dazzle the Spanish gold, and with this gold band, you wed your country to its destiny. This orb the talisman stands for the sun in splendour, whose rays are ranks of angels praising God, and whose officers we shall contact to seal approval.

Elizabeth *is officially crowned in burlesque, mid stage, in the middle of the zodiac. Music, lights.*

Kelly *sits down with a glowing crystal,* **Dee** *with a book.* **Kelly** *stares into the crystal.*

Dee   Now we invite the archangels to witness this, by invoking their subordinates on your behalf.

Elizabeth   Will they answer to you?

Dee   They will; they have blessed the true and simple faith your father re-established when he united Church and throne. Your need for a long and happy reign I have writ here in form round the seal of Solomon, so the proposal is already before them. We seek not to apprehend God but simply to alert his servants. The system I have myself worked out numerically and with my own runes and sigils, to avoid any chance of diabolic interference. Begin, Kelly.

Kelly   (*trance-like*)   The clouds unfold. I see what is revealed.

Dee   Begin with sixty-eight. No, forty-two . . . Forty-two?

Kelly   (*gazing into crystal*)   I have him.

Dee   Who is above?

As **Kelly** *speaks,* **Dee** *moves between his book and the pattern on the floor, with a stick as a pointer.*

Kelly   Eight.

Dee   Too high too fast.

Elizabeth   What's up?

Dee   (*to* **Elizabeth**)   We could not hold discourse coming that suddenly even on the lowest of the entities, else the supplication, like a trickster's cardhouse, tumbles down to a mess of numbers on the floor which even the Court could not rise above.

Elizabeth   Who is eight? Is that below the archangels?

Kelly   Shshsh!

Dee   Their names all correspond to numbers. The good angels allow us to deal with their numbers only, that is how we know that they are good. But I must ask Your Majesty to maintain quiet through this operation for its best success.

Kelly   Nineteen, I can see a nineteen, she pledges. And a seventeen.

Elizabeth   What is the archangel Gabriel's number in the hierarchy? Anon could I speak to him?

Dee   Not if you were well advised. Not Gabriel, not God.

Kelly   Fourteen. Twenty-one. Ten. Ten. Ten.

Dee   We have sufficient to move above ten, Kelly,

Kelly   Ten, ten, ten . . .

Dee   Do not delay, friend, go higher up!

Elizabeth   Since God invested me and I draw my authority from him, why cannot I speak with him direct?

Dee   Quiet, child. Kelly, are you at seven yet?

Kelly   I would be, but she keeps putting me off with her stupid questions. Ten, ten, ten . . . No. I've lost him.

Dee   Start again at sixty-eight.

Kelly   Interfering bitch . . .

Dee   What number was that?

Kelly   I see twenty-six!

Dee   Rest a moment.

Kelly   Elohim, Elohim, where are you?

Dee   What's that? Do not go to one? Did you say one?

Kelly   I forget. (*Pause.*) I'm getting tired.

Dee   One is below the Godhead, which the Magus Zoroaster discovered the symbol for and wrote it as eternity. The zero.

Kelly   (*low*)   . . . Cunt . . . (*Falls over in a trance.*)

Dee This is no great matter, Your Majesty, he will revive anon. At any rate, he was aiming too high. We could not start at one. We should come upon the sacred Ass, like Balaam.

Elizabeth Dr Dee, your assistant has a reputation as a most notorious forger. Is it true?

Dee Your Majesty, he did pass base coinage, before I rescued him. But he has now professed the love of Jesu Christ and clings to the cross with the most touching devotion. He will not fail us.

Kelly Cling? You mean nailed to it, that's how close I am. One of the two thieves, executed with Christ. I don't clip any more. People couldn't understand my good fortune, a poor penniless student and there I was picked up and patronised by the biggest wizard in the land. They see us together and they say, look at him, he knows everything, what's he doing with that thing? But he needs me. He can't see the angels like I can.

Elizabeth So do you help him converse with the spirits?

Kelly That's right, ma'am, I do.

Elizabeth Explain again the precautions you take to see that the heavenly messengers don't play you false. They could be Belial or Beelzebub.

Dee Truly Your Majesty, there is no such thing as a false number. If you are interested, I could show you the expanded keys which are written to bridge numbers with Enochian, the language of the angels.

Elizabeth Are all numbers true then?

Kelly (*mocking*) True to themselves, as true as tennis balls.

Kelly *goes back to the crystal.*

Dee Begin slowly, away from the centre of all things, at eighty.

Kelly I am well up from eighty.

Dee Come back then.

Kelly I saw a forty-love flash by, with a pretty boy put out such a racket . . .

Dee (*to* **Elizabeth**) Sometimes he imagines sports or sees them I know not which, but he can watch for hours some Royal Tennis game. (*To* **Kelly**.) Put boys aside, and seek out numbers only. Sixty.

Kelly I am being borne upwards. I cannot halt the rise.

Elizabeth (*to* **Kelly**) How long have you been scrying for Dr Dee?

Kelly (*to* **Elizabeth**) Seven years. (*To* **Dee**.) I'm going up to primes.

Dee Not yet, we are not ready. Summon twenty-six.

Kelly Too low, too low . . . Ten-nine-eight-seven-six-

Dee We are not ready! Halt the ascent!

Kelly -five-four-three-two-one-

He lets out a great scream and falls down.

Elizabeth Dr Dee your assistant appears unwell. Is he *possessed*?

Dee (*dismissive*) No, he would chew grass and froth green.

Elizabeth Has he accomplished aught?

Dee He has obtained for you the gift of a long and happy reign. These sessions are at great cost to his health. He passed too close to the sun, that great Zero, but he'll recover.

Elizabeth Well Kelly, here is your unclipped reward. Perhaps it will keep you from knavery.

Kelly *recovers from his fit and sits up slowly. He bites the coin* **Elizabeth** *has given him.*

Kelly What's this? I used to lie with a wharfinger for gold. But then he drowned. (*Pause.*) I've done.

Dee   Madam, he is overcome by your generous gift. He is but my assistant.

Elizabeth   You'll not want either if you have done good magic for me and I reign long. You are both required to keep our compact close.

Dee   It will be as unknown, Madam, as our own great orbs travel round the sun. You should have success now.

Elizabeth   Oh – Did my Lord Walsingham not instruct you to obtain the most favourable date for my coronation?

Dee *brings forward calculations and a horoscope chart.*

Dee   It is done. The ripest date and exact time the crown should descend on your head with Mercury trine the moon. Venus however is squared with constellations which could provide some hard dry aspects –

Elizabeth   What means this?

Dee   Taken with Mercury, it would presage an intellectual renaissance under you, if you should graciously permit it. Perhaps the founding of a Navigation Library to speed Britannia's glory through the world –

Elizabeth   Pox on your maps, shall I have children? (*Pause.*) Sir, I employ you to tell truth.

Dee (*diplomatic*)   Either the state will flourish, or your children shall, but not both together.

Elizabeth   That's settled then. I'll not wed. Not worth the candle.

Kelly   An angel just spoke to me on that matter, standing on the same Venus mound that covers your virginity.

Dee   We have done with invocation, Kelly. Your Majesty, I think you should withdraw.

Elizabeth   What did it say?

Kelly   The angel said that should I catch your wandering womb, I'd find it lined with gold.

Elizabeth   No one clips there, sir, and you have your reward already.

Kelly (*another voice*)   'Fuck. Oh fuck . . . Oh fuck . . .'

Dee   Kelly, enough. This is some wild invention on his part. That is not how we invoke, but he is often taken like this after traffic. The Queen is leaving, Kelly, disinfest yourself.

Kelly *pulls himself together, sneezes.*

Dee *and* **Kelly** *bow as the* **Queen** *exits with a royal fanfare. Then they follow her off.*

The **Pope** *comes forward and the others leave unceremoniously as the light goes off them.*

Pope   And so it is settled. The bad fairy Elizabeth ascends to her accursed throne. Giordano Bruno travels to her diabolic court where he resides arrogantly for a number of years before impudently returning to Venice, from whence he is removed to Rome, where we earnestly detain him for seven years before surrendering to the popular cries for justice. Why so long before performing thermal application? Because in the struggle between the demon Queen and the Holy Church, the fate of the world lies in balance. And all that time before we burnt him I was tormented by the suspicion that he had information, that would be of use to save the world against the darkness from the North.

The **Pope** *bangs on the ground three times with his staff. Lighting change.*

Pope   We call before the Papal Court of the Inquisition Giordano Bruno of Nola, accused of heresy on several counts. We wish him to confess his sins and throw himself on the mercy of the Holy Catholic faith. He has chosen to take issue with the holy officers. His ill-founded confidence springs from the seed of pride in his breast, which must be plucked out root and branch for his soul to avoid damnation. I hear the Venetian inquisition will not release him to Rome for further questioning. They are soft in

Venice. Very well . . . Tell them that he has forged his bookplates in order to pass off his wretched offerings as published under their protection.

Bruno *suddenly emerges from behind.*

Bruno   I'm here already, your Holiness. I am Bruno, the Nolan.

Pope   Bruno is this a trick? Have you used magic? Where are your arresting officers?

Bruno   They're waiting outside.

Pope   This is most irregular. You have performed an act to make your arresting officers vanish. How have you accomplished it? (*He looks in the wings.*)

Bruno   I am not a black magician. If I was, I would have slipped the bonds of prison and melted through the bars, leaving an effigy in straw behind. I am flesh and blood. Who would wish to impersonate me in my unfortunate position?

Pope   While I can agree with what you say, I also have to bear in mind that your life's work has been to try to make my authority appear ridiculous. A pact with the devil, yes?

Bruno   I assure you I employed no magic to cross the Italian winter plains. I can remember each step of the journey under armed guards. Morning and evening they religiously searched me for incriminating talismen. Once a black dog sat under my chair at an inn in a thunderstorm and they were so frightened they would have let me have my freedom. But I begged them to continue because I was going to Rome to clear my name. The principal guards were a pair of brothers who claimed distant kinship with great Michaelangelo whom the Vatican so wisely patronised.

Pope   Ah yes, the ceiling painter. To the trial –

Bruno   Another trial.

Pope   You presumably thought I wanted to offer you a cardinal's robe.

Bruno   I know I have nothing to fear, but where are the other judges? In Venice I had three.

Pope   I am both judge and jury.

Bruno   What is the charge?

Pope   There are a number, but I suggest the one you should address yourself to as the most serious is the charge of necromancy that your landlord gave such damning evidence for in Venice. You may speak freely.

Bruno   The black arts. My landlord, Signor Modecino, demanded that I teach him the black arts. He wanted knowledge which I could not give him. I can show you if I can have my books.

Pope   Why do you need access to your books then?

Bruno   Only to refresh my arguments against the black arts.

Pope   There's something else in them, isn't there, beside devotion to God. Perhaps a little code, an acrostic for invocation . . . ?

Bruno   You will have to show me. I know nothing of this.

Pope   Sorcery is a serious matter. There is no time limit, for our investigation, and every exoneration is reversible. But if you should care to unburden your conscience, rest assured the dark arts will be safe with us. You may have your books if you cooperate. You consorted with Elizabeth knowing her to be excommunicated. Does Elizabeth of England use sorcery?

Bruno   No.

Pope   What kind of magic is it then Elizabeth of England uses? You were after all close to her in England.

Bruno   I was the French ambassador's secretary, in return for somewhere to sleep. I spoke no English.

Pope   *She* speaks both Latin and Italian. You were at the court for two years. Somehow she has acquired powers to defeat us. What are they?

Bruno   A navy?

Pope   The winds of heaven were promised to fill the sails of the Armada. What happened?

Bruno   I was a penniless scholar, a catholic, living on the charity of learned men. I never communicated with Elizabeth. Would that I had, for I could have converted her to the true faith –

Pope   Your written address to her is 'Diva'.

Bruno   It is always important to maintain the correct forms of address amongst strangers.

Pope   This testimonial would appear to suggest quite a different relationship.

Bruno   I had always hoped Elizabeth's excommunication could be reversed.

Pope   Bruno, you are being tried by the courts of the Inquisition. This is your second trial. I beg you to be serious for your own sake. Your life is at stake. You cannot believe so strongly in reincarnation that you can ignore what is happening in the world. You come back to Italy. Did you think that the Holy See was in such disregard that you could live out the rest of your days under our nose?

Bruno   Having done no wrong – I did hope that I would be allowed to dwell in Italy. Your Holiness, how long shall this debate with you extend?

Pope   Indefinitely. Unless of course you make your confession now when we would decide if it merited further consideration. We would consider dropping the charges of heresy, completely, if you told us about her powers. I am offering you freedom. You could walk out that door . . .

Bruno   You are as bad as Modecino! I will not deceive you. I have nothing to say. I know nothing.

Pope   We must talk further. Tomorrow. Maybe. Or the day after. No hurry.

Lighting change.

Pope   This is your cell. By day we interrogate, at night you may examine your soul in solitude, beg Christ's protection against the scalding fires of the eternal flames, for these your heavy heresies.

*He gives **Bruno** several books.*

Bruno (*takes them*)   I thank you for the privilege of my books.

Pope   What words does she use, Elizabeth, in her spells?

Bruno   If what I have written is heretical, then perhaps you could point out the spell where it was written down.

Pope   Are you acquainted with Christ's true mission?

Bruno   I ... yes ... I pray to him. He has saved my soul by his sacrifice.

Pope   Then what made you say that Christ wrought miracles by magic?

Bruno   I have never even thought such a thing.

Pope   I have one – no two depositions –

Bruno   Who invented these devilries?

Pope   What is important is not who accuses you but whether the accusations are true. One last time I ask you, what is Elizabeth's secret? Bruno, it is all we want to know.

Bruno   You accuse her falsely of witchcraft, and because you cannot get your hands on her, you burn me instead.

Pope   That's enough! Your brag that death has no terror for you is well known – How about a garrotte?

*The **Pope** sets about strangling **Bruno** with his rosary.*

Bruno   So you are the judge, jury and now executioner.

Pope   No one can stop me now. It's just you and me in here.

Bruno   You and me and the risen Christ, surely.

Pope   How can you dare take his name when you have spit on his harrowing of hell – kneel and beg his forgiveness. Before your name is struck from the Book of Life –

Bruno *prays.*

Bruno   Christ I beseech pity for all wrongs that I have done, you know I have wrought no magic and my sole desire is to see you throned in heavenly glory with the Father and the Holy Ghost, above the archangels who continually do cry Holy, Holy –

Thunder.

Pope   Shut up. What's that?

Music, smoke, reveal **Elizabeth** *regally attired this time.*

Pope   Avanti! Avanti Satani!

Bruno   Elizabeth! My queen!

Pope *is struck by a spell from* **Elizabeth** *and retires.*

Music. Lights on stage. **Bruno** *kneels to* **Elizabeth**, *kisses her hand, she brings him to his feet. Tableau.*

Pope   My attention must have faltered for a vital moment for I did not see how he invoked her. One moment I was interrogating Bruno in his cell, the next my implacable enemy had entered the arena. The witch Elizabeth immediately threw a spell at me and I found myself becoming a maggot in Bruno's filthy straw. She didn't even bother to step on me. She was so confident of having vanquished her old adversary. So I sat there. In a minute I knew that if this maggot was not trodden on I would emerge into a bluebottle. And so it happened. More quickly than you might think. Having carefully dried my wings for the ascent I rose up and settled down next to the remains of a squashed bedbug underneath a small crucifix at shoulder height, on the wall, perfect for overhearing conversation. Many of our Calendar of Saints have levitated, and Christ himself flew up and into heaven, but I believe I must have been the first fly on the wall to carry the heavy responsibilities of the keys of St Peter. Listening to their conversation I rapidly realised that in spite of my own flight control, in matters of heavenly ascent, the Protestants were several years ahead of us. (*Sits.*)

Bruno What, Elizabeth, have they cast you in here as well? Your Majesty you are so much younger than I remember.

Elizabeth Oh, you flatterer! This is my eternal body, not the earthly one which crinkles.

Bruno I am afraid they will come in and apprehend you. I don't understand. If you'd died I would have heard the church bells go.

Elizabeth I am a free spirit. You are to join us shortly.

Bruno Where?

Elizabeth In a place you have described. I was listening to your conversation with the Pope. You haven't changed. You trust men to listen to you too much. It is like pride, it brings a fall.

Bruno God does not instruct us to lie about him. Why should men not be convinced by the truth?

Elizabeth Oh Bruno, you should have been born at a different time. A hundred years ago even Popes were proud to count themselves sons of the Renaissance. They're burning you because none of the intellectual liberties survived from the good old days.

Bruno Why have you come to me?

Elizabeth To rescue you, of course.

Bruno But how have you come – You say yours is an

eternal body?

Elizabeth   Shush. I would not make a window of my soul quite yet. Walls have ears. Do you bring any plays with you? The masque of love of yours performed at Court on earth would not bear a revival, but I'd kill for something new.

Bruno   There is a play not yet performed, *Il Candalaio*. I confess it was not much on my mind tonight –

Elizabeth   Oh, excellent! And you have it here. (**Elizabeth** *takes it out of the pile of* **Bruno**'s *books.*) That's what I came for. (*Reads.*) A comedy? Good! I'll give it to Mr Shakespeare straight away.

Bruno   Shakespeare is with you?

Elizabeth   He is our master of revels. He's still at work of course but even he cannot keep up with our appetite for diversion. He's not quite as you remember him, but I'm sure he'll love your play. Come with me. Are you still all at sea with where I'm from?

Bruno   Your Majesty, your timely arrival banished a creature of the night who was not content with burning me, but had to strangle me as well. My thoughts are all distracted.

Elizabeth   I had forgot your tormentor! Where do lice gather most inside your tunic?

Bruno   Lately, here, on the seams.

Elizabeth *squeezes the seams with her fingernails.*

Elizabeth   I changed your oppressor into an insect, must be one of these. Now we'll give him a royal execution – there.

Amplified popping and squishing as she works.

It's done. There. You're saved.

Bruno   But they execute judgement tomorrow!

Elizabeth Dearest fiery spirit, torch-bearer of the
universal light, do not stay pressed in this dark place.
Come with me. When you join the heavenly host, your
advancement can be swift if you're entertaining. You can
come to heaven right now.

Bruno How come? I'm still alive.

Elizabeth By a mental training through which you said
you were able to leave your body and enter into another
state. You told me that the properly trained soul can
mount by degrees into the Theatre of Universal Memory,
by a system you developed. Have you forgot? Imagine you
are standing in the Theatre of Memory itself. In this room
we go to this alcove which contains a memory or clue, and
then we follow instructions to proceed up the mental stairs
to the roof and the stars. And now we're flying. Apply the
intellect to the microcosm and draw on the pure and
harmless sympathies of nature to rise from one world to
another. The canopy of heaven above the great globe
parts, and we ascend. Come then. The journey can bear
you to the same heaven as Mr Shakespeare and myself
now occupy. There are many heavens, but few as sweet as
ours. If you lose me, look for the one very like England –

Bruno You mean where the turf is close cropped and
dewy, royal swans are constantly being marked and the sun
shines perpetually? I never thought to see it again!

Effects as they 'rise' while staying in the same place.

Elizabeth Stitch your thoughts to the stars and then
follow them up. I hope we shall be more than friends in
heaven. We are close to God already and at night we look
up to see his multiplication in infinity, a countless number
of worlds across the heavens. (*Mocking.*) I never knew you
tongue-tied before Bruno? A penny for your thoughts?

Bruno I beg your pardon Majesty – but I am so taken
up in comparisons with what I had imagined many times
that I had forgot my thanks to you. I have never seen so
many stars. With so much life broadcast throughout the

universe, damnation must be meaningless.

Elizabeth   Not entirely so. Creatures from hell do still visit us.

Bruno   But is not the fear of hell much worse than the reality?

Elizabeth   Oh, infinitely.

Bruno   Just as I thought.

Music, lights, star effects, but not too large as **Bruno** *and* **Elizabeth** *astral travel and talk as they go.*

Bruno   Your Majesty must know that one of the reasons the Inquisition has been so hard on me is that I did not hide my delight when you beat the Spaniard.

Elizabeth   That was not me. That was God. Storms are his handiwork. We have found it is as you said, he dwells in the sun, and heaven is close beneath. Our dwelling place is eternal, invisible to the eyes of men.

Bruno   That's right. Seven years ago I would have sworn that the stars and planets were eternal. But I understand now you can only apply the idea of eternity to the universe.

Elizabeth   Did God preview his doctrine to you that you are so authoritative before you have even reached your new abode?

Bruno   I worked it out for myself actually. Just like the Theatre of Memory. Both rely on maintaining a state of rational ecstasy. Of the two kinds of spiritual ecstasy, one is in the grasp of ignorant people, peasants, the sort of people Christ picked for the bulk of his disciples. The divine comes into them as if into an empty room, a sort of poetic inspiration. But they don't know what to do with their material because their conditioning hasn't prepared them for their insights. The other kind is like me –

Elizabeth *claps her hands as if to kill an insect in the air. She follows its fall to the ground.*

Bruno   What are you doing?

Elizabeth   We were pursued by a common bluebottle from the noisomeness of your cell. There are of course no insects in heaven apart from the blessed scarab beetle sacred to the sun and beloved of the Egyptians.

Bruno   I can't remember what I was saying.

Elizabeth   You spoke of your own unique excellence. I'm sure you will remember to return to the topic. But we are here.

Shakespeare *is revealed, writing furiously at a white cube of a desk. It glows from within. Tableau.*

Elizabeth   Shakespeare's writing. Don't ever interrupt him! If he ever looks up, tell him you have brought your play.

Bruno   Do you mean he has to pass it first?

Elizabeth   He's master of our revels, that's right. And if it is performed here, you never need return to earth to burn, you will stay with us.

Elizabeth *exits.* **Shakespeare** *suddenly examines his inkpot.*

Shakespeare   Ah! There's a creature drowning in there! (*He flicks it out.*)

Pope (*stands*)   Although badly wounded by the demon Queen, I had been still able to fly. I was navigating a course over the expanse of Shakespeare's desk, when the down draught from Elizabeth's passage made me lose control of my altitude. I spiralled down and landed in the ink, which was suffering a constant bombardment from the heretic's pen as he built his glass mountains of lies about the legitimacy of the Tudor succession! I was wondering if I should stay in there till sufficient falsehoods had lowered the level of the ink and I could stand on the bottom, but before that, the so-called Universal Genius condescended to notice me and I was hoist up by one particularly violent flick which enabled me to gain the air. Half blinded with the black juice, which was already dripping the dark night of its delusions over my many single retinas, I made my solitary way back between the worlds, praying I would not fall prey to one of the wild cats of the Coliseum, who were in the habit of taking ants or flies as a little snack after supper. My wings at the end failed completely and I dragged myself into the Vatican leaving an inky trail which I prayed that God could see as his damaged pontiff's signature. Fortunately the Vatican cats had been fed that evening, and I crawled under the door of my bedroom wondering how I was going to explain that I had been changed to a fly and that Bruno was in heaven before we had taken a lighted taper to his pyre.

Pope *stumbles offstage.* **Shakespeare** *continues to write, dipping the pen in the pot furiously.*

Bruno *approaches* **Shakespeare** *writing at a large white table.* **Bruno** *picks up a piece of paper and studies it carefully.* **Shakespeare** *continues to write. He looks up.*

Bruno   What are you writing?

Shakespeare   A play.

Bruno   You write quickly.

Shakespeare   It was going well till a mosquito fell in the ink.

Bruno   Do you write much here?

Shakespeare   All the time.

Bruno   I thought heaven was meant to be a place of ecstasy.

Shakespeare   This is the lower slopes, where we make our own amusements.

Bruno *peers at the blank paper which* **Shakespeare** *is writing on.*

Bruno   Mind if I take a look?

Shakespeare   Not really.

Bruno Do people ask you where you get your ideas from?

Shakespeare Why should they? I've never made a secret of my sources.

Bruno I wondered if you'd read anything of mine.

Shakespeare Oh God, another hopeful! I am plagued by them.

Bruno Do you know who I am? Queen Elizabeth sent me.

Shakespeare I'm afraid up here you're just one more of the would-be writing debutantes that the Queen is always trying to press into apprenticeship with me, in the forlorn hope that I'll fashion him into her ideal poet spouse.

Bruno Why does she want a poet?

Shakespeare It's a long story, but a poet is the only thing in the welkin that she'll consider taking for her maidenhead.

Bruno Down in Nola where I was born, we never set that much store by virginity. Twelve Roman gates to the town, all of them stoved in, one after the other in a perfect example of a historical loss of virtue.

Shakespeare I give up. Which famous Italian are you that Elizabeth has convinced herself once again that she's wet for between the royal legs?

Bruno I've given you enough hints. You tell me.

Shakespeare *completely ignores this and carries on writing.*

Bruno Elizabeth said you'd changed. I can see. Any particular reason? Where are you from, now?

Shakespeare I am still from Stratford in the county of Warwickshire. Yes I'm a woman now, by choice. It's nobody's business but my own and I've still no idea who you are.

Bruno   I'll give you one more clue. I was at Elizabeth's
court. That's how she knew me and why she picked me to
come here. In addition to the *commedia* piece, I wrote a
masque, when I was in England, where the Greek gods all
speak in praise of love. It's one of the things that they're
setting fire to me for.

Looks at **Shakespeare**'s *work.*

Bruno   *Love's Labour's Lost.* Would you like a decent title?

Shakespeare   Not really. The Globe told me to keep my
titles as short as possible. The hook in Love's is in the
alliteration. What's your play called?

Bruno   *Speccio Delle Bestia Trionfante.*

Shakespeare   I'm sorry I don't speak Italian. That's not,
wait – The Expulsion of the Triumphant Beast? (*Pause.*)
Berowne. Brown. Bruno! I know who you are. Giordano
Bruno! What an honour and privilege!

Bruno   No, please, sit down.

Shakespeare   And by an amazing coincidence I've just
written – oh. Have a look at this speech, anyhow, I think it
might amuse you.

Bruno   (*picks up paper and reads*)
   For valour, is not love a Hercules,
   Still climbing trees in the Hesperides?
   Subtle as Sphinx, as sweet and musical
   As bright Apollo's lute, strung with his hair
   And when love speaks, the voice of all the gods
   Make heaven drowsy with the harmony.

Shakespeare   The doctrine of universal love is
unmistakeable, even if I've softened your edges a little. It's
rather clotted, I admit, but it's actually a tribute to your
philosophy. By a character called Berowne.

Bruno   (*sulky*)   Very nice, but my name is not Berowne.

Shakespeare   It is – almost.

Bruno   Is Berowne burnt at the stake?

Shakespeare   No.

Bruno   Then how do they know it's me?

Shakespeare   Because in England everybody knows the great wandering magus! I'm not surprised our dear Queen wanted a play of yours. Can I see?

Bruno *gives it to him.*

Bruno   What do you think of *The Chandler* as a title? Short enough?

Shakespeare   I promise not to steal it. Is it codpiece theatre?

Bruno   It's *commedia dell l'arte.*

Shakespeare   Hmm, probably not for the Globe. Maybe you should try Alleyn's.

Bruno   I haven't offered it anywhere. I was asked to bring it here to you.

Shakespeare   Have you written it yet?

Bruno   Have I written it? I wrote it years ago! You're holding it!

Shakespeare   Don't be too certain. I have a suspicion that this may not be the first time I have attempted *Love's Labour's Lost*. But then it disappears off the page.

Bruno   This Brown – character – You don't make fun of me, do you? I'm seriously concerned about my reputation as a man of ideas. I don't want to be Brown in some footling comic froth – dripping with unnecessary goodwill. Don't drown Brown in your zabaglione! Give me a proper character! Someone with determination who proves a point!

Shakespeare   Ah. Nothing would please me more at this moment to say that Brown proves a point but your ideas have such virility and diffusion that I have not placed the burden of them on any one particular character. Your influence is on every page.

Bruno But you say I am not there on the page.

Shakespeare I think I have been as influenced by you as by any man. It's a generous tribute, from a working author. Can I help you in any other way?

Bruno No, but the Queen would like my play performed.

Shakespeare That's a very interesting suggestion. I know Liz is keen for her own reasons. But it's not as simple as all that. Let me ask you a question. Is the play you have written for the ages? Sometimes satire dates.

Bruno *The Chandler*'s great fun, a good play.

Shakespeare Fun ... and an excellent brief title, but has *The Chandler* been entered as challenger in any theatrical lists? Has it mirthfully slain all nay-sayers and made lady groundlings lose bladder control? (*Pause.*) Has it been performed?

Bruno It has not been played in its entirety, no.

Shakespeare I've set plays in Italy and got away with it. But I'm no Catholic. Could we move it to somewhere neutral, like Bohemia? I should also warn you that since the Armada, plays with foreign characters have been absolutely box office poison. Elizabeth thinks that she can bring in any stray talents to join us here, but this play of yours may not please her enough, and then where will you be?

Shakespeare *takes up the script of* Il Candalaio *which is also on the table with* Love's Labour's Lost.

Shakespeare What manner of play is this again?

Bruno Both learned, and a comedy.

Shakespeare *makes a terrible face.*

Shakespeare So it's a category-smasher, is it? Oh dear. (*Reads from the manuscript.*)

'To the Lady Morgana his ever honoured lady. And to who should I dedicate *Il Candalaio?* To whom shall I send what has by Sirius' celestial influence during these burning, hour by hour more piercing, so-called dog days, made the fixed stars swim in my brain,' blah blah . . . 'The firmament's wandering glow-worms pierce me like a sieve . . .'

– And that's just the prologue. By glow-worms do you mean planets?

Bruno No. Comets.

Shakespeare I thought you might be weaving in a little bit of astrology there. I love it so much the theatre's shareholders tell me to water it down. Hardly surprising, half of them are Capricorns. (**Shakespeare** *picks up the script and continues to read the dedication.*)

'My Lady Morgana, a great gulf stretches between you, happy in Abraham's bosom, and me burning and sizzling in anguish without the solace of your tongue.'
That's a prophetic dedication about your end. How chilling.

Bruno It was a joke. What kind of fire does she put out with her tongue, huh? Abraham's bosom is of course a comic cliché –

Shakespeare I take your point. Absolutely. Fine. I realise fully Abraham doesn't actually *have* a bosom. It's just that sometimes the sword of metaphor is wielded by those who never sharpen its ironic blade. Could I get you a drink?

Bruno Do they serve Lacrima Christi?

Shakespeare (*puzzled*) The tears of Christ? No. (*He tinkles a little bell.*)

Bruno It's local wine from Vesuvius. I used to take a flagon out to the fields with the girls when I was a novice.

Shakespeare This is the English heaven. You can have

anything you like here, as long as it's beer.

Bruno   It doesn't matter. I drank beer in England.

*A Tudor **Barmaid** brings two tankards on.*

Shakespeare   Yes, disgusting habit, isn't it? This horse piss is meant to be Midland Ale.

Bruno   You know, one thing I remember about England above all is its women. Graceful, gentle, soft, delicate, young and slim with fair hair and firm breasts.

Shakespeare   Like the barmaid here?

Bruno *notices the* **Barmaid**.

Bruno   Yes! Barmaid, what's your name?

Barmaid   Oh sir, I'm not going to tell you that, sir. That's personal. Call me 'Barmaid' and have done with it.

Bruno   How can I be intimate with your good parts and still call you Barmaid?

Shakespeare   She'll not give up her name. It has the key to govern her as man should govern woman. Her mother Sycorax does untold harm. She creeps upon young men asleep, pressing their heated dreams to fill her cup then, changing from a female form to male, she lies with a maid all innocent, and warms her drowsy fancy with a kiss. The sleeper stirs to embrace the wraith, and the potent witch cracks home her advantage, spitting the myriad darts of mischief, through Hymen's sleepy door.
And raw young men – as such a one I was – awake from troubled sleep at the altar rail.

Bruno *inspects the* **Barmaid**.

Bruno   I've never been visited by such a succubus myself. Are you quite sure?

Shakespeare   She rides in a coven, each full moon. Ask her.

Bruno   Barmaid, do you fly?

Barmaid Yes sir, when I'm off-duty.

Bruno Will I have to wait a month?

Barmaid Why, no sir, for we are all on Great Helios' doorstep here, and he smiles out upon the earthly moon so bright that it is always full.

Shakespeare What did I tell you?

Bruno Look on this fair maid. Where is her harelip, her anathema?

Shakespeare Her curse is that she bears a bill of fare, writ in a troubled hand across her shame which will never deliver what it promises. She shows it willingly to any traveller.

Barmaid Would you like to look at the menu sir?

Bruno I am not hungry thank you.

Shakespeare I insist. Barmaid, the menu, please.

Barmaid *raises her skirts and* **Shakespeare** *inspects the* **Barmaid**'s *behind upstage.*

Shakespeare Barmaid move over please. That's right. 'Act One' – that must be the starters. French. 'Act Two' – is that cuck, or cake? It's right inside the cheek. I should know it by heart, it never changes.

Barmaid It's all freshly painted on today sir.

Shakespeare Bruno, you're a much travelled man, what's this foreign dish, writ there below the winnets, next her mole?

Bruno *helps him look.*

Bruno I think it has to be 'French toast in her garter'.

Shakespeare Can you conceive of the taste of such a diabolic dish?

Bruno Its seasoning surely depends on how high the garter rides.

Shakespeare   None of this exists except as proof of her unnatural lineage. I'll show you.

Shakespeare *sits upright and the* **Barmaid** *straightens up.*

Shakespeare   Barmaid, my friend of the inflamed appetite would like the Cuckold Pie à l'Anglais. Is it fresh today? (*To* **Bruno**.) Listen to these excuses.

Barmaid   Lawks sir, the Cuckold's all been snapped up tonight along with everything. There was a coach party came through so there's precious little left; one Codpiece à la King, and a portion of woad pudding from yesterday.

Shakespeare   Why couldn't you have told us this before woman? Do you think I enjoy fossicking in your behind?

Barmaid   I don't have to take those kind of remarks from anyone!

Shakespeare   You swiving-pit. You painted mercenary on the milestone to eternity, you sump of stolen essential juices!

Barmaid *smiles.*

Bruno   Barmaid, let me at least pay for the beer. Here are two Spanish crowns, one for each glistening cheek.

Barmaid   Oh, thank you sir, but we got no change for heathen gold.

Bruno   Take it on account, I don't believe I could ever be short-changed by such a heavenly creature.

Barmaid   Thank you kindly sir. At least there's one gentleman in the company, even if he is Italian. Sir, if you would like some more acquaintance with our English customs, I could see you in the taproom after closing time, 'bout half an hour, see to the overflowing of your lower purse.

Bruno   I have no more coinage.

Barmaid (*whisper*)   No – silly – to make up the difference.

Bruno *blows her a kiss, she exits.*

Bruno   Oh. This is the England of my desires.

Shakespeare   Bruno, beware. There's a stickier spread in the cellar than she's letting on. She's looking for an eternal husband.

Bruno   When the subject of marriage comes up, I generally plead holy orders.

Shakespeare   Elizabeth brought you here from earth, and she will drop you down again as far if she finds her magus unfaithful.

Bruno   Why would she deny me a side-dish of such delights?

Shakespeare   Bruno, if you pursue a private entertainment, you will never be able to rise as a courtier with your play.

Bruno   Is she the Queen of heaven?

Shakespeare   She is this one. To your play. (**Shakespeare** *picks up the manuscript of the play.*) 'The main themes of my comedy are triply intertwined. An insipid love, a sordid miser fooled by alchemy, and a stupid pedant.' Yes, I've read it. (**Shakespeare** *looks at* **Bruno** *knowingly.*) Well … what can I say? Giordano … You've created a separate world, which is the first and noblest accomplishment of art. But it's the old problem. *I* like it, well enough. The bawdy is particularly very well done for an ex-monk. But at five and a half hours it's not for us. And as for exposing alchemy – Ben Jonson has been trying to flog that idea for years. I thought your aim should be more the ecstasy of enlightenment and of being at one with the Godhead, if you desire to woo Elizabeth. That's why she brought you here.

Bruno   I wrote a masque on just that subject and she didn't like it well enough to be interested in me.

Shakespeare   But then you were a foreigner, a Catholic and commoner. (*Pause.*) I'm sorry. I can't concentrate on your problems. My work is driving me crazy.

It's to do with a commission for a play I shouldn't have taken. Maybe you could help. We can't substitute *The Chandler* – but all that low comedy you have has given me ideas. What I mean is we could write it together, using bits of *The Chandler*, no? I'll finish up Berowne later, I can't promise to have him burned at the end ... The great thing about your writing is how the naughty bits just sing. Even if the virgin Queen didn't take to you, you would have made your mark in heaven, enough to keep you away from the flames. I've made a bit of a start, so you shouldn't have to do much. You wouldn't have a look at what I've done already, would you? It's just that the deadline is a killer.

Bruno All right. (*Takes script.*)

Shakespeare I should warn you Her Royal Lemonpuss has about as much a sense of humour about her virginal predicament as you'd imagine. So you'll be careful, won't you, dealing with broadness in the writing? I'm going to take a walk. Shout when you've finished.

Shakespeare *exits.* **Bruno** *reads.*

Pope (*to audience*) The fly made a rapid recovery and I was soon able to rub not six feet but two upon the gossamer-thin silk sheets. But I could not stay in bed when the black witch had carelessly shown how to walk between the worlds. This time I took the precaution of leaving a safety line in the hands of six of the Vatican's most trusted bellringers, in the event of a forced withdrawal should *she* appear on the scene again.

Pope *pays out a thick bell-pull as he advances onto the stage. He inches round to where* **Bruno** *is reading.*

Pope (*pious*) Alas, poor doomed soul.

Bruno Fuck off, I'm busy. You have no business being here. Even if you're dead.

Pope (*to* **Bruno**)   If Bruno may dwell here, then the Pope
might visit heaven. I just wanted some vital information.

Bruno   Our last conversation went on for seven years. I
don't have to come with you. I'm writing a script with
Shakespeare.

Pope   Intriguing!

Bruno   It's called 'The Wary Wives of Windsor'.

Pope   I swear I will be brief. I want to find out where we
went wrong with prosecuting you. I want to know where
we went off the rails. It's just a sort of harmless
questionnaire. And the question for which I would give all
the silver and gold of the Spanish Empire, is 'Is the sun
God?'

Bruno   See for yourself.

Pope   Bruno! The Church is founded on the rocks of
faith, by simple fishermen – we are simple people too!
Help us! Should we tell people that the sun is God? I have
responsibilities for millions of souls in the New World,
more every day. Help me from your eminence.

Bruno   There is a godlike action in the sun which is as
near as we will ever get to an understanding.

Pope   So we could tell them the sun is God.

Bruno   No. In the cosmic flux the same sun will die and
where will be your Godhead?

Pope   All right so we don't have to tell them that the sun
is God. What about the son of God? What was Christ?

Bruno   The same as he ever was. The Saviour.

Pope   But you say now his father will die. What does that
make him then?

Bruno   A little more human.

Pope   But is he a miracle worker or a magician?

Bruno   You should weigh the evidence and decide for

yourself.

Pope When John Dee bewitched all Oxford how did he work his spell?

Bruno He did not perform an incantation, he put on a play by Aristophanes, which takes an Egyptian story. A scarab flies up to Jupiter's palace.

Pope What is a scarab?

Bruno A flying beetle which keeps its young in a round ball of dung which it rolls along. They are sacred to the Egyptians. The rolling ball symbolises the fertile sun. When the scarab crawled up the wall there was a riot. They thought it was black magic. That's how intelligent the dons are there.

Pope Let me get this right. The sun, which the Egyptians think is God, is in fact a flaming ball of horseshit full of worms. So this God you worship is a piece of maggoty dung which will burn to extinction shortly? I don't know which is worse. The degradation of the ineffable name, or the fact you deny the existence of hell. Modecino says you don't believe in hell.

Bruno I only said –

Pope You should be in hell for that.

Bruno I only said we have not seen the fires. Fear eats up the soul, and makes it less. We should not cling to God from fear, but love.

Pope Modecino says you have known many females. Have you been familiar with numerous women?

Bruno Not as many as Solomon.

Pope Solomon was not a Benedictine. Modecino says you regard women as an instrument for your pleasure or merely childbearing.

Bruno Plato, not I, says they have no souls.

Pope Does the Queen of England, the one you address

as Diva, have a soul?

Bruno (*shiftily*)   She's different.

Pope   Of course, she's a witch. We have managed to deduce this much. The woman you call Diva in your dedication copulates with Satan disguised as a donkey in a Satanic rite, in order to gain power over the Holy Church. Can you furnish us with any additional information? What does she whisper to the donkey when they are doing it? What are the magic words?

Bruno   Why do you want to know?

Pope   These are dark times and the eye of heaven cannot blink. I have seen myself, in a clouded crystal, scenes come clear of such eternal desolation would freeze the human heart. If she continues to defy us, the future is beyond hope. She's going to live forever, did you know that? She tried to sell her soul to the devil, in exchange for Ireland.

Bruno (*facetious*)   But it was the Irish livestock she was interested in. She was running out of English donkeys.

Pope   Bruno, this is important. As a good Catholic – let's say you are – your duty requires you to divulge evidence of all magical practices. You were seen talking to Dee in an unknown language, our informant says – was this so-called language of angels – or devils?

Bruno   I conversed in Latin with the Doctor and I found him of learned persuasion and open heart. Dee's medium, Kelly, who scried for him was talented, but from the rabble. To him I did not speak.

Pope   What instructions did these so-called angels tend concerning religious belief?

Bruno   They told Kelly that whosoever wishes to be wise may look neither to the right nor to the left, neither to this man who is called a Catholic, nor towards that one who is called a heretic, but that he may look after the God of heaven and earth.

Pope And this science of numbers, does it stand outside the Blessed Sacrament?

Bruno No, Your Holiness, all is one, enfolded in God's love.

Pope I would like to thank you for agreeing to spend this time with a man who has wronged you Giordano. I won't waste any more of your time. I'll go below without you. Your surroundings proclaim your sincerity. You were right, I was wrong.

Bruno Am I to be reprieved from burning then?

Pope After seven years the logic of prosecution has a certain inertia. And Rome is full of cardinals who are looking forward to a visible refutation of heresy in a world shaken by the Reformation, to strengthen their resolve. Retraction at this stage would be most unpopular besides the damage it would render to the Holy See. However, I am comforted by the thought that you will feel nothing. We will go through the forms of burning your body, but we know that it is an untenanted house, and that the true Bruno is already playing in heaven. So that's settled then. Bruno, could I ask a favour of you? It's a delicate matter. I was not sure whether to broach it until I had obtained your trust. May I? (*He sits down again.*) In your dedication to Queen Elizabeth as Lady Morgana, are we correct in assuming a connection between this name and Fata Morgana or Morgan le Fay, the English King Arthur's sister who settled in Calabria, the one who is in fact Hecate, Diana's dark side, the left-handed sickle moon castratice?

Bruno I was born opposite the Straits of Messina, we used to play Fata Morgana games at school. I hadn't met Elizabeth when I wrote it. You would have found it difficult to prove conspiracy.

Pope Of course. It's just that the dedication has suggested a frightening possibility to some of our theologians in the Vatican. It is that at the time of writing

that you have forged an alliance with diabolic powers but
that the powers are cleverer than you in all your
arrogance. It is the dark powers that ensured that you
returned to Italy and took your soul away to this place
until you are burned so that you never saw the necessity of
throwing yourself on Christ's mercy. Come with me. You
are bewitched.

Renounce the demon Queen and I can promise you a
speedy death. On the Campo you will burn unnoticed and
we will later reverse the charge of heresy. You will be able
to go to the true heaven where there are good people, not
like here. How could this possibly be heaven?

Bruno, you are surrounded by phantoms. I tell you what.
Just this once – I'll make a monkey out of Vatican
procedures. We will turn the procession round. There's still
time. I'll say there has been a mistake, new evidence.
Come and work in the Vatican Library. We've got
mediums, astrologers, a crystal ball weighing thirty pounds
– the biggest show-stone in the world – and our Enochian
tables – Dee had 4000 letters. We can give you eight.
That's right, a table of eight thousand Enochian letters.
You can ask the angels anything, that way, anytime – We
need to know more about how she makes the storms. We
need men of your calibre to make a proper breakthrough.
It will be all good, clean magic. The sort you're so
accomplished at. It's your last chance, Bruno. You don't
have to say a word. You can simply kiss my ring, and the
Holy See will spread your doctrine of the sun. Isn't that
what you want? To start a complete religious revolution, in
our time? All right, so you've gone beyond heliocentricity.
The sun will burn out like a candle. The son of God is a
mountebank. Fine! Whatever it is we'll buy it. Come!
Monsignor Bruno . . .

The **Pope** *holds out his hand and the ring.* **Bruno** *takes it,*
examines it. Enter **Dee**.

Dee   A rescue! A rescue! Bruno has been seized!

The **Pope** *grabs* **Bruno**'*s hand and blows a whistle. A loud bell-*
ringing, frantic, starts. The **Barmaid** *and* **Kelly** *and*

Shakespeare *enter masked and cloaked as if for a* commedia *play. They seize* **Bruno** *and start pulling him in the other direction. Deadlock.*

Elizabeth *enters and holds up her hand and the bells die away.*

Elizabeth   Sweet, Shakespeare says you'll not let our new poet alone to read, that he's wanted on the earth. Can he not be immolated *in absentia*?

Pope   No. If he was, life would be impossible. Everybody would come up here, soon as you threatened to burn 'em.

Elizabeth   I see we have a clash of interests here. But this is an English heaven, and there is a happy medium. We will enact the judgement that you crave on Bruno here.

Pope   This judgement of your heaven hands down a mask, and paper flames and asks me to believe that this is justice?!

Elizabeth   Watch, and if you do not believe our justice when it's served, you can have him trussed like a chicken to take back with you. Mr Kelly, please invoke the ritual of Bruno's death, invoking pity at the outset.

Kelly   I cast a shadow in this happy spiritland. (*To* **Pope**.) Sit down, and live through this one, if you dare.

Music, lights change.

Pope *takes a mask and goes and sits. Characters enact parts of the story masked, in dumbshow.* **Kelly** *thumps on the floor three times for silence.*

Kelly   We record a solemn act of justice on an impenitent heretic. At the second hour of night the information came from whence we know not, of the execution of the impenitent friar in the morning. At the sixth hour of the night, the chaplain and the official comforters who had a thankless task, assembled at St Ursula and went to the prison of the Tower of Nona, where winter prayers were offered up. At the conclusion of this ceremony, which was perfunctory, everyone having great anger at Bruno's impenitence, the ex-friar was ushered in, and exhorted by the brothers, all in love, naturally, present being three Fathers of the Order of St Dominic, two of the Order of Jesus, and assorted hangers-on. Everybody made a colossal display of toleration and learning, showing him again and again his error, yet he stood firm through to the end of his obstinacy, which at this stage of the game had a certain tinge of bloody-mindedness to it. Bruno was still enlarging on several different errors in all directions, while being conducted by the servants of justice to the Campo di Fiori – the Field of Flowers. He was chained by the neck and wore a white sheet embroidered on the hem with the cross of St Andrew interspersed and stitched with little red flames. The comforters kept on pushing the crucifix in his face so roughly that it cut his lip. The officials of the Governor of Rome acted as guards. And then, being stripped and bound to a stake, he was burnt alive. There was a certain nobility about the low-cut hem of Bruno's sackcloth as the brothers stood shoulder to shoulder round him to guard against supernatural mishaps, that chilly February morning. The Brotherhood were very anxious because of several upsetting rumours. However, Morgan Le Fay did not come to rescue Bruno and it went off as planned, much to the relief of the long-range policy bureau of the Vatican and the bookies who had her appearance at two hundred and fifty to one. One of the consolers risked a nasty singeing when he reached in to offer Bruno a crucifix yet again to kiss, which was rudely refused by the obstinate impenitent in spite of his dying agonies. Much was made of this in the local news-sheets, which omitted the information that he couldn't have kissed the crucifix even if he'd wanted to: we found out we couldn't stop him answering back, so the last thing we did before we lit the bonfire, us being The Brotherhood of the Pity of St John the Beheaded, the official comforters: The Brotherhood gagged the bugger's mouth. Records show Bruno's burning was the first of twenty-five the Brotherhood supervised during the century, during which we generally sang the following –

The cast all sing a Gloria as they exit, taking **Bruno**. **Pope** *stands to address audience.*

Pope Watching them, I apprehended everything about the fateful dawn of Bruno's last day breaking in marbled pink and grey over the Campo di Fiori, down to the splinters of kindling sticking into the fingers of the woodgatherers as they unloaded their faggots onto the growing mound of wood. At the end, I believed for a moment Bruno had been burned before me. Then I realised that I had been offered a shadow judgement, and the spirits vanished before my gaze as God plunged me, without warning, into a dreamless sleep.

A single bell tolls and the lights die.

Act Two

Begins with **Bruno** *lying down alone. The* **Barmaid** *comes in to collect beer mugs.*

Barmaid Congratulations on your escape. Nice day for it, sir.

Bruno It's perfect. So this is heaven!

Barmaid That's right sir.

Bruno Where are you from?

Barmaid When foolish folks ask, I generally say I be from Mummerset.

Bruno Is Mummerset near Stratford?

Barmaid Lord love yer, zir, It's a make-believe county.

Bruno So you don't come from there?

Barmaid I do and I don't. Can't you work it out? Go on you're meant to be brainy.

Bruno Have you ever been to the real England?

Barmaid No! My mum won't let me go. She says I'm much safer up here what with the wars and plagues and persecutions. It's a pity. It's dead boring up here a lot of the time. You see, really I'm an earth spirit. What have you been doing with Mr Shakespeare then?

Bruno He's putting me in a play.

Barmaid He would, wouldn't he? Did you know when he come here, he was a man? And Elizabeth was that sweet on him but he saw straight through her. That's why he went all like a woman, to stop her pestering him. That's what my dad says. But I know why he went like a woman. Shall I tell you? So he could have more fun. But then he found when he changed over, he'd also changed his mind. I change my mind about plenty of things, but not about that. You still want to

come round the back after? I get next week-end off, maybe
you'd like to come 'ome with me. My dad's Bacchus, he's the
god of wine, you'll like him, course he don't come in here, he
knows they'd look down their noses at 'im, but he'd like to
meet you. When he's had a few, he's always on about universal
love. So much so, that when I goes home I have to lock the
bedroom door. Anyhow, there's plenty of wine to drink. Not
like 'ere. Would you like to nibble on some cheese while you're
waiting? They said the cheese was fresh. I didn't know how to
spell it so it isn't written up.

Bruno I'm sorry to hear that.

Barmaid (*confidential*) It's the 'Crotte de diable'.

Bruno What's that?

Barmaid It's something dirty, innit? French, I think.

Enter **Shakespeare**.

Shakespeare That's right. It's French for Old Nick's poop.

Barmaid I don't know about that, is that it? Anyhow, it
makes your wind go something terrible. I've just had some,
and I wouldn't want you breaking wind before I do, first time
together. I'd be that ashamed, I wouldn't want to start.

Shakespeare In that case, you should get the gentleman
some immediately.

Bruno Please – don't trouble yourself on my account. I am
not hungry for food, but beauty.

Barmaid I expect you're loving it here after all those years
cooped up in prison. All that bright sunlight, yes, and the
lovely little flowers everywhere. You do like mumbly-peg,
don't you? Or will you go along wi' Shakespeare and pour
cold water on innocent copulation? You'll have to watch him
when he's had a few.
He tells such stories you wouldn't believe. He told me my
mum disguised herself as a girl in his village, and seduced him.
I suppose it's possible – she does like eighteen-year-olds. Too
much brainwork, that's his problem. Don't forget our little

game in the taproom, will you. (*Points to* **Shakespeare**.) And don't you go telling tales to Elizabeth, or I'll put my mum on you – again.

Barmaid *exits whistling.*

Bruno   In Nola, if a girl farted during making love, it was called 'driving the devil out'. It was held to be good luck for conception if chaos was banished.

Shakespeare   It's your funeral.

Bruno   If I'm in heaven I must be dead, and that finishes my ordination. You're always writing about good old friars – well some of us have feelings just like the rest of humanity.

Shakespeare   Bruno, if you wish to escape your final fire, you should not treat this heaven as one of indulgence. We know the Pope's going to try and come back. But Elizabeth's agreed to help. I'll write you a part as her lover.

Bruno   That's a good idea, we could perform a Chemical Marriage.

Shakespeare   Please don't.

Bruno   Why not? Mysterium Conjunctis recreates the conditions of the Godhead. We would both become a globe of pure energy. We could start another solar system. That would put me beyond reach of the Pope.

Shakespeare   Can you imagine Elizabeth agreeing to that in her present frame of mind? It was hard enough to get her to be in a play with a commoner at all. Mysterium Conjunctis needs an equally interested and evolved partner. All you will find within at the moment is her fugitive hysteria.

Bruno   She came to get me.

Shakespeare   I have seen her past invitations extend to well-hung asses, geese and swans. In fact she is notoriously chaste. Your elevation as her Latin lover won't lead to a four-legged throne for hymen, let alone an incandescent one, unless I first try out the union in a play. Then if she grows familiar with your manliness, you may essay the fiery transformation. Not before, and you shouldn't be barmaiding it at the same time.

Bruno   I can manage them both.

Shakespeare   Not if you hope for bonding with Elizabeth. The daughter of Sycorax will suck you breathless and a chemical marriage needs every atom of vital air to blaze and fix a higher transformation.

Bruno   I'll bear your advice in mind. I can't promise anything though. Are you writing us into the 'Cheery Wives of Cheapside'?

Shakespeare   'The Merry Wives' does not offer opportunities for initiation into the Godhead. The characters would not know what do with a Mysterium if it branded them on the bum. I have another idea. You would be changed for courtship into an animal.

Bruno   No monkey business. I'm not collaborating. If you had done my play Elizabeth would have accepted me. But no. Instead you wanted to steal the triple plot idea for the 'Merry Wives of Willesden'.

Shakespeare   I plead guilty. What does it matter? Believe me, Bruno, your fame will come from your ideas, leave plays to borrowers.

Enter **Elizabeth**.

Elizabeth   William. Willie. Will. (*Holds out her hands.*)

Shakespeare (*less enthusiastic*)   Your Majesty!

Elizabeth   Approach and kiss us on the hand, the arms, the lips. (*She kisses him and he squirms away.*) My favourite writer! The speech you wrote for me to say at Tilbury has wrought a miracle. When I said I had the heart and stomach of a king the crowd went wild, and buoyed their own hearts to a battlefleet the size to equal anything the Spanish fleet could send. It was *good* magic that you penned, sweet Mr Shakespeare. (*She looks at* **Bruno**.) Look where our latest magus stands. Is he dead yet?

Shakespeare   He has but a quarter of an hour in him, Majesty. (*Aside to* **Bruno**.) Dead men, their tackle stiff and dripping from their sudden taking-off, are endless fodder in her fantasy right now. (*To* **Elizabeth**.) I had thought to make a suitor of the Italian for you in a play.

Elizabeth   Oh, I would love to play with the Italian sage – when he is dead! Oh Shakespeare, will you make something for us with a fairy and an ass?

Shakespeare   I can write it, but whether he will wear it is another matter.

Kelly *comes in and pushes* **Shakespeare**'s *cube off, followed by the Bard.*

Elizabeth   Bruno, you will stay awhile, won't you? Do not leave us yet. The lower slopes of heaven's a pretty place to incarnate a while, and when you fall asleep, you wake a hundred years away downstream, with all these masques forgot. Why seek the shapeless fires of God before you've tasted royalty? For in the play, no social rank, or nicety need stand between you and your prowess. Together, think, we can rehearse your tongue's sweet importuning in the royal ear, the royal garter, and raising the last curtain we will unmask together the sweetest secret of the Royal Zero.

Bruno *is presented by* **Kelly** *with an ass's head which he holds under his arm.*

Elizabeth   But that is something that Mr Shakespeare saves for the final act. We should not blaze before we are hot. You are of course familiar with the gradient of his entertainment? Will takes a scoop to the frozen wrack of time, and scrapes and shapes and arranges it so prettily in the imagination that you never want to leave off feasting on the banquets of his vision.

Bruno (*holds up ass's head*)   And who is to play the donkey?

Elizabeth   Rest your spirit. Mr Shakespeare said that you had noised abroad that the Godhead was an ass. There is no need to strive further since your destination has come to you. Together we will make believe such clangour in the firmament, they'll say the welkin forged another star ... (*Laughs.*)

Bruno   I shall need more than Mr Shakespeare's words for that to happen.

Elizabeth   Before, the world's beginning was only make-believe, then Godhead spoke its word, and we awoke from stellar dust, to find ourselves creatures of Christ and universal love. Here's your part.

She gives **Bruno** *a paper from* **Shakespeare**'s *desk.*

Elizabeth *takes* **Bruno** *off with her.* **Dee** *enters followed by* **Barmaid**. **Dee** *starts marking out the angelic invocation in squares and numerals and Hebrew symbols on the floor busily.*

Barmaid (*to* **Dee**)   What are you doing all that number rubbish for?

Dee   Bruno is far from safety. I need to take counsel from the angelic host.

Barmaid   I'm not allowed to talk to them. My mum give me a thick ear when I tried anything.

Dee   You must know the difference between good magic and ill.

Barmaid   She won't teach me anything. How does yours work?

Dee   There are ten hierarchies of angels. Beyond the angels are the Cherubim and Seraphim, and beyond them there is a mystery, which we are forbidden to touch on, whose symbol is the donkey. Christ who bestrides this unknown thing is our link with Godhead. The sacred letters used by the Egyptians, hieroglyphs, were taken from the things of nature, and by using the writings, the voices of the gods were captured. Afterwards lower forms introduced by a god they call the Ape of Thoth became the alphabet. By the time that Moses took down the Ten Commandments, the writing was in the debased form of Hebrew. The Holy Alphabet should invoke in sound the name of the angels, arranged in their hierarchies, who can be called out by the correct combination of sign, sound or number. But it is lost so I use numbers which are less corrupted. Are you following me?

Barmaid I'm going to work out my own way of doing things, thanks very much. (*Sweeps.*) I don't need counting. I don't need ABCs and I don't need plays to make things I want happen.

Enter **Kelly**.

Kelly Happy the prologue, happy the play. Giordano escapes the flames of the Inquisition, and gets to diddle the Queen of England in the bargain!

Dee He's not safe yet. Kelly, we will enquire of the Elohim how much longer Bruno has to fear his fate. He has to test the fires against his resolve to stay with us.

Kelly (*looks into crystal*) I can see them now – a little group crossing the square towards the stake. Once his body starts to burn, his soul will drop back into his body like a stone – unless we give him the taste of an angel.

Dee You know it is forbidden to enlist entities. Unless through the safety of the blessed numbers, any other invocation will release unchannelled force, and all our work will go for naught. Go fetch the book of Enoch, and do not open it or pry within, except within my sight.

Kelly I'm through with invocation and numbers. Your way won't work here. I know how to get an angel. What have these angels ever done for me? The only time I ever had any fun out of them was when they told me to swap wives.

Kelly *exits.*

Barmaid Go on – Were you instructed in adultery? What number was that?

Dee I'd had my doubts but the angels had caused small gold to appear, books to be restored when they had been burnt in a furnace, and then an angel commanded us to hold our wives in common. On the following day the Elohim asked if Mrs Kelly had been submissive to me, Kelly answered up that he had obeyed their instructions with my wife Jane.

Barmaid You was cuckolded.

Dee   In mitigation I should say, this man reached for me beyond the veil of matter, and through him I had come to such understanding of the sweetness of God's mercies, that I paid it little heed at the time. Later I expunged the report from my spiritual diaries, for fear they might fall into the hands of ignorant puritans.

Fortunately he has no hope of spearing an entity, since they have learnt to fly well out of range.

There's a thump offstage and a cry.
A shower of gold feathers falls down onto the stage.
Enter **Shakespeare**.

Shakespeare   What's that?

Dee   Kelly's mischief. He has somehow found an arrow. Oh pray that it glanced, and he has not made a hit. Quick we must find the poor creature. If I know Kelly he will be trying to perform his unsavoury practices on it before the angel disappears. Kelly – Kelly!

Dee *and* **Shakespeare** *exit. The* **Barmaid** *picks up the fallen feathers.*

Barmaid   Kelly's killed one – Oh my God!

Kelly *enters with a harpooned angel and sees her. He proceeds to hide the angel in the* commedia *box onstage in a furtive way, watched by the* **Barmaid** *from the side.*

Barmaid   It's true what they say. The spot where the fallen angel lies becomes unhallowed. You're going to be in trouble, when the left-handed creatures of the night start doing a dance in here. It's all right, I won't tell them it was you, if I can use these.

Barmaid *sits and pulls her skirts up and starts to stroke the inside of her legs with the angel's feather.*

Kelly   What do you want them for?

Barmaid   I don't want that old Elizabeth to get Bruno . . . I want him . . . you just got to let your thoughts run round them and keep everyone else out and then after a bit, they comes to you of their own accord. Make 'em quarrel . . . it's easy, they ain't got nothin' in common . . . T'ain't magic it's common sense really. C'mere Bruno . . . there's a good boy . . . (*She closes her eyes and pants for awhile. Then she recovers.*) Ever done this Kelly?

Kelly Yes, but I use the whole angel.

Barmaid You dirty little bugger!

Kelly I have to do it quickly, in a minute it'll be gone. Tell me if anyone's coming.

Barmaid (*looks off*) Bruno's coming. He's with Elizabeth.

Kelly Damnation!

Barmaid And if I've done my magic right, they'll be quarrelling.

Kelly *watches as* **Elizabeth** *comes in with* **Bruno**.

Elizabeth What is the matter, Bruno?

Barmaid See? It works!

Elizabeth Did I say something to unman you? (*Pause.*)

Bruno It's nothing! Only – Your praise of Mr Shakespeare is excessive!

Elizabeth Oh, is that what is too much for you? If you stay in this mood, Giordano, I shall begin to think his praise of you is overblown. It was he who revealed the universal shapes of things as well, he was not too proud to use the light of the lamp you lit. I praise his praise of your own rule of love. You should be glad to live through the greatness of his talents.

Bruno He doesn't realise my full significance.

Elizabeth Of course he does. (*Pause.*) You are uphill work, Bruno. This is not the etiquette of courtship I'm accustomed to. Barmaid, fetch my sweet Bottom a drink. Put a love potion in it.

Barmaid Yes Majesty. (*Exits.*)

Bruno   First I am Brown, now I am Bottom. Remember I am an educated man, unlike Mr Shakespeare. I have never been a player like him and do not intend to start now. I am of an equal rank with Mr Dee, with the exception of the areas of conjuration and judicial astrology. And I have written the most remarkable learned comedy of the sixteenth century.

Elizabeth   Really? How fascinating. I'd love to see it, that's why I brought you here, remember? But Mr Shakespeare says it's unperformable and heaven does not admit the second-rate!

Bruno   I am the equal of any here. If not of Christ then at least of his appointed monarchs. I charted the geography of heaven. I am not in any mood to play at donkeys here!

The **Barmaid** *enters with tankards.* **Bruno** *snatches one and drinks angrily.*

Elizabeth   I do not need to take instruction from you about the merits of disguise. I had the wit to avoid religious warfare for half a century, but you're so sure of being right that you go and brazenly sit in the lap of the Inquisition and expect them to listen to your extraordinary theories! Now by some miracle you have escaped but you are threatening to spoil it all through your own stupidity. We are all so well disposed to help and love you. I cannot tell you about our debt of gratitude in opening our eyes up to this new world. But you don't seem to be on the same plane as your imagination. You will not take instruction. You cannot abide the thought of any courtly subterfuge with me. You just want to push me down on a bank of wild thyme. Well go and see if the barmaid will have you!

She throws a tankard of beer in **Bruno**'s *face and walks offstage. Enter* **Dr Dee**.

Dee   Kelly, this is serious. What did you do with the angel? You have taken one to ravish it in a travesty of access to the Godhead. Look at me sir!

Kelly (*innocent*)   Did one fall? I, I never saw one.

Dee   Did any else see aught? Barmaid?

Barmaid   Not I sir, I ain't seen nuthin.

Bruno (*interested*)   What sex are they?

Kelly   All sorts. Divine.

Bruno   What happens when you take an angel's virtue?

Kelly   They disappear. It hardly matters, since there is an infinity of them.

Dee   It's more serious than that. (*To* **Bruno**.) Seraphim now guard the gap between the worlds where last the Pope followed you in, but the place where the fallen angel disappears will become another hole through which he can easily slip in. Kelly, what did you do with the body and where is it now?

Kelly   I am completely innocent. Why should I want to lie with an angel?

Dee   Kelly, if this blessed space is weakened by your predatory nature and misfortune falls upon us, I pray God it lands first on your head.

Kelly   What does he care of me, or any of you here? If God sees all, he'd have come for me before.

Dee   What's in the box? (*Points to the large box on stage.*)

Kelly   Ah, it's, it's . . . a puppet box for Bruno's play. I was inspired to make a little puppet theatre for *Il Candalaio*. It contains a miniature performance of his brilliant play, *The Chandler*, it is of no interest to anyone but myself, and the play's unjustly neglected author. I thought it would make a more pleasing welcome to heaven than the one so far offered by Her Majesty with help from sweet Mr Shakespeare.

Dee *opens the lid. The box opens up in a noisy reveal. Music and screaming, lights and smoke.* **Kelly** *and* **Dee** *try to shut the box. The effects gradually begin to ebb away. Lights back to normal.* **Kelly** *shuts the box.*

Dee   Kelly what have you placed within?

Kelly   Nothing is itself within a theatre. Everything is transformed with this hollow box for words. What you find in there will not be what you think it is . . .

Dee *goes to the box and opens it. It is completely empty and silent. Inside is the Theatre of Memory, the classical theatre. He reaches in and pulls out a large golden feather from the inside of the Theatre.* **Kelly** *closes up the box again.*

Kelly I never laid a finger on an angel. In fact I don't know what you're talking about. The barmaid has been watching me. She can testify.

Barmaid No, I don't know not nothing.

Dee Beneath the box there could well be a fissure now splitting the heavenly firmament. Barmaid – you have nothing to fear from us. But we must know what happened or it is highly dangerous. You're sweet on Bruno, that much we know. Love, even misplaced, is a great redemptive force. Now did you see Kelly put an angel in the marionette box?

Kelly Answer no to the doctor, and I'll not mention how you've been feathering your own nest.

Barmaid I saw him do it sir. He killed the angel and hid it in the box.

Dee Did he practise on it?

Barmaid Not to any purpose.

Dee Very good Barmaid. Thank you. You may go.

Exit **Barmaid**.

Bruno An angel's feather. (*He takes the feather and looks at it.*) Not unlike how I thought it would be.

Dee (*to* **Bruno**) The danger to you is immediate. The Pope has a primrose path here. This leaves no time for masques or for hiding you in Mr Shakespeare's plays. You should leave us all and run from this spot and we will deal with the intruder as best we can.

Bruno After seven years, where else could I run to? Heaven is bounded by a circle like everything else. No, I have trained my mind to ignore the pangs of the flesh. When I burn it will feel no more to me than when a chicken roasts. It is but an hour's torture then I shall be released to join you in earnest.

Dee   Brave words, but your death will go beyond any imagination. Elizabeth dies in the fullness of time. My death is in obscure poverty but with the satisfaction of having completed the work I was sent on earth to do. But yours will be against nature with you out of your body before its time. All your scholarship and remembered will won't hold the dam of your resolve in place, when they light their so-called holy fires. The manner of their murdering you will forever force you to accept the most loathsome contact in their scheme of things, an eternity of fiery pain.

Bruno   What is this magic in the papacy? How can there be an eternity of fiery pain when change is the one thing that runs through everything? They cannot justify this dark dimension. The guardians of my soul are wit and light –

Blackout. Music.

Enter the **Pope**, *in full armour with air raid noises, through the Theatre of Memory, in a blaze of red and smoke. The light level becomes red and smoky. The* **Pope** *puts his visor up.*

Pope   I swear by God I am the Pope, and now God's justice must be served. Where is he? I have come for Bruno. He must burn as other men.

A dull roaring noise from the box, and red light. **Bruno** *puts ass's head on.*

Elizabeth   He's not here.

Dee   God would not allow it.

Pope   God has no reason to usurp my function. I am his appointed messenger here. I know Bruno is here, I had words with the prisoner upon this spot.

Elizabeth   What is wrong Bruno being in heaven?

Pope   It is as natural as a donkey copulating with a woman.

Elizabeth   Very well we will give your proposal due consideration. Tell them to hold off from lighting the fire below.

Pope   No. You will bewitch me again. Already I feel weaker. My head ... (*He rotates.*) Everything's going round ...

Elizabeth (*to* **Dee**, *whispered*)   Can we obstruct him magically?

Dee (*to* **Elizabeth**)   No but it's possible the Pope himself cannot stay; like the fiery comet which glows in the heavens when passing hard by the sun, he's past perihelion. He'll now begin to dim as he whirls from close approach back into the heavens.

Pope (*weakly*)   Comets do not go round the sun.

Kelly   My master was speaking in these heretical terms only to be understood by those dull souls who God has exiled from truth and happiness. It's probably just the long climb in all that heavy armour. Why don't you sit down and have a rest?

The **Pope** *is visibly weakening. He beckons to* **Bruno**.

Pope   Come.

Bruno   I shall not, if you cannot make me. What have I to gain?

The **Pope** *is much weaker.*

Pope   I hear the voice of stubborn Satan sound. You all think you will be safe here. Consider this. I was able to ascend with all my armour as easily as fish are themselves plucked from the sea by a water spout. Until Bruno chooses to descend to meet his proper fate this steep passage will suck up any monsters it happens on from the long nightmare of the world. From the far distant past to deep in the dark maw of the future. This will not long stay a happy place. Things worse than you have ever dreamed of will creep up this sudden drain and make their nests in your green pastures. Bruno, be warned, until you come you are the author of misery's contagion. You owe it to your playmates to preserve their happiness unpolluted. The door to earth is open, till you pass through.

The **Pope** *exits through the Theatre of Memory leaving it agape. The lights onstage gradually brighten and the roaring noise and smoke die away.*

Bruno   Is it possible what he says?

Elizabeth   Alas, it's all too true. All the creatures of the night will start crawling up the pipe. Oh, damn you Kelly. It should be you who gets stuffed in the hole and not this man of letters.

Kelly   You have the same desire for him as I have for the angels. I was only practising my feelings . . .

Elizabeth   At least he is a man. The angels are indeterminate.

Kelly   If you two had managed to get it together properly, the heat of the Mysterium could weld the gap shut.

Dee   Mysterium! There is no one here adept to serve the Virgin Queen, even if she would.

Elizabeth   I would be willing to sacrifice my position if I thought that heaven would be preserved, and Bruno in it.

Kelly   Dr Dee?

Dee   (*shocked*)   Mr Kelly, I have sworn undying fidelity to my dear wife, as you well know.

Kelly   I wasn't going to suggest myself, but Venus cannot conjunct with Venus in a Mysterium. Would you care to bend over the House of Memory with me, Elizabeth? Come.

Elizabeth   You wish to practise your backdoor mischief on me, Sirrah? Do you think to stop up heaven by a criminal and a convicted thief abusing a queen, stealing her virtue and setting her procreation at naught?

Kelly   As you wish. Bruno shall go and burn then. But if he does, then he'll not find his way back here unless he is familiar with the forty aethers, which he knows not.

Elizabeth   Wait! Bruno may save himself with me. Earlier we suffered before from the distractions of a great irritation which came like a cloud between us, from I know not where. We should begin again with the meat of the play since we have

so little time – Mr Shakespeare, please instruct Bruno in his
actions, I have my part by heart.

Shakespeare (*takes* **Bruno** *aside*)   It is not that of which she
is ashamed and all unskilled at practising which will close off
all access from the rude firmament to the vaults of heaven.
You must school yourself. Remember it is not greasy candling
that may raise you in her estimation, you should speak first
and entirely of courtly love to her and then –

Bruno (*interrupts*)   Those are my only thoughts to her.

Shakespeare   Speak them then, but as if a less impatient
mind had wrought them than your own.

Musical cue. Lighting change.
Bruno *and* **Elizabeth**, *their eyes fixed on each other.*

Bruno (*to* **Elizabeth**)   Love. I have already written out my
heart, I loved Your Majesty before the first time I set eyes on
you with adoration born of your report. Fata Morgana!
Arthur's sister, your veil; the sea mist in which you bind your
enemies' sight when they would confound your rule of the
island. Your hospitality now bids a once-proud fugitive
welcome. I beg you, make me rise again.

Elizabeth   In my single reign I dreamed of such a man as
you. The Prospero who they said had raised a storm in the
straits of Messian!

Bruno   Fata Morgana, it was your doing all along. Come,
let's dissolve all ills in the crucible with the heat of alchemic
marriage.

Bruno *kisses* **Elizabeth**. *Music, lights.* **Kelly** *steps forward towards
them but is restrained by* **Dee**.

Kelly (*disappointed*)   Watch; their ship sets sail for fish-and-
finger-land, with only two aboard . . .

Dee   They'll bind the wounds of heaven with their mixed
sweat. Come, we should withdraw.

Dee, **Kelly** *and* **Shakespeare** *exit.* **Elizabeth** *breaks away from
the embrace.*

Bruno   I love you more than I fear my own death. What is the matter?

Elizabeth   The matter is unusual. My person is disqualified for consummation not from the usual cause, or from long habit of thought. But I do not know how to return your love when there is only one of you.

Bruno   I can be changeable as the multitude, stubborn, proud and fickle all at once. Do you not believe me?

Elizabeth   Not entirely. You seem to me to be Bruno, who I should know to be true. And here I am conniving at your death. (*Pause.*) No! I'll not sign that warrant. (*She turns to him again.*) Is it true that in Padua, well-born married women pay to lie with the condemned their final night?

Bruno   They say. I've never yet been kissed in Padua.

They embrace. **Elizabeth** *more aroused.*
Lutes, madrigals on the soundtrack.

Elizabeth   I tell you what. I'll do it if you put on the donkey's head. Don't ask me why. Please. Just do it. You started the idea that God's a donkey. It's your affair if you feel undignified in the part.

Bruno   Very well. Whatever your desire is, Majesty . . .

Elizabeth *starts to kiss his shoulders and hands. She opens his shirt and pulls it over his shoulders.*
The **Barmaid** *appears. She's dressed in ostrich feathers like an angelic chorus girl, she carries a little Gladstone bag. She clumps round them angrily, in high heels.*

Elizabeth   What's the matter, woman?

Barmaid   Nothing.

Elizabeth   Why could you not leave us alone? Where are you bound?

Barmaid   Nowhere. Earth.

Elizabeth   Who's sending you?

Barmaid   I am.

Elizabeth   Why?

Barmaid   Because I can't find no one here will love me back.

Elizabeth   Wait. I know something that could help us both.

Takes her downstage. Whispers.

Elizabeth   You shall take Bruno over from me.

Barmaid   Why would you want to give him to me?

Elizabeth   I was not made for this. I have no appetite for it but I can't let him down.

Barmaid   Will it work if I do it with him?

Elizabeth   He won't know the difference. I'm sure you'll do it royally.

Bruno   Hurry up – what's going on?

Barmaid   I can't talk posh.

Elizabeth   I'll do the talking.

Barmaid   All right.

Barmaid *goes and starts to caress* **Bruno** *and feel him up.*

Bruno   Elizabeth what kept you?

Elizabeth   I was waiting till the barmaid left.

Bruno   Aaah, the barmaid!

Elizabeth   Just take your women one at a time, eh?

Bruno   Have you been with other men, as a matter of interest?

Elizabeth   Millions. I give my fuck in buckets to them all. Their salutations seed the milky way and that's the only canopy for the Queen of heaven, wrought by admirers, her veil of stars, sprung into being from desire.

Bruno   How do I compare? I mean, am I well hung?

Barmaid *gives the thumbs up to* **Elizabeth**.

Elizabeth   Well, it's about average. (*Pause.*) For a donkey.

Bruno   All Nolans have giant tools. My father's was almost as big as mine. (**Bruno** *comes across the* **Barmaid***'s costume*) What's with the feathers then?

Elizabeth   I wanted to be your angel.

Bruno   And your pretty boobies seem different to what I imagined they would be . . .

Elizabeth   That's because I want you so much.

Bruno   It can't be the corselage . . . Just a minute.

He takes off the donkey's head and sees the **Barmaid** *and* **Elizabeth** *standing away.* **Bruno** *laughs.*

Elizabeth   I'm sorry Bruno. Maybe it'll work with her.

Bruno *puts the donkey's head aside.*

Bruno   Maybe. We must continue our desperate remedies with whoever takes pity on us. But I would not have these kisses lead to ignition before I know your name.

Barmaid   Judith.

Bruno   I love you Judith.

Barmaid   And I love you. But I don't know the words of the invocation.

He begins to kiss the **Barmaid**.

Bruno   If Elizabeth will not stoop to action, let her do the talking. Let the Queen of heaven enlarge the announcements that commoners mouth each night, as they jockey down Love Street.

Barmaid   You cheeky monkey! Ask a queen to busk my dialogue!

Elizabeth   I don't mind pretending. What do you say?

Bruno   Speak first of love, then whatever comes to mind to cheer young Eros past the winning post.

The kissing continues. **Elizabeth** *takes a deep breath.*

Elizabeth   Oh darling . . . Oh my sweet put it deep in me
. . . Oh my honey treasure people me, steeple me, I'm the
storm sucking sparks from your spire . . . I love you . . . I love
you . . . you've got such a soft mouth . . . Oh yes yes a
thousand times . . .

Clanking noise, from below the Theatre of Memory. It opens to reveal the
Pope *in a warty* commedia *mask, with heavy chain, keys etc. He starts
strewing straw around. He ignores* **Elizabeth** *and the* **Barmaid** *who
stand aside.*

Elizabeth   Dr Dee! Come quickly –

Kelly *and* **Dee** *arrive, followed by* **Shakespeare**. **Dee** *draws a
chalk circle round the* **Pope**.

Dee (*to* **Barmaid**)   Stand back. That is to contain the
menace.

Barmaid   What about my Bruno? Bruno!

Dee   Bruno is lost. He cannot hear us.

Barmaid   Oh Bruno, oh my honey pet, don't let them burn
you, reach up to heaven Bruno!

Kelly *restrains her.*

Pope   Excuse me, morning Sir Giordano. Before I say
anything, don't tell me, I know what you're going to say. I
thought, what do you give a condemned man on the last
morning of his life. The wife said, two fried eggs, a rasher of
streaky bacon and a double cappuccino, then I can go round
at lunchtime saying the condemned man ate a hearty
breakfast. Leave it out, I said and he's going to be burnt so
he'll probably prefer something cold like cornflakes but I tell
you straight, I didn't get your order last night, so we're going
to have to start all over again. Now, what do you want for
breakfast? Don't remember me, do yer? I'm your new jailer.
Pope said everyone changes round so you don't make friends
with the prisoners and let 'em escape. Name's Chandler,

Alphonso Chandler. 'Lucky' to my chums. Sorry to wake you up so early and so forth but you got two hours left. Priests will be making your life a misery as soon as you step out the door, so what earthly pleasure could I possibly interest you in before bidding you farewell into the unknown? Heaven or hell, who knows which way the wind blows or when your trousers are going to fall down. Not that you'll be wearing trousers again in this life. I expect you're saying, when's 'e going so that I can get back to sleep? Well the answer is, I'm not. Sorry, this is the real world, harsh reality and all that. Even though sleep's the best thing about living. Or it would be for you. I mean, here we are about to be burnt at the stake, and what's on your mind I bet, a nice sexy dream. Now, if I were a donkey at this time of year, middle of February, I wouldn't dream of getting my tool out until, oh, May at the earliest and that's just in Italy, donkeys further north don't copulate at all, round the North Pole, and that's a fact. Which is not to say that Italian donkeys are ignorant of which side their muffin is buttered.

Do you know the one about the lion and the donkey? The lion, noble creature that it is, and the aforesaid donkey had a pact that they would help each other going to Rome. First off the donkey bravely swims across the River Carigliani, it's in flood. The lion's sat on the donkey's back, looks around, sees planks and uprooted saplings borne on the flood of melted snow. He's frightened, digs his claws into the donkey so that they practically hook around the poor animal's ribs, not a word from the donkey. When they get to the other side lion and donkey then go and do their business in Rome. They come back to the Carigliani, still in flood, even worse this time with spring rain. Donkey says, 'It's your turn to carry'. The lion doesn't like it but anyhow the donkey gets on the lion's back. The lion gets in the water and starts across it. Donkey takes the scruff of the lion's neck between his big, yellow teeth. But he still finds himself starting to slip off. So he has an idea. He puts his enormous mangey instrument into the Antipodean parking lot – know what I mean? – beneath the lion's tail. 'Ere, what's goin on?' the lion says. The donkey sadly replies 'My friend, you had twenty claws in me, but this – pardon me – is the only hook I've got.' (*Pause.*) I was born with the gift of the

gab. Life's all luck, believe me. I could just as easily be sitting
where you are. But I've been lucky all my life. Walked out of
plague-ridden cities without a fleabite, out from under
collapsing buildings when everyone else ends up like squashed
flies. I'm lucky because I don't care if I live or die. As a matter
of fact, no one would notice if I took your place. At the stake I
mean. It's a fact. You think that's funny, don't you? Well, it is.
All right, I'll toss you for it, heads I take your place, tails, you
take your own place. Can't lose, can you?

Bruno   What's in it for you?

Pope   A bit of a laugh, passes the time. I got a cold bum, as a
matter of fact. It'll cure that, in no time. (*Laughs.*) Hur hurr.

Pope *tosses during this.* **Bruno** *and the* **Pope** *are examining the coin.*

Pope   Heads it is.

The **Pope** *gives* **Bruno** *his commedia mask.*

Pope   It must be my lucky day. I wander how I'm going to
talk myself out of this one. Here, don't forget the keys. Not
that they open anything. Just for show, you understand.

The **Pope** *passes the keys over.*

Bruno   Why don't they open anything?

Pope   Ah, you're on form, aren't you? Close to unravelling
the mystery of life. In the normal course of events, I couldn't
say. But since we're exchanging jobs I'd better tell you. To tell
you the truth, I wasn't really a jailer at all. I was an actor just
now. Now we've changed over I can tell you I'm pretty well
pleased to get out of the performance of *Il Candalaio* because
you are going to go on instead of me. That's right. I was
playing in there, in your play, up to a moment ago.

Bruno   I thought you were my jailer.

Pope   I was kidding. No. I was playing in that hall. It's got
dreadful acoustics. You're going to die out there tonight. Mind
you, if you're the author I rather think you deserve to.

Bruno   Just a minute. (*He is worried.*) I don't know the lines.

Pope (*he is annoyed*)   What do you mean, you fuckin' wrote it! Don't give me that squire, you're playing the Beadle. 'Pox eat your nose off' and all that sorta stuff. The donkey story. You wrote it for me to say in your play. I'm the Beadle in *Il Candalaio*!

Bruno   Now, just a minute, what's your name?

Pope   You are a joker an' all. What's my name? I'm Bidello, I'm The Beadle, the character you wrote. When I'm not being Bidello, I'm not anybody. You can turn me inside out and you won't find anything else. You think I'm having you on, don't you? I expect it's a bit of a shock at first. Second shock is – You're playing in Nola, your home town, Third shock is – it's a different century. You see, much later on you, Bruno, get to be a big hero for having stood up to the Pope. So local hero gets a patriotic fascist production of his play. Of course out of all the garage mechanics and right-wing plumbers nobody bothered to actually read the play before they put it on. Result, half an hour after it crawls onstage, is that about three-quarters of the blackshirt audience fall fast asleep.

Bruno   Blackshirts?

Pope   Fascists. Boots, short back an' sides, concentration camps an' straight arm salutes. Nasty people. But all they know is that you're a hero for your stand against old redsocks. So they put your play on. Bingo. Ironic twist of fate – you get to play in it in its first production in 1943 which will be towards the end of the Second World War. You have got a lot of catching up to do. That's another reason I'm glad to be out of that play because Nola's in the middle of an air raid. Know what an air raid is? Know what an aeroplane is? Never mind. They've locked the theatre doors, see, because the fascists naturally don't want anybody leaving. You don't need to know much more about the twentieth century. I'll tell you why. In about five minutes there's going to be a direct hit on the theatre from the aeroplanes and the first casualty is you. You are going to be burnt alive on stage and there is no escape. Have a look at that coin, check it for yourself, it's not weighted or anything. It's just bad luck. But as they say, this is your five minute call. OK? Keep your pecker up. Break a leg – Cheeribye!

The **Pope** *disappears into the Theatre of Memory and throws the* **Bidello** *mask to* **Bruno** *as he goes.*

Elizabeth Poor Bruno. They can come in any disguise to trap you to this cruel fate.

Bruno If I am still in heaven, I shall go up and throw myself on God's great mercy. If I could touch his face, he would pity me!

Shakespeare Bruno desist. You would never get there.

Bruno I have no quarrel with the Cherubim. They'd let me pass.

Elizabeth If the Seraphim should move aside for you, which most assuredly they would not, you'd incandesce.

Dee Besides, we have no conjuration which would lift a mortal.

Bruno What of the golden scarab once you made to rise against the Oxford walls?

Dee I brought it not to this place.

Barmaid What's this then?

On the back wall is projected an icon of the golden scarab. Lighting change to spot on **Barmaid** *as she moves behind it.*

Bruno It is the golden Egyptian chariot of the Sun!

Dee Yes! This is indeed the vessel that Hermes Trismegistrus saw in-dwelling, in the founts of nature. Whence came it?

Barmaid It came as an answer to this maiden's prayer.

Dee It needs ropes to rise.

Bruno *is sitting on the scarab.*

Kelly Not this one. This creature can take you up, Bruno! Judith knows how to make things live.

Dee   She does not have the spells, she's steeped in low desires and ignorance.

Barmaid   I know how to get it to take a living weight. Take the feathers of the Seraphim and stroke them on its mandibles, look, it lives, it blinks. It's ready for us now, Bruno.

Bruno *and the* **Barmaid** *sit astride the imaginary scarab.*

Bruno   Elizabeth, though worlds decay and perish through the incessant infolding of the absolute through nature to itself, I record my eternal salutes.

Elizabeth   Bruno you must make haste or the flames will reach you!

Bruno   Goodbye, sweet William whose o'erflowing mind poured out of the world soul, illuminating all, not least the gift of England and her Queen who sheltered me, both are dear as my own eyes. Judith, will it take us both?

Barmaid   I'm not leaving you.

Siren. The **Pope** *pops up inside the theatre.*

Pope   It is time.

The **Barmaid** *threatens the Pope.*

Barmaid   Don't you dare lay a finger on my Bruno! Let's go!

Blackout. Music. A small golden scarab starts to ascend the walls of the set.

Pope   Come back! Bruno, come back!

Kelly   He's going too high.

Dee   Slow down Bruno, down.

There is a distant boom and feathers flutter down.

Elizabeth   The fool! He's gone through the Cherubim. (*Calls.*) The Seraphim, watch out for the Seraphim.

There is another boom, even louder.

Oh my God, he's gone straight for the donkey.

A third, final, dull boom as an amazingly bright light flares all over the stage. It slowly fades away. The golden scarab has disappeared. Exit all.

Lights as the **Pope** *gets out of the Theatre of Memory to come and speak to the audience.*

Pope   At the nightmare's end, I get my man. I awake before dawn in my own bed in the palace to find myself cool as if my fever has abated. I rise from my bed feeling almost weightless, a symptom I attribute to renewed health. I can just make out the servant's thick bodies sprawled in the doorways. But it is deathly quiet. Angelo! Angelo! Bring light! I go to him. I cannot hear him breathing. Is he dead? I give him a little kick and my foot goes straight through him. I now have serious cause to be concerned.

Gradually the realisation comes. It is not Angelo who is a ghost, but me. The poison he poured for me gnawed through the cord between soul and the body, and now I am an ex-Pope. What next? I can only give you the benefit of my personal experience.

I am standing in a galleria, wide, dark. The only light that I see shines from a doorway, far ahead. I pass down that long passage under the familiar astrological roof which my predecessor Alexander VI ordered, towards a door in a wall that I do not remember.

Have I been condemned to spend eternity in some forgotten earth closet? Oh no! Inside I see hung up on hooks, all the different *commedia* masks. It is not an abandoned convenience. It is a far livelier place. It is a theatre!

Gradually my body falls from me till only the face remains, and I take my place at the end of the row. I realise judgement has been served on me and I am now permitted a limited existence in the afterlife – as a player's mask.

The **Pope** *puts the mask of* **Bidello** *on again. Music.*

I have become the mask of Bidello. I, who in reality once held the keys of St Peter. I exist – now and forever only in Bruno's Theatre of Memory. Which does not exist. And so – goodnight!.

Darwin's Flood

Foreword

Producing Snoo Wilson's plays presents a challenge, and has been deemed a risk by many, but a risk that always seemed to pay off in our case. Surreal, vibrantly theatrical, endlessly intelligent, well-researched and informative, Snoo's plays are overlaid with coarse gags and jousting humour – he is a playwright who fucks with your mind and jovially assaults your senses.

Darwin's Flood is, without doubt, one of Snoo's very best plays, providing triangular philosophic opposition between Darwin, Christ and Nietzsche, borrowing from and subverting history in true Wilsonian fashion. In this play Snoo anticipates the big scientific and metaphysical questions – Is life ordered or chaotic? Creative or destructive? Governable? Containable? What is the worth of knowledge? Or belief? And while your brain begins to hurt, the drooling Nietzsche is wheeled on in a barrow to be revived by a sado-masochistic crucifixion, administered by Mary Magdalene who, in zipped hooker-PVC, has abseiled from the helicopter apparently hovering above the Bush's twelve-foot ceiling. Or – in a grand *coup de théâtre* – the Ark explodes from under Darwin's lawn where previously he had discovered only worms.

Snoo's voice is completely original and his themes are vital, epic and provocative. He needs a designer of experience and vision, a director who can distinguish baby from bathwater, resourceful and courageous actors and an audience who are 'up for it'.

Simon Stokes
Plymouth, 1999

Darwin's Flood was first performed at the Bush Theatre on 6 May, 1994, with the following cast:

Charles Darwin	John Kane
Friedrich Nietzsche	Bob Goody
Elizabeth Forster	Rosemary McHale
Bernard Forster	Paul Bentall
Emma Darwin	Alex Kingston
Jesus	James Nesbitt
Humboldt/Mercator	Paul Ritter
Mary Magdalene	Barbara Barnes
Mrs Muller	Paul Ritter

Directed by Simon Stokes
Designed by Robin Don
Costumes by Katie Birrell
Lighting by Chahine Yavroyan
Sound by Simon Whitehorn

Act One

A spotlight on **Charles Darwin**, *an aged, genial and eminent Victorian, as he talks to the audience.*

Darwin The night I died, I had the most extraordinary dream; I was in our house at Down, where my wife Emma and I had lived for so many years. My wife was formerly a Wedgwood: in each generation Darwins of either sex always seem to marry Wedgwoods. When I returned from the voyage on *The Beagle* and married Emma, I could not abide the excitements of living in London so our immediate search had been to find a country nest where we could settle down and I could write, without being overexcited by visitors all day. I was never a bright light, socially, and though I could flare up occasionally, it took me days, sometimes weeks, to recover from the rude assaults of social intercourse. And so it was, for the forty years after my voyage. I wrote my books here and we never moved again.

Gradually the lights come up to reveal Down, the **Darwin**'s *home. We see a large, comfortably furnished Victorian drawing room, with a view to the outside garden at the back, now dark, and stairs leading up out of sight at the back. Part of the ceiling of the room is present as* **Darwin** *describes it, a lowering amorphous presence, like low cloud cover, with a bas-relief of a large stylised face looking down.*

Darwin I have such happy memories of Down. I remember the house filled with experiments, writing and children. People have held me responsible for the abolition of God, and the subsequent ruin of the family. But in the dream, my dear, long-dead father's face had somehow replaced the ceiling, from which it glowered down like a giant cherub's. It was my father, no doubt, and no one else. My grief, when one of my little ones died, was so great it quite crushed the belief in me of a benign creator of the universe.
It was said by the godly that my many nervous disorders were a punishment from God for denying His existence.

When I was not confined to bed I would throw myself into
my work. But when ill, I used to feel rather like a tortoise
I saw once, with a hole bored in the tail of its shell, which
cruel boys had attached to a stake with a length of elastic.
Unable to escape, the tortoise scrabbled endlessly towards
the horizon only to be dragged back and back, and back,
for days upon days.

In the dream, it was as if this stake had been pulled up for
ever, and the tortoise found itself suddenly free. But just as
I was experiencing the first flush of healthy release, into my
house, all uninvited came – (*Noise off of door being rapped,
smartly.*) Here we begin.

Darwin *goes to a writing stand, takes up a quill pen and dips it
as a wheelbarrow comes on, pushed by* **Elizabeth Forster**, *a
bossy, dominating woman. Seated in the barrow is a lean, sprawled
figure in a dirty white suit and a sun hat, with a walrus moustache;
her brother* **Frederick Nietzsche**.

Elizabeth Dear brother, you have no idea how tiring it
is pushing a wheelbarrow all day through a landscape with
such a hostile attitude. The hail spits, the mud sneers at
our efforts, and plucks at the boots. It makes me wonder if
our proposal to go to Paraguay and form a colony of
racially pure Germans is what nature intends. (**Elizabeth**
tends to **Nietzsche**.) Our twelve Saxon families had never
been in a town before, let alone out of Germany. Their
stout hearts are bearing them through a world which is so
maliciously contoured. They look to you for inspiration.
They are farming folk, not clever like you, but their blood
is pure.

Enter **Elizabeth**'s *husband* **Bernard**, *in lederhosen and carrying
an alpenstock and old-fashioned binoculars.*

Elizabeth You fool Bernard, you have got us lost again.
You are leading one hundred and forty-four Swabian souls
without a toe-nail-full of black earth to call their own.

Bernard Lost? On the contrary. I have a box of
German soil which I will scatter over our new country
when we get there.

Elizabeth Do you believe that something picked up from a roadworks by the Brandenburg Gate would serve for a country?

Bernard My tongue tells me where we are. It is the land of our Teutonic cousins. I know when I fall on my face, I taste firstly a distinctive English accent in this soil. Then when I stand up again, to the north-east, I see far away, the silhouette of St Pauls, wreathed in the smoke of the capital. And so, from the hawthorn breaking out its blossoms in the hedgerows here, under that last shower, I deduce unequivocally it is springtime, in Kent!

Elizabeth Oh very clever! And what year is it?

Bernard Last night the sun set in 27 degrees Aries, and Saturn and Jupiter followed in Taurus. So now it ought to be the evening of April 19, 1882.

Elizabeth Yesterday you said it was August the first. Why is time travelling backwards?

Bernard I do not see why you are worried. Most women would be happy to discover that they are getting younger. I'm sure Professor Darwin will be able to feed us supper. After all, we Nietzscheans are his intellectual heirs. And then the bugles will blow, and we will set off again, with our merry marching song to Nova Germania!

Elizabeth Perhaps Professor Darwin knows why time is travelling backwards.

Bernard We do not need to know why, before we share this useful news with your brother. (*Goes to* **Nietzsche**.) Herr Professor Nietzsche! It is no longer the year of tragedy, the year of your madness, no, so there is no call for you to be diminished any more. You are sane and we are carrying out your ideas in the world. (*Goes to a bookcase and pulls out a book, licks page.*)

Elizabeth Bernard, are you mad?

She tugs at his sleeve and points at **Darwin**, *who stares at them, then continues writing.*

Bernard   The further we travel back in time, the more tasteless libraries become ... I'm not going to look at the title, but I guarantee that if it was written before your brother's influence, it will be insipid ...

Elizabeth   – They must have proper food here. Frederick, what would you say to a hearty English tea with muffins?

Bernard   Rather dusty, this volume; Teutonic, with Francophile undertones, possibly Fuerbach's negation-of-negation. (*Looks.*) *Das Kapital*, von Karl Marx. I was close! And listen to what's written on the flyleaf! (*Reads.*) 'To my admired good friend Prof. Charles Darwin with heartfelt good wishes.' It is a signed second edition! Our host I see, has left most of the pages uncut. Sensible fellow. I'm sure Professor Darwin will greet us with open arms. His ideas and the theories of your brother are in accord, the cornerstones of modern thought!

Bernard *puts the book aside, gets field glasses out and stares through them.*

Bernard   One family at least is coming this way. The others seem to be making their way into a sheep pond.

Elizabeth   That is serious.

Bernard   Yes, but they should have followed the marks on the trees I made on our way along the ridgeway so it is their fault entirely.

Elizabeth   None of them can swim! Go and rescue them!

Bernard   It is better to take one's time. If we lose a few, the survivors will be hardier. (*Exits.*)

Elizabeth (*to* **Nietzsche**)   You know dearest, that it is you that I really love. I married Bernard for what he can do for us. Nothing more. I could not lead an expedition on my own. Take whatever is in my heart, it is yours. (*Coquettish.*) I am only a woman, the poor creature that you could only visit holding a whip ... Even when you are speechless, you can still feel the updraft of your mighty intellect, bearing the human spirit like an eagle tirelessly up over the cols and glaciers, sometimes swooping down with beak and talons with nature's justice for a tender lambkin. (*Pause.*) It is warmer than Poland here. You were cold in Poland, weren't you dearest, in all your extremities? What will the Professor say when he hears we are from the future? Frederich, does time travel not contradict the laws of natural selection? (*Pause.*) Luckily I lined a suitcase with a newspaper the day we left Berlin, so there is scientific proof . . . (*Produces battered piece of newspaper.*) . . . (*Reads.*) October 1890. (*Panic.*) That can't be right. We left in 1885. It should read 1885. It must be a misprint. (*Looks on the other side.*) It's on both sides. I should be brave. Perhaps it will be reporting the triumph of your philosophy, Frederich. That would be pleasant, no? (*Reads.*) 'German Colonist Leader Dies.' (*Horrified.*) Oh no! (*Reads.*) 'Bernard Forster, who led a colonising expedition to Paraguay was found dead in his boarding-house room on the anniversary of his arrival, a pistol by his side. Forster lived with constant accusations of sexual misdemeanour and financial fraud. A farewell note said he did it for the fatherland. His wife Fräu Elizabeth is said to be returning to Germany with his remains.' (*Pause.*) The fatherland! As long as you are not harmed, dearest . . . (**Elizabeth** *tears the newspaper.*) There! We don't need newspapers to prophesy. The future must look after itself. It will happen, when it happens.

The phone rings. **Elizabeth** *is startled.*

Oh! Don't be alarmed! It is only a 'far-speaker'! There was a similar device on the quayside in Danzig, remember? As for this one, crying its eyes out – it cannot be for little me, or you or your genius.

Emma Darwin, *a beautiful dreamy young woman in a négligé and tousled hair as if she has just woken up, comes in, hurriedly putting on her dressing gown.*

Emma   Doesn't anyone here know how to answer the telephone?

Elizabeth (*aggressive*)   Yes we do, but no one knows we're here yet. Stupid person!

Emma *blithely goes to the phone and picks it up.*

Emma   Down House. Emma Darwin speaking. Oh my
husband. No you can't speak to him. He's about to be
interrogated in Westminister Abbey by his beloved worms,
shortly. He and I were kissing cousins, true. I can't speak
as an expert but we had almost a dozen offspring by the
end, and they didn't show any dramatic signs of
inbreeding. The girls in particular are quite ... You're
doing what? (**Emma** *puts the phone down.*) Not *another* one.
What is it about bereavement that I should suddenly be
like a bitch on heat to all the men out there? But then
animals are wiser than we are, they wouldn't try to mount
the telephone.

Darwin   Would you get rid of these visitors, darling?

Emma   Of course dearest. (*To* **Elizabeth**.) Excuse me,
I'm Emma Darwin. I don't know your name – Charles
does – did not like surprise visitors.

Elizabeth   I am Mrs Elizabeth Forster-Nietzsche, and this
is my brother the famous philosopher. We have a problem
for Herr Professor Darwin. If time goes backwards, what
happens to natural selection and survival of the fittest?

Emma   I'm afraid I'm not a scientist and my husband
will not be able to answer the question – he's dead.

Elizabeth   Not for long if we are correct. When we left
Germany, it went to 1886, then all of a sudden it was
1885. I would have turned back but Bernard said we
would explode when we met our dopplegängers. So we
caught the ferry to England, and it seems it is even earlier
here.

Emma   You're going backwards in time, but it doesn't
mean that anyone else is! Both Charles and I would have
loved to come with you. We could have got off at our
wedding day, and lived it all again! How I envy you! But
for now, Charles does not like surprise visitors interrupting

his routine.

Elizabeth   Professor Darwin cannot refuse us hospitality.

Emma   I'm afraid he could.

Darwin   Darling Emma, just tell them to go please.

Elizabeth   My brother is a philosopher, who has devoted his life to the perfection of man.

Emma   There must be some misunderstanding because, my husband maintains there is no such thing as perfection. Species change all the time. 'Not a single living species will transmit an unaltered likeness to a distant future.' His words, not mine.

Elizabeth   What of the sacred flame in the heart of higher man, which sets us apart from the animals?

Emma   As a Christian I'd have to agree, but Charles would say there's nothing unique about human's social organizations. He said guilt is the basis for social life and he could make his dog feel guilty, so there was nothing very special about it. It's sometimes very upsetting living with a scientist if you love them and are afraid of their ideas. Tell me, where are you bound for?

Elizabeth   South America. We will reach our new land, with a bridge of music, christen it 'Nova Germania' and breed pure Germans there.

Emma   I wish you Godspeed, then, as any Christian would. You say you aim to breed. The half-wit presumably has been neutered?

Elizabeth   The half-wit – is my brother!

Emma   *covers her mouth with her hand.*

Emma   I do beg your pardon. And his! If he can hear.

Elizabeth   He hears every word we speak. *He* has understood your husband's writings. He is a philosopher who we are co-opting from the Fatherland, because one philosopher is worth more to a rising nation than a dozen battleships.

Emma   They say biologists are useful, too.

Elizabeth *goes to stroke* **Nietzsche***'s brow.*

Elizabeth   But this is the greatest man who ever lived. When Pan and Apollo come together in him in a burning flash, the thunderbolt splits the oak, ecstasy overwhelms him and he becomes whole again. If we stay you would see.

Music of a brass band distantly playing Deutschland Uber Alles. **Elizabeth** *deeply stirred.*

Elizabeth   Oh! Bernard must have found them all! I can hear the full brass band! Each family playing its instrument, the cornets and the fluglehorns, the serpent and the clarinet! No bastard saxophones or lewd French horns poison the music with semitic counterpoint.! It must be the Swabians, and they are pressing on!

Elizabeth *pulls herself together and starts to push the wheelbarrow off.*

Elizabeth   It is getting fainter – They are marching away and we must catch them – (*Calls.*) You are leaving your brains behind you, dumkopfs! Oh, wait for your philosopher, you bovine rabble! Let us all bear our standards bravely towards The Future!!

Exits pushing the barrow with **Nietzsche** *in it. The music dies away.*

Darwin   What nonsense she talks, about music for a start!

Emma   Darling, you can hardly argue, since you cannot even keep time.

Darwin   I know when I am moved. Your playing moves me, dearest. It always has!

Emma   Shall I play something soothing for you now, dearest?

Darwin   That would be so kind.

Emma *sits down to pluck music from an unlikely source, an invisible piano: we hear a recording of Lizst's* Liebestraum, *for the piano.*

Emma You've always liked this one.

Darwin It sounds marvellous, as fresh to me as if you were playing it for the first time.

A beating at a door, off.
A weird, strangulated cry, off.

Darwin What was that?

Emma Don't worry, Cook was standing by, to bar the door as soon as they left, and no one can get by her!

Jesus *enters, a dark-haired muscular man dressed as a competition bicyclist, carrying a racing bike on his shoulder.*

Jesus (*perky, Belfast accent*) – Except him who rolled aside the stone. That cook of yours is a pushover. (*Hints.*) Kyrie Eleison. (*Slow.*) Kyr-ie El-eison . . . Either of you speak Greek?

Darwin I can just about read it.

Jesus (*translating*) 'The Lord have mercy' . . . Are you getting warm? And not just any Lord.

Emma Christ! It is Christ, Charles! I think I recognise him from my prayers!

Jesus She's right, I'm Christ. (*Pause.*) But I'm not pushing myself forward, Professor. I'll only believe it if you do.

Darwin Are you aware sir, of the laws in this country against trespass?

Jesus Just a minute, who do you think you are talking to? Your lovely wife needs me, Professor, even if you don't. Her heart could stifle itself in mourning, if it doesn't get some of my balm. It's only the same make as I use when I get calf-muscle cramps but it's really good stuff for bereavements.

Darwin   Emma, do you really recognise this man?

Emma   Something about him tells me that he is not an imposter, Charles.

Jesus   Her instincts are correct. Christ is not just a man of *that* time. Christ is a man for all time. He's been to the end of history and back again. So tell me, Professor, what gear for me to wear would *not* be an anachronism? (*Pause.*)

Darwin   Are you the son of the God that takes little children?

Jesus   Not that little. I was thirty-three when Da dropped me in the shredder. Emma, I think your husband would prefer to have me pounding round Kent in a pair of authentic Roman sandals: is he aware you can't fit Jesus Boots into a modern pedal assembly?

Emma   Can he stay, Charles? I think you are being a little selfish denying your wife the comforts of religion. You're popping off, round about now, after all. What have I got to look forward to, apart from . . . ?

Jesus   No offence! I can see I'm not required. I'll shake the dust of the driveway of unbelievers off my pedals and go. I believe it's a wee derailleur problem. I could fix it if I had a cross-head screwdriver.

Emma   Charles – have we?

Jesus   Woman, it's no good asking him, they've yet to be invented. I'm just stalling for time here. (*Pause.*) Give me another five minutes with the Professor here, and we could bag another soul for Jesus.

Darwin   I'm sure you think you would win me, but my mind sir, is indifferent to you.

Jesus   Oh really? I know a great deal more about your inward workings than you think. I happen to know your dear wife sends seismic shivers down your spine when she plays the pianoforte. And you have noted this reaction has happened on nine separate occasions.

Darwin (*astonished*) – How on earth –

Jesus Precisely. I know it, even though you never wrote
up your paper on the use-value of beauty in evolution, did
you now? Was it the same kind of excitement as that
which you had when you first stumbled across the rude
beginnings of your unfortunate theory?

Darwin When I came upon the idea of natural selection,
it's true I was filled with a sense of a glorious unfolding
discovery, a possible order in the universe – it was a
similar excitement.

Jesus Ah well, then you are probably beyond
redemption.

Emma (*distressed*) Oh Charles!

Jesus You see, your husband did not bring order, but
disorder. If there is an order, you're looking at it. The Son
of God. Let's set the triptych up. Left panel! On the day of
creation, Dad personally places the fossils in the rocks
wearing white cotton gloves, to guard against fingerprints.
Middle panel! A bearded old git comes in, as God is still
bent over and tries to give him one up the bum with a
geologist's hammer. Frame three – the pay-off – bearded
old git dies, and thence to meaty and unending torment,
because God is not mocked. What's that, good old chum?
Do I see a heart secretly panting for the cooling streams of
repentance? Did you not think for a moment, you loved
me, just then?

Darwin You lose all sympathy, when you insult the
intelligence of your listeners with such coarse arguments.

Jesus Listen to the man! Do you think that nature, red
in tooth and claw, is any more dainty? Very well, I will
adjust my sermon so that it may be appreciated *above* the
salt. Brace yerselves. (*Pause.*) There have been miracles! To
those who say religion is a screen for grossness and
hypocrisy, I say, let them turn the celestial clock back, till it
points to Bethlehem and they hear the ox and the ass
yapping it up – actually talking – on the night of my birth.

To those who say that the sewers of religion are backing up on the laboratories of science, flooding the typhoid of bigotry into the scientific way I say, turn back the clock, and let them come to Bethlehem. Let the time travellers behold that blazing confluence of planets right over the very stable there where I was being born.

To your generic sons, Charlie, the scientific tinkerers of the future, who presume they can cobble a genetic aristocracy of man, greater than me, I say, let them get in their time-machines and find Bethlehem, Judea, before it even had a postal code! Then let these time travellers witness a pregnant woman, married to an impotent old follower of some bastardised monotheism which his tribe got thrown out of Egypt for adopting, this hopeless case of a young woman, schizoid, prone to hallucinations, unlettered, landless, suddenly – right in the middle of a population census by an occupying power – she gives birth to the SON OF GOD (*Pleased.*) How does that sound? Are you believing, yet, or are you stuck at the lych-gate, mid-funeral, waiting for the corpse to miraculously rise? Better hurry up, Charlie boy, the corpse in this case is *you*!

Darwin   *Mister* Jesus, my calling tells me that when I am witness to the unexplained, my first duty is to attempt to understand it.

Jesus   Ach, you're too smart for the likes of me. I'll just bang the dog shite off the brake shoes and be on my way, and rejoin the race outside.

There is a loud, unearthly cry offstage.

Jesus   Oh, damn and blast it!

Emma   What was *that*?

Jesus   The same cry that arose at my first death, that the sailors heard, rolling out over the empty sea. The cry seeks out suffering. The daughter in her abortive fever, curses the drunken whoremaster, her infected dad. Or, hear it from the mouths of sick, bruised slaves.

Emma   What does it stay?

Jesus People have heard it say, Great Pan is dead. Or
the universe is cracked, the architect deceased. This time, it
was a reminder of pastoral duty. Be comforted, Emma,
Christ your defender stands in the room.

Emma It would comfort me further if I knew Charles
will not be punished for his opinions, in the afterlife.

Jesus It's not so much cynical unbelief with Charles.
What comes up again and again with him is – incest.

Emma Incest?

Jesus You're his first cousin. How many times did you
. . . You had ten kiddies. How many other times, Emma,
did the purple wound of your shame give entry to his virile
member?

Emma It was after he won at whist.

Jesus Do you not know?

Emma He kept count.

Jesus Did you allow him to win a great deal?

Emma It made him happy!

Jesus Not for nothing do they call cards the devil's
picture book, Charlie.

Darwin Mr Darwin.

Jesus Mr Darwin, very well, no 'Christian' names. I
know where you are bound, for the pit! It's not just the
dubious muff-diving after an evening's gambling. God's
forgiven a lot worse than that. The clincher is the ungodly
life's work, a protracted assault on Biblical truth.

Emma He was not always so fixed. It was when Annie
was taken away from us, that Charles lost hope. Her death
toppled any remaining faith Charles had!

Jesus Annie's death was something of an own goal
though. Your husband, if not you, should know that
interbreeding with a first cousin makes for weaklings and
imbeciles.

Darwin   I realised I had lost all hope when I took Annie to a clairvoyant, and she diagnosed Annie's sickness very accurately.

Jesus   There's consistency for you! The great scientist went to a clairvoyant! Tell me something Charles. What could my dad have passed on to my children through my loins? What characteristics of his would the little snappers inherit? Would they go round wanting to flood the world?

Darwin   We don't know if heredity transmits unfulfilled wishes. Lamarck believes that the giraffe's struggle to reach the higher leafy treetops translates directly into longer necks for its descendants. Lamarck is a favourite amongst social reformers who see the working classes as a species which can transform themselves by trying harder.

Jesus   You haven't even cut the pages of Karl Marx's little book. What do you know about class struggle?

Darwin   I know more than I wish to about struggle. The Church of England and *The Times* have made war on me for thirty years. Recently the local vicar closed down a night-school for parish labourers which I set up, because of my alleged godlessness.

Jesus   What do you expect?

Darwin   I never said God was dead. But it seems hasty to assign creation, when there is so much that we do not understand.

Jesus   You don't have to understand creation! Just accept! Come, Emma, let's see if I can get to wash out this grief of yours. I'm wasting my time with him! Bang your bones, man!

Jesus *exits with* **Emma**.

Darwin (*to audience*)   'Bang your bones' was how I used to express my excitement when close to winning, playing Emma at whist. Then Emma would gracefully concede defeat, and we would retire upstairs. Thus each of the ten children's conception depended on a lucky fall of cards. I won 3,456 times in all and I lost 1,486. The shadow of my father's exacting memory has descended on me and I am ungratefully mindful of all those games of whist lost. I mean the 1,486 times I never . . .

Enter **Elizabeth** *pushing* **Nietzsche** *as before, both much torn as if having gone through hedges backwards. Vegetation clogs the wheel of the wheelbarrow.*

Elizabeth   We missed them. We will never see them again. We will shrivel anonymously in these English hedgerows, and become forgotten, racial relics, figures of fun and spite for the locals when drunk. Nova Germania cannot be founded without us and so existence has lost its reason. I think my heart will break.

Darwin   You could try to catch them up on Christ's bicycle.

Elizabeth   I am exhausted and my brother would never agree to ride on the handlebars of Christianity.

Darwin   You can both rest outside, in the stables.

Elizabeth   You take him there. I am tired. (*Sits.*) I will come later.

Darwin *obediently goes and takes the barrow with* **Nietzsche** *in it.*

Darwin   The doctor said I shouldn't do anything like this, but it is only a few yards – anything to get these people out of the house . . .

Elizabeth   Professor. Who is that fat stupid man in the ceiling?

Darwin *halts and abandons the wheelbarrow.*

Darwin   That is my father, who was the wisest man I ever knew. It was like the tide coming in when he entered the house. He also became immobile in late life and we had a special wheelchair made, and sitting in it, he looked

exactly like a stranded elephant seal. He caught me
laughing at him once and to avert his wrath, I began
reciting my own illnesses to him – numbness of the
fingertips, giddiness, insomnia. He cut me off quite before I
had finished. 'Quite so, dear boy, quite so. Neuralgia.' I
suggested that he could be winched up and lowered into
his pony-cart, so he could take the air, as he did in the old
days, when he had practised medicine. He shook his head,
and replied, 'There is not a road out of this town that does
not have painful memories.'

Nietzsche *stares at him balefully and belches, contemptuously.*
Jesus *comes down the stairs.* **Nietzsche** *starts inarticulately
snarling and drooling at him.*

Elizabeth   Quickly! You should put some distance
between my brother and Christ, or Frederich will have a
seizure.

Darwin *wheels* **Nietzsche** *off as* **Elizabeth** *lies on the floor
fanning herself.*

Jesus   Was that feller in the wheelbarrow Frederich
Nietzsche?

Elizabeth   The same.

Jesus   I was hoping to have some crack with him. I
heard he is something of an intellectual atom-splitter, with
each sentence whacking the void harder than a brickie's
hammer, breaking meaning into particles of pure energy,
etcetera.

Elizabeth (*modest*)   He is a genius and I am his
inspiration.

Jesus   A philosopher in a wheelbarrow! This follows a
noble tradition of alienation. It was the cynic philosopher
Diogenes, was it not, who used to go round dressed in a
barrel, preaching a return to the simple life?

Elizabeth   Bernard stole the wheelbarrow in Margate.

Jesus   Oh really?

Elizabeth The Polish wheelbarrow had collapsed.

Jesus Diogenes *paid* for his barrel. Otherwise no one would have listened to him.

Elizabeth You should not stay or Frederich will organise for your destruction.

Jesus He doesn't look to me in much of a position to defend himself, physically or verbally!

Elizabeth In his books, it is not the philosopher who kills God, but the people. We have a hundred and fifty followers arriving shortly. I will order them to set about you.

Jesus I suppose they might oblige you and tear me to pieces, but what about the Christ in the mind? When two or three Christians are gathered together, there I am, in the midst of them. The chances of ridding the place conclusively of me, with a hundred and forty-four devout Lutheran farmers present, is pretty slim. What I will do for your farmers, since they've walked such a long, long way, is wash their feet. (**Elizabeth** *snorts disbelievingly*.) It's a chore, Elizabeth, only if your heart's not overflowing with love. I know you think I'd be spoiling them, but permit me this once. All right, let's compromise. I'll just wash sixty-two pairs of feet.

Enter **Emma**, *glowing but dishevelled*.

Jesus Thirty-one? Seventeen? Eight-and-a-half pairs, call it nine? All right – I'll just do the Professor's, his lovely wife's and yours.

Emma Oh yes please!

Jesus I could throw in a massage, with spikenard, very costly.

Elizabeth And now you are trying to bribe me!

Darwin *enters from the direction of the stables*.

Jesus You're a hard woman to please, Elizabeth.

Emma   Charles, you must try it. Christianity. I feel a glow. A definite warmth.

Jesus *ducks away.* **Darwin** *moves to separate them.*

Jesus   He couldn't. He's totally against my works.

Darwin   Not totally. Christian missionaries greatly reduced cannibalism in the Pacific, although I always felt that the Tahitians, with their naked tattooed bodies, must have formed a finer picture of man before missionaries discovered them. What is going on, here?

Jesus   Elizabeth is trying to prevent the slave religion from fatally weakening the collective will. Everyone's going to bed in their boots tonight, according to her.

Elizabeth   I do not permit Christ to wash my feet! As my brother says, it is a charade and you are the foremost hypocrite!

Emma   If Christianity is hypocrisy, I can do without truth; it feels wonderful!

Jesus   I came here for a job. It's not suitable that I'm going to be embroiled in useless arguments –

Elizabeth   – Coward – !

Jesus   – I'll be in the bedroom, when you want me again, Emma. (*Exits.*)

Emma   Now, I know you don't like visitors but what would you say if you knew we were going to have a hundred and fifty people to supper?

Darwin   Anything you want dearest. We must offer these poor people shelter, if they are in need. Elizabeth, I wonder if you would like to go and discuss a menu for our guests, with Cook. The kitchen's through there.

Elizabeth *exits.*

Emma   You don't mind, do you?

Darwin   There's something rather serious come up.

Frederich has spilled the beans to me about the so-called expedition they are all on, in quest of racial purity. He is a prisoner of his sister Elizabeth who has taken all his papers and is editing his books so that they reflect her own cracked ideas about race. Since the expedition ran out of money, her husband has been sexually exploiting all the female members of the farming families, who of course are effectively prisoners.

Emma Oh, monstrous!

Darwin Lock up the silverware.

A scream and crash of saucepans, off. Enter **Elizabeth**.

Emma Is there something the matter Elizabeth? (*Peers off.*) There seems to be a lot of soup on the floor. Why is Cook crying?

Elizabeth She was not giving me any respect so I taught her some. You pretend this is a Christian country. Now prove it to us! (*Exits, angrily.*)

Darwin It looks like the end of the mock-turtle soup.

Emma I don't know how we'll feed everyone now. I'll go to the village, and see what I can buy.

Darwin Darling, you realise it's foul weather, and dark outside –

Emma Fear not – for perfect love casteth out fear.

Emma *kisses him and exits. Music. Enter* **Nietzsche**, *in a mighty, oversized and old-fashioned wheelchair, throne-like, pushed by a man with two heads,* **Humboldt/Mercator**.

Darwin (*to audience*) I immediately recognised *two* criminal convicts – I had last seen one at a dinner party in Tasmania – who had somehow formed a working symbiosis!

Music swells. **Humboldt/Mercator** *is introduced by* **Darwin** *as a fascinating specimen, as the wheelchair moves about the stage.*

This sixpenny thief had stood behind the Attorney

General's shoulder with the port decanter, while the excrescence growing on him I seem to remember had taken money from me outside a tent once, for a too-brief union with an exquisite Melanesian girl. Now they have conjoined and taken service to the philosopher who was seated on the throne of my father's old invalid chair! (*The music fades.*) What fragile, provisional creatures we are indeed, that a mere chair can wrack us so! (*Sniffles.*)

Nietzsche (*stilted*)   Why is the food ... taking so long?

Darwin   We are doing what we can. (*Pause.*)

Nietzsche   Then why are you laughing?

Darwin   I'm not laughing, I'm crying. (*Laughs.*)

Nietzsche   Are the little German farmers still alive?

Darwin   They strayed into a small sheep pond. I imagine they would be able to find their way out again.

Nietzsche   I told you how I am tired of being carried as the inseminator for this wretched expedition. Even if my revulsion for female flesh was removed, any progeny would be cursed with my venereal disease. I have just had a notion that would set me free. Professor, will you please castrate me?

Darwin   I beg your pardon?

Nietzsche   Remove the testicular sac with a sharp blade?

Darwin   I'm not your man. I cannot stand the sight of blood.

Nietzsche   All right, I'll do it myself then. I can have control of my hands now for a few moments after sexual release.

Darwin   And how do you intend to obtain that, exactly?

Nietzsche   When you were a young man did you not visit prostitutes?

Darwin   The idea excited me enormously, but I never did.

(*The footmen both cough noisily and shuffle their feet.* **Darwin** *recants.*)

– Except once, in Tasmania . . . .

Nietzsche   I take it you were more fortunate than I, and were not infected. I want you to get me a male prostitute.

Darwin   London is teeming with unfortunate females, but I wouldn't know where to start looking for a male catamite.

Nietzsche   Very well since time is running out get me a girl.

Darwin   I suppose I could ask in the village . . .

Nietzsche   No no. Open the large book with yellow pages, with alphabetical listings and look up a woman.

Darwin *juggles with the Yellow Pages section and the phone.*

Darwin   There's nothing under 'W'.

Nietzsche   Of course. As an ex-philologist, I know better than to look for something under its name. Try L for lady or P, for philanthropist.

Darwin   Nothing under P–.

Nietzsche   Come – the English have buried their lust as usual, but it will be somewhere in the alphabet.

Darwin   The sailors on the ship used to refer to them as cunts, or brasses.

Nietzsche   No, no. Let us first ransack the obvious word pockets, and then evolve to the argot of the picturesque. E, for Eros.

Darwin (*looks*)   Nothing . . . What about escort?

Nietzsche (*laughs*)   Yes, yes, I will take an escort. Pick up that thing and put the flat end to your ear.

Darwin *listens to phone.*

Darwin It sounds as though there might be a gnat or a small insect trapped inside.

Nietzsche Everything is in order.

Darwin When the proboscis is too short they can sometimes climb inside an unfamiliar plant and become trapped –

Nietzsche The thing you are holding is a growth from the brain of man. On no account try to water it. Copy the sequence of numbers printed in the advertisement onto the corresponding raised squares of the instrument.

Darwin *does this.*

Darwin (*listens*) The insect's died. No, it's in regular spasm now.

Nietzsche When the other person's voice comes, it sounds little. But you don't have to shout. Just speak to the end which –

Darwin (*shouting*) Hello! Can you hear me!

Nietzsche *cringes with the noise. He gestures with weak hands to* **Darwin** *who takes the phone over.* **Nietzsche** *props the mouthpiece on his shoulder.*

Nietzsche Hello . . . Any boys? I thought it was universal amongst the English. Then a girl, for one hour. If she is paid some more, would she cut it off? It's going to be hard to see what I'm doing, without a mirror. (*Indignant.*) Why ever not? Vatican choirboys are still castrated. (*Pause.*) Full bondage only then. Down House. Professor Frederich Nietzsche.

Darwin *takes phone and replaces it.*

Nietzsche You see how Christian hypocrisy filters down so it can be found even in pimps and panders. He says she cannot so-called 'hurt me'. (*Pause.*) You have no faith, have you, Darwin?

Darwin My dear friend Huxley coined the word for

what I am – agnostic.

Nietzsche   How fortunate, to have such inventive friends!

Darwin   I used to believe in God straightforwardly. When I was a boy, I could run very fast, and at class if I was late, I would pray to God as I ran. I was amazed at how often he helped me.

Nietzsche   So when did you kill him?

Darwin   Did I? I am not convinced he was ever there. I console myself in his absence with the magnificent puzzles of the physical world, and the endless accumulation of evidence, millenia on millenia.

Nietzsche   Evidence for what?

Darwin   Evolution.

Nietzsche   And what does evolution tell us?

Darwin   That the only constant is change. There is a small circular stone on my lawn outside which I placed there on my fifty-fifth year as an experiment. I have observed it has now almost had its burial in fourteen years – exclusively from worm-casts. There are no footprints in eternity.

Nietzsche   How peculiar to preach nothing but slow change, invisible to the rest of us, when the real truth is so violently different.

Darwin   The scientist is seldom in a position to observe extreme transformations.

Nietzsche   Tidal waves follow earthquakes and volcanoes blow mountains into dust.

Darwin   When I was in Peru, and the shoreline was raised several feet by a recent earthquake, I remember thinking how fortunate I was to witness such an unusual occurrence.

Nietzsche   The unusual is the norm, Professor. I give you this example. Giant rocks regularly slam into our planet

with such impact that your pat-a-cake theories are doomed
to second place! Catastrophe is the mother of creation!
Only the nimble survive!

*Music, effects. The face in the ceiling starts to moan eerily, while
vapour puffs from the gaping mouth.*

Voice   Charles – I cannot be with you much longer.

Darwin   What is it? What is the matter, Papa?

Voice   I have to come down.

Darwin   But I was just getting used to you being a part
of the ceiling.

Music. Ominous rumbles. **Jesus** *comes on stage, followed by*
Emma, **Bernard**, **Elizabeth**, *forming a rough chorus.*

Nietzsche   Darwin you're asleep
                Leave off counting sheep
                If you desire to stay alive
                Don't stand where the dead men dive.

All   Stand back from catastrophe
                Stand back from catastrophe
                Stand back from catastrophe

Jesus *pushes* **Darwin** *away from below the face.*

Jesus   The trumpets called down Jericho's walls
                Your father's image is cued to fall,
                And then up there, there'll be nothing at all

Humboldt   Your summons the voice of the football
                   crowd,
                Hear our warning all out loud,

All   Step away Darwin, or step in your shroud!

Exeunt all except **Darwin** *and* **Jesus**. *Mighty rumbles and
subterranean groans.*

Voice   Look out!

Darwin's *father's face drops out of the ceiling and smashes on the
stage. A roar, like that of a football crowd when the team scores.*

Lights to normal. **Darwin** *stares up through the hole, joined by* **Jesus**.

Darwin   I can see open sky – I thought my bedroom lay directly above.

Jesus   Over the years, it must have *evolved* to somewhere else. I'm sorry, Professor, I shouldn't make jokes at your expense. Don't worry, I can confirm your bedroom's still up there *some*where, because I've been in it with Emma, comforting her.

Enter **Emma**, *voluptuously dishevelled as before.*

Jesus   She needs it! She's taking your death hard. (*Pause.*)

Emma   Look at that sky!

Jesus   Aye, and the speed on them raggedy black clouds now, scrimping the dark across the stars.

Emma   Unless the Swabians turn up in the next ten minutes, they're going to get soaked.

Jesus   To think, I put dry-weather tyres on the bike this morning. But that's neither here nor there, since someone nicked it from the hall.

Darwin   Someone stole your bicycle, sir from under this roof? We should question the servants, dearest.

Jesus   You'll have to find them first.

Darwin   What does he mean?

Emma   He's right. Elizabeth got loose in the kitchen again so Cook, the butler and the 'tweenies gave in their notice and fled. Then I was going to leave and buy ready-cooked food but the coachman has taken the carriage and horses out.

Darwin   Why?

Emma   To stop Bernard requisitioning them. The only thing left in service, as far as I can see, waits on Mr Nietzsche, and it claims it is a footman, and refuses to scrape salsify or peel so much as a potato. So what are we going to do when the Swabian hordes turn up, expecting their dinner hot on the table?

Helicopter noise.

Darwin   What is that?

Jesus   Don't worry, it's not the last trump, yet.

Helicopter noise, loud. Lighting change and through the hole left by the fallen face, a woman exquisitely dressed in smart military fatigues is lowered. **Mary** *steps out of the harness, which is withdrawn upwards and the noise of the helicopter recedes. She takes off her military gear to reveal a bondage outfit underneath.*

Mary (*brightly to* **Darwin**)   I'll just phone in, if that is all right. (*She takes out a cellphone. To phone.*) Hi, this is Mary Magdalene. I'm at Down House now. (*To* **Jesus**.) Oh, hi, Jesus, long time no see! (*To phone.*) Yeah, I'll hold.

She embraces **Jesus***, and exits.*

Emma   She's very striking, Jesus . . . Is she an old girlfriend?

Jesus   Not for a long time now.

Emma   So what is she doing here?

Jesus   I honestly don't know. It's a terrible shock to the system seeing her.

Emma   Did you really not know she was coming?

Jesus   I may have asked for many things from my father at various points, but I've never asked for an airborne whore! (*Pause.*)

Emma   I do believe you're blushing!

Jesus   She's not my type, at all. I don't know what I was doing with her, in the first place. Honest. We weren't together for long. Look – I was on the road, and you don't get to meet decent women when you're touring.

Darwin   I thought Mary Magdalene was forgiven

everything because she loved you!

Jesus   It was what she did before she was forgiven that's the trouble!

Emma   Gentle Jesus, we have a hundred and sixty people coming to dinner, and no food. Perhaps it would redeem your reputation a little to –

Jesus (*interrupting*)   If I did everything people asked, there'd be nothing left of me, honest.

Emma   Is that a no, to charity?

Jesus   It's nothing to do with charity. It's profile. After the feeding of the five thousand, it's non-productive to become involved with smaller-scale catering efforts. So I'd like to keep this visit specific to its original aim of comforting the bereaved. Is that all right, Emma?

Emma   Up to a point. But I can see now it is not just me who needs comfort and succour from you. So what are we to do?

Jesus *takes* **Emma** *by the arm.*

Jesus   Why don't we go upstairs and we'll pray together, Emma.

Emma   I want to be alone to pray. You can stay down here with your fancy woman, and sort the world out, Jesus!

Emma *throws her dressing gown at* **Jesus** *and exits up the stairs.*

Jesus   I'll never understand women. Not in a million years. Is this just before her monthlies, or something?

Darwin   I doubt if anyone knows, including her. Emma has never bothered to note her own cycle. We once had to cannibalise an unread copy of *The Times*, as her period had started in the middle of a picnic.

Jesus   All the same, she's a very attractive woman, your cousin. A cracker. You know what I like about her? It's the way she never quite manages to tie all her hair up.

Darwin It's true she's not the most organised of ladies in her dress.

Jesus There's more to it than that! It draws a harmony from her which sings through the infinity of all her dimensions.

Darwin Save your poetry. It's wasted on me.

Jesus Do you really not like poetry at all?

Darwin Not at all. Not any more.

Jesus (*affecting shock*) What! Do the words of the Song of Solomon mean nothing to you, man? 'Beloved, thy breasts are like – gazelles – Two *twin* gazelles, nested together'?

Darwin I cannot see the point of gaudy and empty pieces of phrase-making which obscure any point the characters are trying to make.

Jesus Spoken like a scientist, Professor. A *dead* scientist.

Jesus *exits up the stairs.*
Nietzsche *is pushed on by* **Humboldt/Mercator**.
Enter **Mary**.

Mary (*identifying him*) Mr ... ? ... Neat-chur ...

Nietzsche (*pronouncing it*) Nietzsche, Nietzsche. Professor.

Mary Got it! Professor Frederich Nietzsche!

Nietzsche Let us begin.

Mary Money first.

Nietzsche There is a two ounce bag of gold in the desk.

Darwin It's mine!

Nietzsche Darwin will pay.

Darwin I certainly will not!

Nietzsche This may be your only effort to practise eugenic birth control, Darwin.

Darwin Young woman, your client told me he has

syphilis.

Nietzsche   Nice try, Darwin. But I do not require her to touch me.

Humboldt/Mercator *comes forward and opens the desk, takes out a bag with the gold in it, and passes it to* **Mary**.

Darwin   That is daylight robbery!

Nietzsche   Nonsense. In a robbery, criminals are involved in theft. This is the murky kiss of Christianity, the debased currency of pity. You are giving money because you feel sorry for me.

Mary *cracks the whip.*

Mary   Tie the slave down!

Humboldt/Mercator *takes* **Nietzsche** *and spreadeagles him under the hole in the roof, using ropes round his ankles and wrists.*

Nietzsche   Don't forget to spit on my face.

Mary   Shut up you little worm!

Nietzsche   Whip me please Miss.

Mary   I don't think so. (*She yawns.*) I'm tired. Someone else can whip you.

Nietzsche   No, no, please.

Mary   Why should I whip you? You're not well hung enough. No, as for whipping, that can be done by servants.

She tosses the whip to **Humboldt/Mercator** *and walks away to* **Darwin**.

Mary   Excuse me sir. Could I help myself to a glass of water?

Darwin   Certainly. Would you like wine? Or there's some Irish whiskey.

Mary *goes to a table and helps herself.*

Mary   No thank you. I don't drink alcohol. I have to piss on someone in about two hours. (*Drinks.*) It's good water.

Darwin   It's from our own well. A fortuitous arrangement of strata below the house.

Mary   Is this your house?

Darwin   Yes.

Mary   God, it would be my dream to have a house like this. It's huge. You have a lot of books – are you a writer?

Darwin   Yes.

Nietzsche   Whip me please.

Humboldt *snarls at him menacingly.*

Darwin   Shouldn't you be attending to your client?

Mary   Being ignored gets them hard too. Anything I do. I think it's the fact that they're paying for it or something.

Darwin   *I'm* paying.

Mary   Yeah, but he stole it from you. But with his Mercury opposing Uranus, whaddya expect?

She takes another run at **Nietzsche** *and pretends to grind her heel in his groin. Then she goes back to* **Darwin**.

Mary   These dominatrix gigs are so weird. Sometimes I can catch myself getting into it.

Nietzsche   Yes! Get into it! Yes!

Mary   For about thirty seconds – and you think – hey! Where *was* I??

Mary *turns and takes the whip and starts whipping close to* **Nietzsche**, *yelling at him. Then she drops it abruptly and goes back to* **Darwin**.

Mary   Have you written anything I would have heard of?

Darwin   A couple of steady sellers. In fact I could have made my living as a writer, if I hadn't sat on the book like a dodo for twenty years. *The Origin of Species* was intended to be an abstract, an introduction to a larger book, which remains unwritten.

Nietzsche Nietzsche's law says that it will stay as a great book, as long as it remains unwritten. Only the mediocre prosper.

Mary Did I ask you to break into this conversation you butt-sucker?

Nietzsche (*speculative*) I want to come on my belly button.

Mary You hold onto that jissum unless you want another smack! You'll come when and where I tell you!

Nietzsche ... So ... I am forbidden to come.

Mary (*to* **Darwin**) Would you excuse me one moment, sir?

Mary *takes the whip and starts menacing* **Nietzsche**.

Nietzsche I'm think I'm coming. All pleasures want eternity. Deep deep eternity. Oh dear it's not coming. You have to be ruder and INSULT ME!

Mary Who cares? Shut up you little worm. (*She goes back to* **Darwin**.) Why is it guys like this kind of stuff?

Darwin All courtship patterns have their own separate momentum in evolution.

Mary I have met guys whose idea of total bliss is to blow smoke up my ass. Now would you explain that?

Nietzsche Untie me.

Humboldt/Mercator *untie him and he gets up rubbing his wrists and walks over to* **Mary** *and* **Darwin**.

Mary Did you come yet? (*Pause.*)

Nietzsche No. I stood on the lofty crags of sensation thinking; why am I not borne upwards faster? But thoughts are not to be compared with the blaze of feeling, thought is the shadow, dark and empty. Then I realised there is a perfect moment missing, one thing left to repeat in the eternal repetition and that is for God to drown us all. That would be the time to achieve full sensation. He's sworn not to drown us again, but we can always test him against his word. (*Shouts.*) I spit on you, God! (**Nietzsche** *spits upwards.*)

Mary Would you do that somewhere else? You are covering me and this dear old man.

Nietzsche You spat on me only a moment ago.

Mary That was work. I thought we were through.

Nietzsche I paid you for forty minutes. If I want to insult God I will.

Mary Sorry.

Nietzsche Don't apologise. Start ordering me about too.

Mary (*changed tone*) Creeps like you ought to be tied up.

Nietzsche If you say so, Miss.

Nietzsche *goes and lies down under the hole, staring up through it. Distant thunder.*

Nietzsche Here I am Miss. Come and do it to me, please. Don't make me wait please. (*Pause.*) Aha! God was thinking just what I was thinking. The storm clouds are gathering. The little cuckolded farmers and their ugly pregnant wives are about to be drowned.

Mary (*to* **Darwin**) If the weather gets any worse I could be stuck here with my schedule totally destroyed.

Noise of growling thunder, off.

Nietzsche I want to die by lightning strike. I challenge God.

Mary Then you should take a walk.

Nietzsche Tell the little shit upstairs that if his father wants to kill me he can do it right here in Darwin's front room!

Mary (*to* **Darwin**) Why do people want to die? It

doesn't seem natural.

Nietzsche   Man is an animal whose nature has not been fixed. Who else but Man would say; How much do I have to pay God to fuck me in the arse with a dildo as he kills me? The only creature ever worth being fucked by is a graceful dancing god. But Great Pan is dead, his forests are cut down. I am the town crier for chaos. The day after tomorrow belongs to me. But I was born too soon. (*Pause.*) Something's happening! His spies are reporting back! I have a feeling that somewhere, a cosmic telephone is going to ring!

More thunder and noise of the approaching storm. Drops of water splash down through the hole onto **Nietzsche**.

Nietzsche   More, more. Can't you do better than that, God?

Enter **Elizabeth**, *drenched*.

Elizabeth   My brother! Where is my Frederich! Thank God you are safe, Frederich –

Nietzsche   Stay away from me, sister.

Elizabeth   Why?

Nietzsche   STAY AWAY! I am taunting God! I can feel him getting angry! Yes!

Bernard *comes in soaked.*

Bernard   Elizabeth! It's me, Bernard!

Elizabeth   Where are the Swabians?

Bernard   I was fording a river when it suddenly started to rise, and we were separated.

Elizabeth   Go and get them!

Bernard   I'm not going out again. They had been sheltering under a tree, and just after I led them away it was struck by lightning.

Nietzsche   None of you will be safe in here! It's coming!

It's coming! It's going to come through that hole!

Bernard   You madman! What is coming?

Nietzsche   God's reply! I have thrown down the gauntlet! I challenge God!!!!

Nietzsche *laughs wildly and points upwards. The stage darkens and lightning flashes off around. Wind noise. Suddenly a blinding flash of light and a bang as* **Nietzsche** *is struck by lightning through the hole.*
Elizabeth *screams.*

Elizabeth   Frederich!

Bernard   What was that?

Mercator   Mr Nietzsche got struck by lightning sir! Are you all right Mr Nietzsche?

Humboldt/Mercator *goes to* **Nietzsche**.

Humboldt   His heart's stopped.

Elizabeth *throws herself on her brother, howling.*

Elizabeth   No, no, no!

Bernard   Is there a doctor in the house?

Darwin   The nearest one is the village.

Bernard   It's already cut off –

Mary *(calls)*   Jesus, come on down, step on it, we got a high voltage dead one!

Jesus *and* **Emma** *emerge from upstairs in scant attire.* **Jesus** *goes to the body.* **Mary** *is opening his shirt.*

Jesus   Look at you standing round – a whole bloody roomful of misguided higher education and not one of you with enough mother-wit to learn elementary heart massage!

Jesus *kneels to* **Nietzsche** *and starts a heart massage.*

Elizabeth *(to* **Jesus***)*   Get your dirty Jewish hands off my brother! That is a humiliation worse than death!

Jesus   Woman, I am whoever I am but you are never going to be anything but trouble. This is the one man who had the courage to articulate chaos. He goes out, the likes of you go in. He is spirit, you are poisoned clay.

He works on and then stands up. **Nietzsche** *is still on the floor.*

Jesus   He'll live.

Elizabeth (*kneels to* **Nietzsche**)   Liebchen! Silly boy! Don't ever do that again. Don't leave me. Don't ever leave me. Come, Bernard, let us put him in the rolling stool and take him away from that bad man Jesus.

Emma (*to* **Jesus**)   You saved him! Even though he reviles you, you saved him!

Elizabeth *and* **Bernard** *help* **Nietzsche** *into the wheelchair and wheel him off.*

Jesus   The real miracle is not that I saved him. It's the utter uniqueness of each human. One individual can conduct voltages harmlessly through their body at a level which would turn another body to charcoal and steam. I haven't met any 'scientist' who could explain that, yet.

Thunder and lightning outside.

Mary   How am I going to get out of here?

Jesus   You won't be going home in a hurry. Old dad's really making it come down.

Darwin (*to audience*)   I suddenly realised that a disgraceful desire had arisen in me to bed Mary Magdalene. I fancied I saw a similar understanding in her eye, too. As in many dreams, I found myself like some Tahitian savage, quite bereft of restraining morality. I even experienced a quickening glee, as the prospect of a round juicy debauch arose in front of me, with someone who was not, and had never been, a Wedgwood. (*To* **Mary**.) You will be welcome to stay here, my dear. I could show you my library.

Mary   Oh I'd love that sir!

Jesus Make your visitor welcome! That's the spirit!

Music, Gounod, St Cecilia Mass, 'Credo'.

Emma Jesus – I feel I have heard this music in my heart already.

Jesus If not already, then you will, Emma! It's for us to dance together, in the rain.

Emma Is that all right, Charles? It seems hardly fitting . . .

Jesus Emma, ignore the unbelievers. Do you believe in the one God, the Father Almighty, maker of heaven and earth? Then come! The Lord of the Dance desires you: come. Be his only partner tonight!

Jesus *takes* **Emma***'s hand in a ceremonial fashion, and leads her off, followed by* **Mary** *and* **Humboldt/Mercator** *as* **Darwin** *watches.* **Humboldt/Mercator** *take* **Mary Magdalene***'s hand and exit. Blackout. Music swells.*

Act Two

Outside, crazy silhouettes of dancers in the rain, caught by the lightning. The sounds of a ceilidh band. Thunder and lightning. **Darwin** *and* **Humboldt/Mercator** *on stage.*

Darwin (*to audience*)   The rain continued, though no more fell inside the house.

Mercator (*interjection*)   – It's raining cubic miles of water out there, every second, and that's a fact, amen –

Darwin   – Then the downpour turned into a deluge, so violent that it finally even drove the dancers back indoors and Christ retired upstairs with my wife. The rain continued so hard that after a while, I felt as if the heavens were preparing to wash the dear, ugly old house clear off the face of the downs.

Humboldt   Water level's rising.

Mercator   Water's rising fast!

Humboldt   'Tis a second flood. A great body of water now stretches to every horizon. (*Points.*) And look down! Humble cottages are bein' abruptly submerged, in the 'ollows. See as their little rush lights first go green, and then they is extinguished utterly as the waters bust the windows in and engulf the family round the supper table, before they 'ave time to eat the bread they have blessed.

Mercator (*pleased*)   The whole village, drowned like a litter o' kittens.

Humboldt   The barmaid was carrying your child, I heard tell.

Mercator   Aye. Poor Rose. Drowned. Amen.

Humboldt   Very soon there will be no land uncovered all over the world, amen.

Mercator   Amen.

Darwin   But my dear fellows, that can't possibly be true, if you go by the Bible as you seem to. God promised, with the rainbow. He said he wouldn't do that again.

Humboldt   There was to be one flood, but then Man did not stop at one wickedness. This is the second inundation, on account of how wickedness in Man has evolved.

Mercator   Every word in the Bible's true.

Darwin   Come come. The fossil record nowhere shows that there was anything as dramatic as a first flood.

Humboldt   Rose said she heard tell in the bar, that the fossil record is incomplete.

Darwin   Rose was correct, as far as it goes but –

Humboldt   She also told me you had found clamshells and oysters four miles up in the Andes. Proof of the first flood!

Darwin   Not so. It is simply that the Andes used to be on the seabed, and very slowly they rose.

Mercator   That's a ridiculous idea.

Darwin   Where is all this extra water going to be coming from, to cover the Andes now?

Humboldt   It's coming from somewhere! Look out there, it's bucketing down.

Darwin   But there's only a finite amount of water available, even if the polar ice-cap melts. You think that God has a big tap in the sky, and turns it off when the level's high enough to cover the land, like you do with a bathtub?

Mercator   I don't know, because I ain't ever had a bath. But I do know that everybody in the whole world's going to drown except for those who get in the ark, two by two.

Darwin   Has God provided a second ark?

Humboldt   Matter of fact, he has. Just like the first.

Darwin (*giggling*)   Is it still – let me see if I remember – with an upper, middle and lower deck, three hundred cubits long?

(*Pause.*)

Mercator Roughly.

Darwin Why? There are fewer creatures today. The Polynesians made dozens of species extinct before white men arrived in the Pacific. The dodo, the passenger pigeon and the austral wolf have all disappeared in the last hundred years. You would have thought God could have shrunk the specifications, this time. (*Pause.*)

Humboldt (*grudgingly*) Maybe there are more beetles this time. Or ants.

Mercator Maybe he's got to make room for the Swabians.

Darwin So where is this mighty ark?

Humboldt/Mercator *weigh up the question.*

Mercator Reckon it's safe to tell him?

Humboldt Aye. (*To* **Darwin**.) You're standing on it. It's right here beneath your feet.

Darwin Nonsense. This house stands on the earth.

Mercator This house is a house no more. It is the cabin. While the Ark is set underneath it, in the earth.

Darwin I've never heard anything so preposterous. I have only yesterday drawn water from our well.

Mercator Oh aye, the Ark carries enough sweet water in her as well as supplies. Do you not remember seeing two great posts in the ground behind the stables? They are the Ark's twin sternposts.

Darwin I do remember something now, but, bang my bones! No one can have buried a complete ship underneath the house without my noticing it!

Mercator The God who hid your bedroom now, he can do anything.

Humboldt Underneath the house now, ready to bear it up as the waters rise, is a great twin-keeled frame, with mighty beams, and ribs of heart of oak.

Darwin   I shall investigate.

Mercator   I wouldn't do that. If you go doubting God, and start poking and prodding, he's not going to like it at all. He'll sweep you overboard, and there aren't no lifebelts on this trip. I'd stay inside if I were you.

Enter **Elizabeth** *and* **Bernard**. **Darwin** *conceals himself.*

Elizabeth   We are bankrupt. Bernard! Why is there no money in the money box?

Bernard   The Schwartzes could not pay in advance; the Schmidts likewise. The Schimmelpennicks and the Müllers also have problems. That is why they came with us, Elizabeth. That is why they are not behind a plough in Schleswig-Holstein. They did not have land. In order to found the new fatherland, I agreed in some cases to defer payment.

A flash of lightning, nearby. A loud cry, off, from **Nietzsche**.

Darwin   Whatwassat?

Mercator   Whatwassat?

Elizabeth   One of you, go and see what Mr Nietzsche wants.

Exit **Humboldt/Mercator**.

Elizabeth   Mrs Schwartz's two daughters are both pregnant. The youngest told me you had an arrangement with the family. Now I see what the arrangement is; you are to be whoremaster for this expedition.

Bernard   They are very fertile Germans, yes, that is why it is important that they should come.

Elizabeth   And Mrs Müller is out to here! (*Gestures.*) She can hardly keep up!

Bernard   I had to do something about your broken promises. You promised them that their stock would be upgraded with racially enhanced children, from your brother, the genius. He has not performed. Some idealist had to make an effort.

Elizabeth (*to* **Bernard**)   I *know* my brother is potent. Almost every time the lightning strikes now, he has an orgasm. He could father the next generation of Swabians.

Bernard   You should thank God he did not. He is diseased.

Elizabeth   You are a penis. All one big lying penis. I am never again going to let it inside me. Never!

Bernard   Lizaveta, *carissima*, we both know your brother is a genius. But making his ideas come true in one lifetime is hard. And my penis is a good, German penis!

Elizabeth   How can I possibly put his ideas into action, working with dross like you! We now don't have enough to get tickets to Buenos Aires, let alone a plough or seedcorn when we get there.

Bernard   Don't let's quarrel. This place could be a gold mine.

Elizabeth   The silver is mostly plated rubbish. They don't live grandly at all. I thought he was a great man!

Bernard   I can smell money, somewhere. Look at these first editions. (*Points to books.*) Audubon's *Birds of America*! That is worth enough for a steerage passage for five.

Elizabeth   Not if you start licking it.

Darwin *decides to break in. He coughs.*

Darwin   I didn't realise, Mr Forster, that you were something of an expert on rare books. But I don't lend out my books. I would be obliged if you put them back.

Bernard   This signed copy of Marx – Why did he not give you a first edition of *Das Kapital*?

Darwin   He wanted to dedicate the whole volume to me but I refused. It was never clear to me how he collected his facts.

Bernard   I am so glad you are against Herr Marx. He is a spiritual poison, a Jewish canker in the German soul. Herr Professor, your breeding experiments have inspired us to think that it is not only desirable to breed to the perfection of true conquering Germans, but possible.

Darwin If that is true, then I am responsible for as much mayhem as Mr Marx. But you have completely misunderstood me. In evolution, it is clear there is no such thing as perfection. There are only nature's blind strategies.

Elizabeth The will is perfect, and it is present in the Nordic races.

Darwin How can you measure will?

Elizabeth Will is measurable in humans, by territorial conquest.

Bernard You have said that if giraffes strained once to browse on treetops, then the necks of their offspring with longer neck vertebrae would provide an advantage.

Darwin There is no evidence so far that species knowingly contribute to the next generation's inheritance. Nature is blind, proceeding by trial and error. Whatever noble aspirations the giraffes have as they reach up, long-necked offspring have been favoured while shorter giraffes, produced by the same parents die out.

Bernard Is that 'The survival of the fittest'?

Darwin Yes. But 'fittest' does not mean fiercest, or blondest. And I didn't write anything so potentially misguided. Followers of social Darwinism attribute it to me, but its originator is a man called Lyell.

Bernard Why are you against us?

Elizabeth Why are you disowning your own ideas?

Darwin Throughout my life I have made every effort to pursue the truth, separate from all Christians, Mohammedans, and the lunatic fringe. My reverence for life has enlarged with every plant and living creature I have studied. Every night I drink to our cousins the plants and our brothers and sisters in the animal kingdom. I can hardly be expected to applaud when complex issues are vulgarised and politicised by barbarians.

Bernard   So what is the difference between a German and an ape, to you?

Darwin   The same difference as an Englishman and an ape, and a Chinaman and an ape, and an African and an ape. All humans have a common ancestor, who most likely peopled the world in the last million years, by walking out of Africa!

Elizabeth   Are you saying that my brother's ancestors were *Schwartzes*? That is worse than the Polish ones he claims!

Enter **Nietzsche**, *on his wheelchair, pushed by* **Humboldt/ Mercator**. **Nietzsche** *claps slowly, three times, with limp hands.*

Nietzsche   Bravo, sister. Best applaud while I still can. Prepare my bath for me will you, Humboldt.

Humboldt   Are you sure you'll be all right sir?

Nietzsche   Quite all right. The peak of the storm is past, and so I do not anticipate any more genital perturbation. There have been so many lightning flashes now that I can relax.

Elizabeth (*of* **Humboldt**)   Is that an ancestor? No! – Things like that should be put down without mercy!

Humboldt/Mercator *exits.*

Nietzsche   Humboldt is not as stupid as he looks. He knows about the lost Book Four of Aristotle's *Ethics*. The one that says that comedy rules, not *Germans*. Listen. The horde of Swabians are almost upon us, hot for vengeance.

Elizabeth   Vengeance? We are their saviours!

Nietzsche   In your absence, you have both been voted deposed.

Elizabeth   Frederich – whose side are you on? (*Pause.*)

Nietzsche   Aristotle approves of the slave class as a faithful rendition of natural order. Provided we lose our heads, sister, I shall be on the side of the aristocrats.

Elizabeth   We must teach them a lesson Bernard. Pretend to parley, then shoot the ringleaders. Where is the gun?

Bernard   This way –

Bernard *and* **Elizabeth** *rush off.*

Darwin   Who told you they were coming?

Nietzsche   This sly fellow with horns and a tail came to me, saying he was forced out of his basement, beached and half-drowned in a field of winter wheat. (*Phone rings.*) Don't answer it! It will be him, but these deformed creatures of the brain finally wither if you ignore them.

Enter **Jesus** *at a run, undressed, and goes to the phone.*

Jesus (*to phone*)   Hello, yes, Jesus here. Of course there's such a personage as the Devil. He visited me. Old Nick. We were together up this mountain, where you could see all the countries of the world. The world was flat in those days. Well he's a perfectly pleasant fellow on the surface. Likes a joke. (*Pause.*) Oh, no it's you again, Satan. You frigging gobshite! Don't waste my time, man! (*Phone down.*)

Nietzsche   Come off it! You boys pretend to piss in each other's pockets. But you all need each other to exist.

Emma *appears.*

Emma   Jesus? Oh, there you are! What are you doing? I thought you had left me . . .

Jesus   I'll be with you in just a minute Emma! (*To* **Nietzsche**.) The trouble with you professor types is that your brains have gone to your head. Before you dismiss me as some hairy-arsed Stone Age hitch-hiker, it might surprise you to know that I'm with the most radical spiritualists who want to knock the whole superstructure of established religion on the head. It was what I was trying to do in the so-called Holy Land – to wind the whole thing up – everything!

Nietzsche   Why?

Jesus   The end of the world was a dead cert., I thought. I was wrong there. Instead of stopping history I found I'd started some more.

Nietzsche   Rather trashy history, too. I believe your cult was a success because there are only bad instincts praised in the New Testament.

Jesus   Oh, crap, man. If you're half-man, half-God, how can you have instincts?

Nietzsche   Ask Professor Darwin!

Emma *tugs at* **Jesus'** *sleeve.*

Emma   Come and comfort me, as you did before. Jesus, don't be angry, please.

Jesus   I'm not angry!

Nietzsche   Tell that to the money changers whose stalls you wrecked.

Emma   Is this what he deserves for saving your life? Really, there's not a bone of malice in his body.

Nietzsche   He's a duplicitous little cheat. This is the same Jesus who claims that with bread and a little sweet wine we can pretend we are tearing his limbs and sucking his blood.

Jesus   Yours is the one miraculous cure I'm beginning to regret. If you were able to stand up, I'd knock your soup-strainer through your arsehole.

Nietzsche   Why don't you make me stand up? It's in your power.

Emma   Don't listen to him Jesus!

Jesus *is about to strike* **Nietzsche**, *but thinks better of it and exits with* **Emma**. **Nietzsche** *snatches round with his head trying to get a whistle on a chain round his neck.*

Darwin   What's the matter?

Nietzsche   I can't use my hands any more. Put the whistle in my mouth.

Darwin *does it for him and he blows a long blast on a football whistle.*

Nietzsche   Sham religion of slaves. Charade of Dionysus. False joys, false salvation, the cuckolding God who lies his way into the bedchamber like everyone else.

Darwin   I am not a Christian – but he is offering Emma a comfort she would not get elsewhere, when I am gone.

Nietzsche   You only pretend to feel sorry for her.

Humboldt/Mercator *comes in at a run, covered in bubbles, with a towel.*

Humboldt   Bath's ready sir! (*Pulling wheelchair off. Sings.*)
   Scrub a dub dub
   Three pigs in a tub –

Humboldt/Mercator, *blithely humming, exits pushing*
Nietzsche. **Darwin** *goes to his books, starts pulling them out and putting them into a large Gladstone bag by his desk.*
Enter **Mary**.

Mary   Can I help you?

Darwin   Thank you my dear. I need one copy of every English edition of all my books.

Mary   You seem upset.

Darwin   I am. All my life I have striven for truth, although in writing, sometimes I have felt that the simplest expression was beyond me –

Mary   You write beautifully!

Darwin   I told you I was planning a big book, after *Origin of Species*. Well I think that the world needs such a book. But I can't write it here! It's a circus! I refuse to believe that my house is the new Ark, and it's going to float away on an outer hull of two-inch Scots pine, sheathed with copper.

They start to pull books out of the shelves.

If I stay here, with all these people, I shall contract neuralgia.

Mary   Where are you going to go?

Darwin   I'm not sure. To a calmer and more scientific atmosphere. The potting shed out by the sandwalk. If I cannot work there, then perhaps rooms in London.

Mary   I think it's just so great that at an age when most people would be wanting to enjoy their retirement and what they have left of their life, you are still working for the good of humanity. Can I ask you something? Why don't you take any account of courting rituals in genetic selection?

Darwin   Probably because I feared I would be mocked even more than I have been.

Mary   When did you start getting out of step, not believing in God?

Darwin   When I lost Annie, it destroyed the vestiges of my belief.

Mary   But you had other kids.

Darwin   Ten.

Mary   Ten pregnancies, nose-to-tail?

Darwin   I made a study of each of their expressions, before they could speak. I was doing similar work in a local lunatic asylum, run by a friend, to find the connection between feeling and expression. Mad or sane, at whatever age, we're very like chimpanzees, for the most part.

Mary   So – ten little chimps! Did you not take *any* precautions?

Darwin   Emma simply had to lose at whist. Or I had to win. And she is very vague about her fertility. Caught short on a picnic, I recall, she used *The Times* as a sanitary towel. It was never referred to and we simply stopped taking the paper afterwards. I was glad, because the paper never missed having a cheap shot at Darwinism.

Bernard *and* **Elizabeth** *enter from opposite sides,* **Bernard** *with* *gun.* **Darwin** *takes up bag of books.*

Bernard   Where are you going?

Darwin   Outside. I can't think in here. I want space, to work soberly, away from all this religious nonsense.

Enter **Emma** *and* **Jesus**.

Emma   Oh do be careful, darling! Have you seen the weather? You could catch your death! You could be swept away!

Enter **Nietzsche** *pushed by* **Humboldt/Mercator**.

Bernard   Darwin! There are fleas in my manger. Common fleas! Biting and sucking aristocratic Polish blood. What kind of hospitality is this? Come back, and reorder your house.

Jesus   Darwin! Nothing will be the same after crossing this threshold!

Mary   Don't worry, I won't let anything happen to this lovely old man!

A lightning flash and thunder offstage again as the rest of the cast changes the set around **Darwin**, *forming a rough chorus, as the set changes to outdoors.*

Chorus
　　Beware the rain, the sightless architect of change,
　　One step outside, you'll not return the same.
　　Confront the elements and in no time
　　You will dissolve to protozoic slime

Thunder and lightning.

Jesus
　　Out there, creation is in flux!
　　Instance, old men who dare beneath God's angry glare
　　To bare to youthful girls their love,
　　Have of a sudden turned to three-toed pigeons
　　Startling their panting swains, who in their turn,
　　Turn turtle-dove!

Chorus (*Sung*)
　Darwin don't
　Darwin don't
　Don't take that step outside
　A chilling blast will wash the flesh
　From your old bones
　As you step from home
　The very stones will cry.

　Life's a greaser, Charlie boy
　You've become unstuck
　You aim to fuck sincerely,
　Sincerely you are fucked

　Appreciate that it's getting late
　Though character creates our fate
　Even though you meet and mate
　Out there you'll surely die.
　A shame there is no one to blame
　After the storm, no one to curse.

　No first cause no eternal name
　Given time, and given clay
　We all fade away.
　Fade away, fade away.

Etc., and fade. All withdraw at the end of the set change except **Darwin**
and **Mary**. *A star cloth at the back. A huge prow of a mighty ark breaks*
slowly through, with massive effects. **Darwin** *examines it.*

Darwin　The original was made from gopher wood, covered
in pitch. This does seem to fit the description.

Mary　A truly beautiful night.

Darwin (*to audience*)　It was indeed a magical night. The
clouds had moved away, leaving a mysterious silvery
landscape. Hedges and houses were showing blackly against
the moonlit sheen on the water, half a mile away. It was a
flood and no mistake. But the water needed to rise at least
another hundred and fifty feet if it was going to reach the
house.

Mary　Mr Darwin. I would consider it one of the greatest

honours ever paid to me if one of the greatest minds of the
nineteenth century, not to say of all time, allowed me to – I
can't say it. I'm too embarrassed. (*Pause.*) Do a lot of people ask
you to do this? Emma need never know. I'll make myself
invisible.

Darwin   As long as you don't become invisible to me as
well.

Mary   It's not really invisible, it's more like the dress turns to
a sorta camouflage . . . It's just we're awfully close to the path.
God, you're old enough to be my great-grandpa! But you have
such a reputation!

Mary *lays the books out on the prow to make a large mat.*

Mary   Don't want to catch a chill now do we. (*Reads a book
spine.*) '*The Various Contrivances by which British and Foreign Orchids
are Fertilised by Insects* by Charles Darwin MA, FRS etc.'

Darwin   Oh dear. I had an experiment set up on this part of
the lawn. (*Angry.*) Do you see what has happened? This has
come through right underneath my worm stone! That's fifteen
years research down the drain! Bang my bones!

Mary   Wooo! So this is the notorious Mr 'No footprints in
eternity', on the rampage. (**Mary** *consults a book.*) 'One of the
moths which fertilizes an orchid with an unusually deep cup
has evolved an *eleven inch* proboscis . . .'

Darwin *joins* **Mary** *on the books. They embrace tenderly.*

Mary   Is writing science books hard?

Darwin   I think a great deal of my nervous ailments are to
do with it. Sometimes, when I cannot pen a sentence correctly
I begin to suspect that clear expression to my fellow creatures
was out of reach for me.

Mary   Would you say you are socially progressive?

Darwin   I've tried and failed. When I tried to introduce a
working man's study group in the village, the vicar sabotaged
the enterprise, complaining that the working men smoked in
the school room. Of course they smoked. There wasn't much

else in their lives.

Enter **Emma**, *arm in arm happily with* **Jesus**, *in the dim light.*

Emma   Charles, why are you lying there, all alone?

Darwin   The worm stone's been moved!

Jesus   Charlie – don't worry about the worm stone. Take the word of one who's been to the end of eternity and back. The good news is that Emma's persuaded me to do what I've said I would never do, with her womanly wiles. (*Pause.*) I'm going to make dinner for you and the Swabians. Before you can push your legs under the tablecloth it'll be there, steaming hot in front of you, abracadabra.

Emma   What will we be having?

Jesus (*confidential*)   Tell me – Are you at all partial to Ulster Fry?

Emma   I am not familiar with it.

Jesus   Well it's thick slices of blood sausage curled in their death throes round fatty, back bacon, laying on corned beef in batter, with mountains of soda bread deep-fried in proper beef dripping.

Emma   What about vegetables?

Jesus   What d'yer want vegetables for?

Emma   Charles has rather a weak stomach.

Jesus   It's Ulster Fry or nothing.

Emma   Surely it would be kinder to give the Swabians something they are familiar with, say boiled beet and sauerkraut? (*Stiffly.*) Charles' haemorrhoids were never the same after the naval diet, on *The Beagle*.

Jesus   Away with you, woman! If I have to endure the grapes of wrath, so can he!

Jesus *exits with* **Emma**.

Mary   What's the most sublime moment you've ever had?

Darwin   I was twenty-one. I was in the Brazilian rainforests, with the great canopy of green above me. I was all alone. It was as if I had been given the secret of creation.

Humboldt/Mercator *pushs* **Nietzsche** *on to see* **Darwin** *lying with* **Mary**

Nietzsche   Oh no! There are things I do not wish to see, things I do not wish to know, and here is one of them. Don't stop. It's not happening. Disgusting heterosexual acts!

Exit **Humboldt/Mercator** *pushing* **Nietzsche**.

Mary   If you were able to go into the past and future, what one piece of information would you seek out to bring back?

Darwin   The process whereby species' characteristics are inherited. Pigeon fanciers know more about it than the so-called experts. We still have no real idea.

Mary   They do find out, after your time. It's called DNA. The keys to heredity.

Darwin (*excited*)   Oh, I knew that someday someone would find it – How does it work?

Mary   It won't be discovered for almost a century. It's this long molecular spiral of a programming code which all species have. It's really teeny – you couldn't see it through a conventional microscope. But it governs the replication and subsequent interaction of cells –

Darwin (*excited*)   I knew it!

Mary   It shows we seem to come from the same bit of Africa . . .

Darwin   I have such endless mockery for my belief that Man originated from a primate in Africa.

Mary   But it's not just we're kissing cousins of chimpanzees. DNA shows we've got an awful lot in common with sweet peas.

Darwin   This gets better all the time. The vindication of our cousins in the vegetable kingdom! (*Ecstatic.*) I was right. God, I was right! Oh! Mary! If I died now, I would die happy!

Triumphant music. **Darwin** *and* **Mary** *conclude their lovemaking.*
DNA spirals arrive magically, effects. Exit **Darwin** *and* **Mary**.
Humboldt/Mercator *enters with tray and glasses. A table is laid*
out.
Enter **Jesus**.

Jesus (*to* **Humboldt**)   What are these for?

Humboldt   Pudding wine, sir.

Jesus (*scorn*)   Pudding wine? Did I say I was going to make
pudding wine? Take up those glasses.

Humboldt/Mercator *collects up the glasses sulkily.* **Darwin**
arrives, collects books feverishly.

Jesus (*to* **Darwin**)   What are you looking for?

Darwin   Future generations will have the key to heredity. If
you can find and alter the key process, it would mean no more
hereditary disease.

Jesus   There's nothing you will be able to do about it. It's
too late.

Darwin   Why is it too late? I am on the scent of a new
discovery which will crown my expanded version of *The Origin*
of Species.

Enter **Emma**.

Jesus   This house is your temple, right? You stepped outside
your temple. This is a split between soul and body. And so,
farewell and goodnight!

Emma   We can clear the tables back and have dancing at
the end. What do you say, Jesus?

Jesus   Dancing? I hadn't heard you wanted dancing, Mrs
Darwin.

Emma   Mrs Darwin! We've got very formal suddenly!
Darling, you can call me Emma! I want to see you bounding
like a satyr, like you did outside, lit by flashes of lightning!

Jesus   I'm sorry, Mrs Darwin but I shan't be dancing any more, with you or anyone, tonight.

Emma   I thought we had become close. Is that not true?

Jesus   It can never be. Things have to end, and so we must look round for reasons. Your husband has been encouraged by our own free and easy behaviour to behave in a similar fashion. I cannot stay in any case, in this day and age. Apart from being an anachronism everywhere, socially I am not in your class.

Emma   Charles taught me to value people for what they were, not where they came from. This is not too smart a house I hope for you . . .

Jesus   It's not that – it's good and homely here. The carpets are worn but I know the circles you move in. Do you really want a semi-professional cyclist with no GCSE passes, when the historian Carlyle comes by, or when the great Huxley visits, or when, God help us, Prime Minister Gladstone drops in for tea?

Emma   I need someone, Jesus. I thought you were bringing me comfort. Why can't you stay now?

Jesus   It's the rules of the game. I am the God you desire, only when I'm in transit. On the road, I can be that thing, but tied down anywhere, I'd have the Godhead squeezed out of me, I'd be as lively as a kite in a dead calm. It's . . .

Emma *cries.*

Jesus   Believe me, it is the newel post and hub of my agony that I cannot stay with you. But what you don't realise, my pet, is that the Christ is only completely himself when he is puking his hiatus hernia up the final stage of a tough hill-climb, sitting on his mutinous piles, at four o'clock on a winter afternoon. That is my model of existence! Easy yoke be fucked! (*Long pause.*) Excuse me.

Emma   Can you bring Charles back to life for me then?

Jesus   Woman, there would have been no point in my

coming to you if I could have. Bloody hell! Be a bit reasonable!

Emma   I see I shall have to be brave. Shall you be staying for supper?

Jesus   Maybe ... I'm on call, though. I'm off as soon as my prayers are answered for a working bicycle.

Emma   I don't think we should sit together in that case.

Jesus   Oh, don't be like that, Emma, I mean, Mrs Dar-.

Emma   I do see now that you are a horrid, common little man.

Jesus   Emma! Don't be like that! All right, I'm common! But I'm common because I have to be! Common to everybody! Isn't that what you saw in me? And that's what you saw in me, your own spark of divinity!

Emma   I've been taken advantage of, and I never want you to speak to me again.

Jesus   Forgive me for loving you. But in my bowels, I have to be who I have to be. I've got races to lose, out there.

Emma *exits, slams a door, off.*

Jesus   I hate this bit of the job. Charles, could I ask you a very great favour? I need some haemorrhoid ointment.

Darwin   My dressing-room cupboard.

Jesus   Bless you. Sure, the westward hill slopes will be dry enough by midnight to give me a run down some lonesome road.

Enter **Humboldt/Mercator**. **Mercator**'s *face is missing, just a red smear with a dangling eyeball.* **Darwin** *is fascinated.*

Humboldt   Hallejulah! The Swabians will be arriving shortly. They were saved, every single one, when the waters swept over them, in an airpocket of a blessed slaughterhouse they had taken shelter in, delivered from God's wrath, by the tender mercies of our Lord Jesus Christ who redeems all sin and all sinners.

Darwin I say, your friend seems to have taken a bit of a bashing.

Humboldt It was during a discussion with Mr Nietzsche, sir. Mercator holds his soul was saved by a belief in the literal truth of the Bible. He was unfortunately challenged to demonstrate 'If thy right eye offend thee, pluck it out' But then he went and tore – feels like his whole face off.

Darwin It must hurt frightfully.

Humboldt He whimpered a bit at the time, but he's gone all quiet now. To be honest I don't feel a thing. I would have asked Jesus to help, but this Jesus is not our Jesus, but an inferior Jesus who we do not recognise.

Exit **Humboldt/Mercator**.
Enter **Bernard** *who starts to collect* **Darwin**'s *books.*

Darwin Damnation! You don't give up easily, do you, Mr Forster! He's trying to take my books again!

Elizabeth *enters from another door and goes directly to him.*

Elizabeth Bernard what are you doing? Put Mr Darwin's books back.

Bernard Tomorrow I will go to the famous Charing Cross Road in London and sell them. Then we can go and sail to Buenos Aires from Southampton. He does not need them any more.

Darwin I do so! The moment I saw you, I knew you were of a criminal bent!

Bernard (*to* **Elizabeth**) He knows nothing of the kind of man I am. Neither do you. You only like me because I am dangerous.

Elizabeth When the Swabians arrive what will you tell them? That it is *good* to steal from your host? You must put the books back, Bernard. I have had enough of your games.

Bernard The game is the fittest survive, Elizabeth.

Elizabeth *produces the revolver.*

Elizabeth You think I like you because you are dangerous? Now who is more dangerous? Put the books down.

She advances on **Bernard** *and pursues him off.* **Mary** *rescues* **Darwin**'s *books.*

Mary There, they're quite safe.

Darwin (*looks in the bag*) Oh dear.

Mary Is there something wrong?

Darwin He's right, I have mistreated these wretchedly. We should have not lain on them. My mother always said I should not leave books out in the grass. I've always treated books badly, ever since I was small. Torn them down the spine so they wouldn't crush my chest as I read.

Mary Don't blame yourself for it. Were you very fond of your mother?

Darwin As to what I remember . . . Mother died when I was eight. My sister taught me, then a little later, I was sent away. I craved affection from my schoolfellows . . . I see a woman's face . . . then it's gone. I remember nothing more of her. (*Pause.*) . . . I am afraid when knowledge is lost. If sleep should come on me after the meal, will you guard the books, Mary?

Mary Of course.

Darwin I knew you would.

Enter **Nietzsche** *also in evening wear, pushed by* **Humboldt/ Mercator**, *who lifts* **Nietzsche** *into his place at the table.* **Nietzsche** *examines his place.*

Nietzsche 'Herr Doktor Professor Nietzsche, Chair of Classical Philology, Basel, and –' uppercase '– Genius'. Boys, whatever your beliefs, you have scored a bull's-eye here! I'm right in front of my name.

Exit **Humboldt/Mercator** *with the huge wheelchair.* **Jesus** *enters down the stairs, in a smart dinner jacket, still with Lycra cycling shorts underneath.* **Nietzsche** *hoots and points laughingly.*

Jesus This is a gesture to placate the missus of the house whom I fear I have mortally offended. Underneath, I am still that uncouth modern man, more familiar with steel and stress, than wood and woe.

Darwin Would Jesus know about DNA?

Mary Whaddya know about heredity, Jesus?

Jesus Not a lot, and it's mostly depressing. Dog breeders say that it's the bitch who has the upper hand. I've been recently confronted with the fact that I could only be twenty-five per cent divine. But here's Her Highness!

Emma *comes down the stairs in a white wedding dress with a long train. It has a large bloodstain on the front of it.*

Nietzsche What is this, Emma? You look a picture. A picture of a woman on her own, smeared with the evidence of dreadful deeds, the fearful, sacrificial bride conquered in the bloodbath of the wedding night by the blonde groom's superior, brutal strength.

Emma Not so, Professor. It is just that, distracted as ever, I have omitted to use *The Times* again. But even so, I must be a merry widow. I will dance with everyone tonight, except for Mr Jesus. Even you, my infected snarling cripple.

Nietzsche Emma, you should know by now, that is unlikely. There are only a few minutes, after *le petit mort*, that I can move at all.

Emma I'm sure that if someone made water on you, you could achieve satisfaction and then you'd be able to move your arms and legs for a while. We could do a horrid little parody of a polonaise together, no?

Nietzsche Oh, excellent. This is splendid. Emma's true character has emerged, a daughter of Dionysus.

Emma No, it is not 'me'. I don't mind fitting the role though. It's what women have always done. But in order I may oblige you later, my Polish prince, this lady must drink deep.

Emma *goes to the sideboard and pours herself a large drink and drinks it off.*

Nietzsche   Bravo! Bravo! (*Pause.*) I never thought, Darwin, tonight that I'd be in a wetter place than you ever laid up in.

Darwin   The wettest place we ever laid up? Without question, the Falkland Islands. I was there – it must be oh, fifty years ago. Lord it was a bleak piece of land. At first I thought I would never stay at a place with so little for my journal. Then we lost a man, drowned retrieving a duck he'd shot on Beaver Island. I knew it was a foolish death, although I was but twenty-one. For what came after? I was an idle young man, addicted to camaraderie and killing . . . but the taste for it suddenly left me. I would have never made a surgeon. When an operation was begun on a child in Edinburgh, I could not stay to see such suffering. (*Pause.*) It's thirty years now since Annie . . .

Darwin *breaks from the table and goes to window, weeping.* **Jesus** *goes to put his hand on his shoulder.*

Jesus   There now man. I'm with you.

Darwin   I've had enough of your promises.

Darwin *knocks* **Jesus***' arm away.*

Emma   (sotto voce)   Charles could not bear to go to her funeral for fear of breaking down completely and losing his mind.

Darwin   Where is my Annie, Jesus? (*Long pause.*)

Jesus   We're all with you. We've all been scarred. But better times are to come.

Humboldt/Mercator *brings on a racing bicycle with a label on it addressed to Down House, Down. He leans the bike against the side.*

Jesus   (*cheerier*)   Prayers are answered, see? There's a point I've been trying to get across to everyone all evening, but I'll have one last try before I leave. (*Pause.*) Who among you *entirely* believes that I am the Christ? (*Pause.*) No one? (*Pause.*) Good. Because I don't, either, and that means that you are not in the hands of the deceiver yet, where the voice and face and gesture finally overcome all inner resistance in the speaker and he becomes what he is not.

Nietzsche So, in yet another bid for our affections, you are now claiming to be not what you are, am I correct?

Jesus Shut up a minute, clever-clogs. I'm talking about the deception of inspired rhetoric. It happens in stages. First the speaker is overcome by a false belief in himself, then when this miraculous belief which comes from nowhere wells up in him, he transmits it to others. 'I say it thus, therefore it must be thus.' Finally the deceivers end up owning reality. Except they have made it worthless, a devalued currency. (*Pause.*)

Nietzsche The pale Galilean is a plagiarist.

Jesus You don't have a monopoly on scepticism.

Nietzsche I distinctly remember writing that.

Jesus Does that mean you don't want anyone else to think it, as well?

Enter **Bernard** *majestically down the stairs. He has the revolver.*

Jesus Bernard, get Elizabeth, will you.

Bernard Get Elizabeth? I've just done that. (*Laughs.*)

Jesus Get her in here for supper. I don't want to start till everyone's sitting down.

Bernard Don't bother to serve me. I am going to kill myself. (*Pause.*) I have lost the expedition's money. So I am going to show Elizabeth that I am sorry, in the only way I can afford. It is the decent way. The Prussian way.

Nietzsche (*calls*) Bravo, Bernard!

Bernard *walks off through the main entrance, with measured tread.*

Jesus I really don't think self-slaughter is the answer.

Nietzsche Oh yes you do! Except you never dared do it yourself, you got the Romans to do it for you and the whole world has been saddled with the guilt ever since!

Enter **Elizabeth**, *down the stairs, clothes torn and wide-eyed. She comes downstair slowly into the room.*

Emma   Elizabeth! What's happening?

Elizabeth   It's all right. It's all right. (*Pause.*) Does he still have the gun? He said first he was going to blow my head off with it, so I was lucky. He only raped me.

Emma   What!!

Elizabeth   He said he wanted to show his complete contempt.

Gun explosion, off.

There. It's over.

Nietzsche   Come on! This sort of thing is catching and if our host suddenly follows Herr Forster's notable example, there will soon be no one left to eat the food.

Jesus   Point taken. I'm going to move it right along. Take your places, everyone. Though I expect Mr Darwin will say I hid it up my sleeve.

Darwin   It is no matter to me, now. When I was a child I believed such things, but then in so many respects I was an ordinary boy . . .

Jesus   Let's hear it for the trinity: one, two, three!

Jesus *spreads a tablecloth, but there is nothing on it.*

Emma (*to* **Elizabeth**)   Do you want to lie down?

Elizabeth   No, no. Frederich will need help.

Elizabeth *lovingly tucks a napkin round* **Nietzsche**'*s neck.*

Nietzsche   Elizabeth, get away! You've got lumps of blood and skin under your fingernails.

Elizabeth   I'm so sorry. Why are men afraid of women? It should be the other way round. My brother is terrified of me. In his dreams, I obtain his emission in my mouth while he sleeps and then in the night he wakes in dread. When I hear his screams I run in to him, and he tells me he can see a naked succubus with my face, upon the floor, its mouth to a rubber tube which disappears between its feathered legs – kill it, he says – and when I hold the lantern up, saying, Frederich, there's nothing there, just me in my nightdress, he points to some dark stains upon the floor, and says, look – the first cell division – incestuous twins! –

She is wiping her hands under her armpits.
The doors slowly open and **Humboldt/Mercator** *comes in pushing* **Bernard** *who has shot himself in the head. He is still sitting in the wheelchair.* **Humboldt/Mercator** *positions him at the table as if he was alive and about to eat. Round his neck is hung a placard; SUFFER BITCH, THIS ONE'S FOR YOU.*

Emma   Who put that on him?

Humboldt   It was there when we got to him. (*Exits.*)

Darwin   I can only speak for Mr Forster's character which was, from what I was able to observe, deficient. But I am astonished it should come to this.

Nietzsche   'Suffer bitch, this one's for you!' What a singular legacy Bernard has left you with, Elizabeth. Unlike someone I could mention who didn't let a single one off.

Jesus   I'm going to send you out of the room if you carry on like this, Professor. I mean it.

Nietzsche   The whole of humanity got fingered with his suicide, eh, Darwin?

Jesus   And now, the wine! (*He produces a goatskin, or plastic simulacrum.*)

Nietzsche   His own piss, I expect. (*Calls.*) Get me something drinkable from the cellar, Humboldt.

Jesus   Fetch it yourself, Professor.

Elizabeth   Are you mocking my brother?

Jesus   I've never been more sincere. I'm curing him.

Nietzsche   For how long?

Jesus   That's for me to know, and you to guess.

Nietzsche *stands, unsteadily.*

Elizabeth   Oh Frederich! Look everyone! His genius rises again!

Nietzsche   I shall summarise: Darwinism is stupid because it presupposes a state of chronic distress everywhere. Darwinism is the enemy of affirmation and joy. Humans are not pigs or any other kind of animal. The will to power is the rocket fuel of consciousness. That is where we should be aiming. Up, up, among the stars. Not with the worms, underneath the stone.

Nietzsche *starts to walk off unsteadily.* **Elizabeth** *goes to help him and he waves her away.*

Nietzsche   Humboldt will catch me when I fall shortly. Recovery will be a makeshift event, like everything else the saviour performs.

Exit **Nietzsche**. **Elizabeth** *blows kisses.*

Elizabeth   Bravo! Bravo!

Jesus   He's a chancer, that man.

Mary *takes the pourer from* **Jesus**.

Mary   He's going to miss the best vintage. Hey, whyn'cha let me do that Jesus?

Jesus   Just like the old days, eh?

Mary   I miss hostessing for you. Here it comes! (*Passing out plastic cups.*) From the perfumed hands of the one-time hot favourite, something straight from the holy goatskin.

Jesus   Mind you, I should confess that there's actually a kernel of truth in Professor Nietzsche's criticism about the wine's origins. I confess I *have* pissed some of it.

Everyone puts the glasses down, horrified.

Jesus   But so have you all. If we believe Professor Darwin, with his elongated notions of planetary longevity, the water would have also passed through dinosaur's rear ends, for some sixty million years, and then spent ice-ages immobile, in glacial sheets a mile thick. In the future, if I can still use that word amongst you sophisticates, some of its molecules will dilute the battery acid of a seven-year-old Ford Cortina I will part-own, in Strabane. (*Reassuring.*) This offering generally comes with a bouquet, a light dry Sauternes. Tonight it's . . . (*Sniffs, suspicious.*) Just a minute. (*Misgiving.*) We seem to have something rather unusual, here.

Mary This is one of those moments when I'm *really* glad I don't drink.

Jesus (*amazed*) It's Irish whiskey. This is Ulster ambrosia! Old Bushmills! – brewed by Protestant loyalists for everyone, including Catholics. Twelve years maturing, almost long enough to sink a worm stone! Stickin' out!

Jesus *raises his glass to the company and drinks it off. A clock in the distance starts to strike twelve.*

Darwin I thought the bells had drowned. For a moment there I heard Annie's voice. The church clock in the village must still be above the water. (*To self.*) Yes, that's it.

Mary I'd like to propose a toast, to Charles Darwin.

Jesus I'll second the scarlet woman. Anyone who's had to stand up for truth against those pillocks in the Church of England and the Establishment, for thirty years –

All To Charles Darwin!

Darwin *rises to acknowledge and sits at a battering at a door, off.*

Jesus Don't anyone move – I'll let this one in! Here's one last joke before I go. Why are there no footprints in eternity? Because – it's a merry-go-round! Thank you and goodnight! (*Exits.*)

Mary (*applauding, to* **Darwin**) Speech, speech!

Darwin *stands.*

Darwin Thank you. To seek after truth is hard. I am who I am because my father showed me to never lie. He was a great man. Destitutes would turn up at the door in rags, but the money he lent out to them would always come back. He could tell, you see, who was telling the truth. He also knew that in the struggle for survival, it is not necessarily the higher type that survives. There is no one to take his place, now he has gone. If Darwinism has illuminated anything in the world, it is because my father –

A mud-blackened pregnant figure appears. It advances to the middle of the room and collapses.

Mrs Müller   Mrs Forster! Help me, help me please.

Elizabeth   Oh it's you, Mrs Müller. Where are the others?

Mrs Müller   I don't know, ma'am.

Elizabeth   Do you mean they are dead?

Mrs Müller   I fear so, ma'am. (*Sees* **Bernard**.) Oh no! Bernard is dead too. And he swore he was going to marry me. Bernard! Dead!

Elizabeth *threatens her with the revolver as* **Mrs Müller** *is helped onto the table.*

Elizabeth (*to* **Mrs Müller**)   Tell me – stupid bitch – what's happened to the others?

Mrs Müller   Ooh, my contractions! Ooh it's a breech birth – I know it – runs in the family –

Elizabeth   What happened to the rest of your party? Tell me where they are or I'll blow the bastard's little head in before it has time to come out!

Mrs Müller   Gone, gone.

Elizabeth   Where have they gone?

Mrs Müller   I cannot say. We were all coming to Herr Professor Darwin's house, directed by the slashes on the trees along the ridge. We were going to have a little rest, a sit down in an apple orchard of a garden of a little cottage. There weren't any railway tracks around the cottage, but there were noises, train noises coming from inside the garden. We were tired. Everyone went in, not realising. It didn't look dangerous. It looked abandoned. But it wasn't. The cottage was all broken down. I was last. I could see people going up to the gate. One by one as they stepped into the garden they – disappeared. And there was a little voice, saying, 'Schnell! Schnell!' And I got close and there was no one there, no one at all just the sound of trains in a big station although there weren't no big station. I got frightened, and I didn't go in through the gate – I ran, and I ran, and I didn't know what I was running from, and my waters broke as I saw the house on the hill . . .

Elizabeth   So – there is only one German left. Very well.

Emma   Elizabeth, why don't you go and boil some water in the kitchen?

Elizabeth   Do you think I can make a nation from one? No. But I am not defeated. I know my future. It is strong. It surprised me when I found it in the newspaper of the future. But it says I am to go back to Germany and make a book, from my brother's ideas, and I will of course correct them where they are incorrect. The book will be called *The Will to Power*. Every German soldier will have a copy in his knapsack, in the final battle of the nations. Between battles, I will be nominated for the Nobel prize, many times. When I die, I will be given a state funeral, as big as Queen Victoria's. You say, 'Boil some water!' Before I am finished, I will boil more than water!

Elizabeth *exits.*

Emma   We'll need to sterilise some dissecting scalpels, Charles. If you could just look them out for me, before you go.

Darwin   Before I go? I'm not sure I am going.

Emma   Jesus said that you just need to walk to the end of the sandwalk, where the waters begin.

Darwin   And then?

Mary   There's no particular ferry. You just step onto the first one that you see.

Emma (*to* **Darwin**) I shall miss you, dreadfully. I know you leave me with the purest heart of any husband.

Mary That's such a beautiful thing to say. You married a lady, Professor!

Darwin (*to* **Emma**) You flatter me more than you know, dearest. But thank you for looking so beautiful tonight.

Emma Beautiful? Covered in blood, and my hair is not right . . . ?

Darwin Of course you are beautiful. Always.

Mary (*to* **Mrs Müller**) It's going to be a little Pisces if it gets a move on. If not, it will be an Aries. Did you plan to be astrologically compatible with your child? Did they ever teach you how to push? (**Mrs Müller** *moans.*) Never mind. I'm going to put some water to heat on the stove, and I'll be right back. (*Exit to kitchen.*)

Darwin (*to* **Emma**) I remember when you first wore that dress. You were thirty-one when we married. A year older than me. You have been so good to me. I have been the luckiest of men. So lucky to find you . . . incredibly fortunate, to have a fulfilled heart . . . the merest chance.

Emma *helps* **Darwin** *on with his coat.*

Emma Just remember that Annie will be there for you, on the other side.

Darwin These hopes are folly. You know I would not dare aspire to anything like that.

Emma Oh, you will find heaven, if anyone will. Dearest, it was your love for the children that made me certain you were a truly good man. Remember once when you were going to London, the children said they would give sixpence if you would stay and play with them?

Emma *goes to* **Mrs Müller**. *Lights are going down.*

Darwin That wakes so many memories, Emma. But the children are all grown now . . .

Mrs Müller*'s stomach slowly starts to flash, brighter and brighter, the speed of a heartbeat.*

Darwin   ... And I see now, I should not stay.

The women bend over the glowing form. Slow fade over other lights: tableau, finally blackout.